Bakumatsu

From Samurai to Soldiers – Japan in the 1860s

Till Weber

Kateba kangun, makereba zokugun -
"Conquer, and you are the Emperor´s army; lose, and you are nothing but a pack of rebels."
(Japanese proverb, second half of the 19th century)

Author:	Prof Till Weber
Artwork:	Sascha Lunyakov
Additional Graphics:	Peter Bunde
Maps:	Bernhard Glänzer
Editing (German edition):	Michael Danhardt
Translated by:	Dr Jan Eschbach
Layout:	Stefan Müller
Publisher:	Zeughaus Verlag GmbH
	Knesebeckstr. 88
	10623 Berlin, Germany
	Telephone: +49 (0)30/315 700 30
	Email: info@zeughausverlag.de
	Website: www.zeughausverlag.de

All rights reserved.
Reproduction, translation, and photographic reproduction (including extracts) are prohibited. Storage and distribution including transfer onto electronic media such as CD-ROM etc. as well as storage on electronic media such as the internet etc. are not permissible without the express written permission of the publishers and are punishable. All violation is liable to legal prosecution.
Bibliographic information from the Deutsche Bibliothek. The Deutsche Bibliothek lists this publication in the German National Bibliography; detailed bibliographic information is available at http://dnb.ddb.de
Printed in the European Union
Originally published in German as "Bakumatsu. Wie Samurai zu Soldaten wurden. Japan in den 1860ern" (Berlin: Zeughaus Verlag 2023) in the Heere & Waffen series number 46. This edition based on the German original.

© 2023 Zeughaus Verlag GmbH, Berlin, Germany
ISBN: 978-3-96360-051-7

Cover
Battle of the River Oze, 1866 (detail)
See pages 104/105

INHALT

Introduction — 9
    About this book — 9
    Internal conflict and civil war in 1860s Japan — 10

The military revolution – Japanese military reforms between 1841 and 1868 — 14
    Reform of the Shogunate – The new Takashima academy — 14
    Tentative steps towards rearmament — 22
    The Shogun makes a clean sweep – the new army — 23
    Command structure under the Tokugawa — 25

The antagonists – Satsuma and Choshu — 30
    Satsuma — 30
    Choshu — 34

Firearms – from matchlock to Gatling Gun — 37
    The example of Yonezawa — 37
    Foreign arms and Japanese armies — 40
    The influence of foreign arms dealers — 48

The Shogunate, Imperial forces, and allies – an overview of the most important domains and their banners and insignia — 54
    The Tokugawa and their allies — 56
    Satsuma, Choshu and their allies — 61
    Other mon and standards — 68

The combatants — 75
    Shishi – men of high ideals, or unmitigated lunatics? — 75
    Shinsengumi – shining heroes, or gang of thugs? — 77
    Samurai – the last battlecry of the old feudal élite — 82
    Modern Infantry — 91
    Shotai Militia — 100

Campaigns and battles of the 1860s — 106
    The second punitive campaign against Choshu in 1866 — 106
    "In this sign, conquer!" – the Battle of Toba-Fushimi (3rd–6th January 1868) — 111
    The first day (3rd January 1868) — 114
    The second day (4th January 1868) — 115

The third day (5th January 1868)	117
The fourth day (6th January 1868)	122
Why did Tokugawa Yoshinobu lose the battle despite a numerical superiority of three to one?	123
Aftermath	124
From Kyoto to Edo	125
The Battle of Ueno, 15th May 1868	127
The Hokuetsu War in Nagaoka (May – August 1868)	130
The bloody siege of Aizu-Wakamatsu (6th October – 6th November 1868)	138
Sendai, Yonezawa and Shonai in the Boshin War	142
Last stand of the Shogunate party in Hokkaido – the surrender of Hakodate on 27th June 1869	142

Important characters of the Bakumatsu period — 151

Choshu´s Young Blades	151
Katsu Kaishu and Saigo Takamori	153
Jules Brunet, true "Last Samurai"	157
After the battle, or the experiences of Dr William Willis	160
Imai Nobuo (1841–1918) and the long road to an ordinary life	163

Sources and further reading — 166

Gatling Gun operated by Kawai Tsuginosuke, leading vassal of Nagaoka domain (line drawings by Sascha Lunyakov for KLIO-AG SHOGUN). See also pp. 147-149.

INTRODUCTION

About this book

The volume at hand is the third part of my series of publications in the Zeughaus Verlag that concerns itself with the history of Samurai warfare. The books published in the years 2009 and 2012 respectively (revised and augmented English editions appeared in 2022) covered the apogee of the 16th and 17th centuries, when the fate of Japan came to be determined by a feudal samurai élite. This third volume brings the story to its conclusion by focusing on the events of between the middle and the second half of the 19th century which took place in the context of the so-called Meiji Restoration. What had become of Japan´s warrior class after a two-hundred-year period of peace, and how did the proud samurai react to a new age in which technologically superior colonial powers appeared on the horizon, armed to the teeth with the most modern warships and weapons industrialization could produce? It is surely not anticipating too much when saying that the Japan that finally emerged after 1868 had not much left in common with the Japan of the year 1841. This is particularly true in military terms.

The editorial guidelines of the first two volumes have been consistently maintained to facilitate orientation and cross-referencing. To improve readability, diacritical marks (e. g. for vowel elongation) have been omitted. Japanese words and phrases are explained in context wherever possible. We have also sought to avoid excessive footnoting by only employing these to provide links to other parts of the book also dedicated to the topic. A full bibliography is given at the end of the book. Japanese names have been given throughout in the traditional manner that has a person´s surname precede their first name.

In spite of this, reading may prove slightly demanding at times, since territories, institutions as well as individual samurai often had far more than just one name. It was common for a member of the nobility to change their name several times in a lifetime, adding titles and nicknames, some of which were even given posthumously. The present author seeks to consistently employ the most frequent and widely established name combinations throughout this work; occasional deviations from this rule are unavoidable however, as for instance referring to one and the same princedom by a variety of different names was common practice: Saga was also referred to as Hizen, Kii as Kishu, and Hiroshima was also known as Aki or Geishu. Wherever necessary, name variants are given to provide clarity.

Princedoms, fiefdoms, or domains were called *han* in Japanese and ruled by hereditary princes called *daimyo*, as they will be referred to throughout the text. The Shogunate and its administrative authorities were known to contemporaries as *bakufu*. Samurai were often referred to as *bushi* (or simply *shi*), while *ashigaru*, the warriors who ranked lowest in the samurai hierarchy, were frequently called *doshin* by the Tokugawa. We choose to refer to them simply as *samurai / ashigaru* in order to clearly distinguish them from the regular soldiers who fought in the modern armies that emerged in this period. Japanese nomenclature was a source of bafflement also to foreigners of past times. In the middle of the 19th century the Emperor and the Shogun were often erroneously referred to as *mikado* or *taikun* (cf. English *tycoon*) respectively instead of by their proper titles, *tenno* and *shogun*. Such misnomers often occurred simply because many Europeans did not understand the manner in which political power was distributed in Japan. It would not be out of place to add that this seems often to be the case even today.

Another important word in our story is *koku*. The term denotes the amount of uncooked rice necessary to allow one person to subsist for one year (c. 180 litres). In the period under examination, incomes of both daimyo and samurai were were calculated by *koku*, even allowing for the fact that not all was actually consumed but exchanged for money. The gap between Lord Tokugawa, the Shogun, and a small-time provincial lord is best illustrated by comparing the annual millions of *koku* due to the former and the ten thousand the latter required to be able to call himself a daimyo. The amount of *koku* at a samurai or a prince´s disposal determined the number of samurai he was expected to contribute to his lord´s army, and how much financial liberty he enjoyed for example when it came to acquiring foreign military equipment.

The traditional Japanese method of time computation also occasionally has its snags for the Western scholar. The year 1867 was known to its Japanese contemporaries as Keio 3, since it was simply the third year of the Emperor Keio´s reign. 1868 consequently began as Keio 4 but promptly turned into Meiji 1, when the young Emperor Meiji mounted the throne. The ancient Japanese calendar worked according to astronomic principles and allowed for twelve or thirteen months, each numbering 29 or 30 days. The new year commenced in February, which is why the Gregorian calendar, which was introduced in Japan in the year 1873, is actually ahead of its predecessor. Days were also counted differently. The Battle of Ueno thus took place either on 15th May 1868 according to the old Japanese calendar, or on 4th July by its Gregorian successor. For some unexplained reason, some sources even give dates according to the Julian calendar (although these may admittedly simply be conversion errors). This would actually move Ueno to 22nd June. This work seeks to adhere to the Japanese calendar, and any resulting mistakes are entirely the author´s.

Heartfelt thanks goes to Professor Masuo Kataoka for his kind cooperation, and also to Rod Johnson, John Cruikshank, Werner David as well as the museums and individuals who generously contributed images and knowledge to this volume. Among these are the Samurai Museum Berlin and Alfred Umhey (Lampertheim, Germany). Japanese institutions who assisted in the making of this book include the Miyasaka Koukokan Collection in Yonezawa, The Yonezawa City Uesugi Museum, the City of Nagaoka, and the Goryokaku Tower in Hakodate. Cooperation with the illustrating artist Sascha Lunyakov was as exciting and enriching as ever. Peter Bunde and Bernhard Glänzer drew the other graphics, maps and diagrams featured in this work, and Jan Eschbach provided a state-of-the-art English translation. As always, special thanks is due to Stefan Müller and his team at Zeughaus-Verlag, Berlin.

Internal conflict and civil war in 1860s Japan

After gaining political supremacy over Japan at the beginning of the 17th century, the powerful Tokugawa dynasty achieved lasting peace and prosperity for the country following almost one and a half centuries of fighting. Both peace and a measure of economic stability were ensured by the permanent and inflexible institutionalization of the social, political, and military order, and by almost completely isolating Japan from abroad. The only means of access to Japanese trade for Europeans (though not much of the country itself) existed in the form of the Dutch trade post of Deshima, a small artificial island in the port of Nagasaki. The Shogun resided at Edo (modern Tokyo). This powerful office was held by fifteen members of the Tokugawa family in succession and comprised feudal control over more than 250 daimyo. These princes presided over fiefdoms of varying size and were divided into two basic groups: the *fudai*, ancient and traditionally faithful allies of the Tokugawa, and the *tozama*, who had only eventually yielded to their Tokugawa overlords. The lords of the two large renegade princedoms of the South-West, Choshu and Satsuma, who were later to instigate the 1868 coup, belonged to the latter category and even after two centuries had not lived down the humiliation of playing second fiddle to the almighty Shogun.

Japan had no national armed forces in the conventional sense, but since the Shogunate controlled the country and wielded the largest financial resources, its power remained unchallenged as long as the most important *fudai* retainers remained loyal. The Tokugawa had succeeded in permanently freezing the military balance of power prevalent in the 1640s, as this benefited their political position.

Only members of the samurai caste were permitted to carry arms, but these only accounted for less than 10% of the overall Japanese population. Until the mid-19th century the main weapons were lance, sword, bow, and the matchlock arquebus. These were supplemented by a few superannuated bronze cannon. This sufficed perfectly since military conflict in the the long Tokugawa peace was restricted to local peasant risings. As a consequence,

many formerly warlike samurai gradually became civil servants, whose military experience and training dwindled to occasional fencing bouts after a day´s work.

Every member of Japanese society knew their place. Samurai, peasants, artisans and merchants each formed their own class, that of the samurai ranking highest. Priests, minorities and outsiders and outlaws existed independently of this social hierarchy and were excluded from it. The samurai class itself was subdivided into a rigid caste system – members were either born into one of the rich and powerful upper castes of feudal retainers if they happened to be a blood relative of a daimyo or major retainer, or they ended up one of the large numbers of increasingly impoverished and socially irrelevant ordinary samurai or *ashigaru* foot soldiers. In any case, both the individual´s life and career were rigidly predetermined from birth by this regimentation, but in the 19th century many young samurai were beginning to question these long-established but increasingly unpopular social conventions.

At the beginning of the 19th century, the foundations of the long peace which many had begun to perceive as in fact tiresome and obsolete, began first to faintly tremble, only to rapidly disintegrate as the century progressed. Natural disasters, famine, and a growing income gap between a few wealthy princes and merchants and the majority of minor samurai began to cause discontent and unrest among young samurai who for themselves saw no real chance of social advancement. Frustration at this common lack of perspective was also spreading among the rest of the population.

The Japan of the 1860s was determined by massive insecurities, to which a number of movements claimed to have found solutions, thereby promising what was generally called *yonaoshi* ("healing the world"). Some proved bizarre; for example, the followers of the popular *eejanaika* movement (*eejanaika* simply translates as "So what?") were wont to suddenly erupt into a flurry of lurching dance movements in the street, frequently driving the authorities to distraction. It was these developments along with impending economic crisis which became inseperably associated with a period the Japanese still refer to as *bakumatsu* – the final phase of the Shogunate, from which finally there emerged a new age. This was to be called the Meiji period, taking its name from the Emperor whose reign created a new world (1868–1912).

The great change that had been in the air for some time manifested itself with a bang when a squadron of four American warships commanded by Commodore Matthew Perry (the Perry Expedition of 1853) anchored in Edo Bay and forced Japan to give up its centuries-old international isolation more or less at gunpoint. The other major industrial and colonial powers followed suit and quickly gained footholds in Japan, thereby causing concern that Japan would share the fate of so many countries humiliated and exploited by the Western powers. Not only the samurai began to remember the ancient duty of the Shogun expressed in his complete Japanese title *sei'i taishogun* – to expel barbarian invaders from Japanese soil. Widespread demands for the Shogunate to meet increasing foreign interference with more determination became impossible to ignore. The Shogunate

After the Battle of Toba-Fushimi, January of 1868. (*Nishiki no mihata* 1907: plate XXII)

saw itself caught in a double bind. It was obvious that any attempt to contain what was perceived as foreign intrusion would result in the complete colonisation of Japan. The country was simply too backward to offer successful resistance. One could not fight breech-loading guns with sword and lance. The Western powers meanwhile urged the Japanese government to admit more foreign traders, presenting the Japanese with the infamous "unequal treaties" containing highly unfavourable conditions. At first, the Shogunate tried to play for time, but eventually it was forced to comply.

The political climate had meanwhile become decidedly heated, and by what was deemed surrender to the alien the Shogunate became a traitor in the eyes of many young and fanatical samurai. The South-Western domains which for so long had been denied political influence, among them Satsuma and Chochu, finally saw an opportunity to strike. While the Shogunate and other rich and influential domains became embroiled in a frantic process of industrial and military modernization (the Western powers were only too happy to provide the latest technology), the hopes of many disgruntled and disaffected samurai became focused on a personage who for centuries had been without any real political influence – the Emperor himself.

Since the 12th century Japan had been ruled by the warrior élite of the samurai with the Shogun ranking highest in the military and political hierarchy. The Emperor and his court resided in the capital at Kyoto. The Emperor possessed few sources of income and commanded no troops of his own. He kept well aloof of the political intrigues of his age and remained politically impartial. It was this political "purity" which was shortly to become the Shogunate's death trap. Because the Emperor stood for no specific political faction, anyone could instrumentalize him for their own ends. Since the Shogun had failed to drive out the foreign barbarians, the rebellious samurai (and eventually also many powerful domains) turned to the Emperor, demanding that he decree the expulsion of the foreign invaders from Japan.

Having suffered several military reverses in the course of the 1860s, the rebels realized that this was simply not practicable. Changing their strategy, they now called for the replacement of the Shogun. They invariably professed unfailing loyalty to the Emperor, yet their true motive remained a longing for profound change in politics and society. The Emperor, they declared, was to reclaim the power which in truth he had not possessed since the Middle Ages. Yet the Shogun officially owed his office and legitimacy to none other but the Emperor. Since the 17th century the judicial and ideological foundations of the power of the Tokugawa Shogunate had rested on Imperial approval, despite the fact that this had long deteriorated into a mere formality. He who represented the Emperor could claim legitimacy for whatever actions suited him. He who controlled the Imperial court was able to determine what was considered good and right. Conversely, any person declared a public enemy (*cho-teki*, an "enemy of the court") became an outlaw devoid of rights and without personal honour.

Thus the 1860s became the period of an incessant struggle for influence at court and the Emperor's favour. At court and in the streets of the capital Kyoto the Shogun and his allies fought to contain the mounting number of enemies, which at first had only consisted of *ronin* (freelance samurai bound to no particular domain), and a handful of courtiers. All parties who could afford to do so began to modernize their private armies. This modernization however spelled the gradual abolishment of the old samurai fighting units in favour of infantry and artillery equipped with rifles and guns. The foot soldiers and artillerymen serving in the new units were no longer required to be samurai themselves. This development entailed a number of interesting experiments and enterprises, which form part of the fascination this period holds for the military historian – Japan became a virtual laboratory where old and new clashed with unprecedented and unpredictable results. The Boshin War of 1868/69 can thus be considered an equivalent link in the long chain of military conflicts in the late 19th centruy reaching from the Crimean War (1853–1856) and the American Civil War (1861–1865) right down to the Wars of German Unification until 1871.

This volume cannot discuss in detail the numerous political turns of events which occurred in Kyoto, Edo, and at the courts of the provincial capitals. The conflicts erupted briefly into open war in 1863 and reached a first climax in 1866, when the Shogun's feudal army of 150, 000 samurai failed to defeat a force of 4, 500 Chochu soldiers trained, armed and equipped in the Western fashion. As the failing power of Edo became increasingly apparent, the powerful princes began to ponder the future. Meanwhile at Kyoto, the court factions fought over whose strategy was to be approved and officially declared Imperial policy. In 1867, Shogun Tokugawa Yoshinobu resigned his office and placed it at the Emperor's disposal. One year later, old political scores were settled at the four-day Battle of Toba-Fushimi, where Satsuma and Chochu along with their allies defeated the army of Tokugawa Yoshinobu. At the same time, Kyoto declared for the rebels, who could now proudly claim to be acting in the Emperor's name, while the unfortunate former Shogun and his retainers saw themselves declared enemies of the court.

Kateba kangun, makereba zokugun – "Conquer, and you are the Emperor's army; lose, and you are nothing but a pack of rebels" was a phrase coined in these times of great unrest. Henceforth, a combination of political and military success was to bring about the country's change. The majority of domains threw in their lot with the new Imperial government, but many daimyo in the eastern and northern regions of Japan chose to remain loyal to the Tokugawa despite the fact that Tokugawa Yoshinobu himself had quickly given up and submitted to Imperial authority. The Boshin War, which had begun on the fields and in the streets of Toba and Fushimi, was to last for another one and a half years until June 1869. Battles took place in central, eastern and northern Japan, and in the final weeks the fighting even spread to Hokkaido. Daimyo faithful to the last, individual groups of samurai, and even a few French military advisors refused to give up and fought to the very end. In the course of the war, the old samurai fighting techniques gradually vanished to be superseded by the exploits of units of skirmishers armed with modern firearms and highly efficient artillery pieces. Only the old fighting spirit of the samurai remained as a reminder of more glorious times.

In the end, the new Imperial government proved unstoppable. In 1868 the old Shogunate capital of Edo was renamed Tokyo, and the young Emperor Meiji took up residence in the former castle of the Tokugawa. Changes occurred at breakneck speed and were not restricted to military matters, also comprising politics, society, and the economy. In the course of 1870s both the old domains and the samurai as a distinct social class were abolished. All Japanese were subjects of the Emperor forthwith, in whose name a new oligarchy mostly consisting of the victors of 1868/69 ruled supreme.

This book will first examine the various major stages and components of the Japanese Military Revolution which determined these fateful years. An overview of the most important parties involved in the Boshin War will be provided, and their organization, weapons and battle insignia explained. All of these had changed significantly since the 16th and 17th centuries. A look will be taken at the combatants, whose appearance ranged from regular samurai to fanatic *ronin* and modern rifle-armed infantry. The fifth, most extensive chapter will analyse eight defining campaigns and battles, all of which occurred between the summer of 1866 and June 1869. Since history is always made by human beings, a number of short biographies of the most important and interesting protagonists will conclude this work. The period we are concerned with abounds in fascinating characters with dramatic biographies, of which unfortunately only very few can be told here. Any reader who may wish to conduct further research is commended to the bibliography at the end of this book.

View of Tokyo (Edo) castle, which was the seat of the Shogun´s feudal government until turned into the Imperial palace under Emperor Meiji in 1868. The modern Seimon stone bridge in the centre was built in 1889 and is a powerful symbol of the changes in Japan resulting from the conflicts of the 1860s.

Takashima academy students drill in front of high-ranking representatives of the Shogunate government in 1841. (public domain)

THE MILITARY REVOLUTION – JAPANESE MILITARY REFORMS BETWEEN 1841 AND 1868

Reform of the Shogunate – The new Takashima academy

Black powder weapons, which had been introduced in Japan in the mid-16th century, contributed a great deal to the political process of centralisation which reached its conclusion with the victory of the Tokugawa and their allies at the beginning of the 17th century. Although Japan never completely abandoned firearms (contrary to Noel Perrin's thesis published in his widely known yet factually incorrect work *Giving Up the Gun. Japan's Reversion to the Sword 1543–1879* [1979]), those firearms that remained in use at the beginning of the 19th century, mostly matchlock *teppo* arquebuses (*teppo* or *tanegashima*) and a few artillery pieces, were either leftovers or of the same design as they had been at the beginning of the Shogunate. The art of shooting was taught by hereditary masters at special academies (*ryu*) scattered across the different domains. True to samurai mentality, individual marksmanship was considered a prized asset. Modern tactics, for example concerted firing by platoons, companies or even battalions, was a topic known only to the few specialists who had read the more modern Netherlandish manuals available in Japanese translation.

One of these few was Takashima Shuhan (1798-1866), a samurai son-turned-civil servant who also ran the Ogino shooting academy, an institution whose methods were based on the ideas of the 17th century. A high-ranking public official involved in the administration of Nagasaki, Takashima Shuhan had access to the latest Dutch know-how, since the United East India Company's trade post of Deshima was located in Nagasaki Bay. From the books he had read and conversations with Dutch experts Takashima concluded in the 1820s that in war individual marksmanship counted far less than unit organisation into large bodies according to Western standards (platoons, companies, and battalions). Such troops had to be armed with modern firearms and move in rigid and concerted

Takashima academy students in 1841. Detail (public domain)

formations to achieve a maximum effect on the enemy, as the Napoleonic Wars had shown. Also, the military had to be organized into specific branches of service (infantry, cavalry, artillery, and support troops).

Takashima proceeded to put his ideas into practice. He purchased dozens of books on military subjects, hundreds of European muskets, and even a few artillery pieces (field guns, howitzers, and mortars). In 1839 he opened his new academy, which although it followed Japanese time-hallowed tradition in admitting individual students to be taught by a master, was in fact a school of infantry and artillery with a Western curriculum.

The First Opium War (1839–1842) sent shock waves across the Chinese Sea. No one in Japan had reckoned with the ease with which Western forces had defeated the great Chinese Empire. Takashima decided to act and drew up a petition in which he recommended to his lord and master the Shogun the ideas and tactics taught at his school. He proposed that these were suitable to drive the "Western barbarians" from Japan. Traditional Japanese marksmanship, he claimed, was "uselessly ornate or archaic [and] esoteric", mocked by Western observers (Jaundrill 2016: 23). Takashima´s petition struck a nerve at a time when emotions were running high at Edo castle. Reformers and traditionalists in the Shogunate administrations argued bitterly over which approach to take. One of Takashima´s opponents was inspector (*metsuke*) Torii Yozo, who wrote that such ideas would not stop merely at marksmanship, but profoundly change marching, tactics, and ultimately even custom and education. How right he was to prove.

In June 1841 Takashima received his chance to present the results of his teachings to the Shogun´s assembled military experts in the northern outskirts of Edo. Takashima had meanwhile managed to attract students not only from the southern domains in Kyushu, but also from the eastern provinces around Edo. He duly paraded 129 of his students, most of them infantry, but there were also three gun crews and even three cavalrymen. The display's climax was reached when Takashima and his students discharged several salvoes from their flintlock muskets in close-order formation, thus making clear that such tactics were far superior in range and effect than anything traditional Japanese marksmanship could hope to achieve. Takashima's "soldiers" were uniformly clad in blue jackets and wore a peculiar new type of tall headdress which Takashima had himself designed: the *peloton-gasa*, or *tonkyo-gasa*, was more suitable for riflemen operating in close formation than the traditional broad-brimmed *jingasa*. All commands were given in Dutch. Such dress and the language of command were of course a provocation to traditionalists, but Takashima had won the first round. With government support he opened two more academies in the east of the country and was told to pass on his knowledge to two high-ranking vassals of the Tokugawa, Egawa Hidetatsu and Shimosone Nobuatsu. Takashima's ideas were to be taught all over Japan. Not only the Tokugawa and their retainers were to benefit from them but all samurai, since repelling the Western barbarians was after all everybody's affair. The ideas and conflicts leading to the 1860s civil wars were still far away.

However, the traditionalists were not idle. For generations, all black powder weapons had been the responsibility of the Inoue and Tatsuke clans, who were something akin to the Shogun's armourers (*teppo-gata*). They had no intention of letting an upstart with foreign ideas like Takashima ruin their subsistence. They found an ally in Torii Yozo (aptly nicknamed *yokai*, "demon"), who managed to get Takashima Shuhan placed under house arrest from 1846 to 1853. This did not stop the spread of his ideas however, since Egawa and Shimosone took over Takashima's schools and continued to develop his methods and theories. The main branch of Takashima's academy was situated at Edo, which attracted tens of thousands of underemployed and idle samurai from domains all over the Empire. Many of these men spent their time attending martial arts schools (swordsmanship holding pride of place), and thus Takashima's ideas gradually spread to the most distant corners of Japan. The Shogun would have been well-advised to prevent this from happening to preserve his own power, for these ideas were to prove the breeding ground of a military revolution which eventually removed the political headway which the Shogunate had enjoyed for two hundred years.

Egawa's academy was at rural Izu in Nirayama to the south-west of Edo, where there was plenty of space for military exercises. To counteract the criticism Takashima's Western methods had evoked, Egawa changed the language of command to Japanese and conceived a new form of headdress which complied more to Japanese tastes and was named *nirayama-gasa* after the school where it was designed. This hat was made of stout lacquered wickerwork with a high comb and sides that covered the ears so that the wearer was not impeded when handling the the rifle and bayonet. The traditional *jingasa* had proved unsuitable especially when the man stood at attention or in the shoulder-arms position.

In spite of these innovations the samurai were still loath to abandon their individuality. They continued to wear a multitude of headdresses which never ceased to amaze Western observers. Thus, the correspondent of the *Tokyo Gazette* was able to write after reviewing Imperial troops in 1868:

"As for the dress of these men, it would require a quick artist's eye for each samurai. They represented all the colours of the rainbow. Their hats alone were as diverse as the nations on earth. Some wore black cone-shaped wooden basins, some a Chinese winterfelt hat, others glazed plaited cotton the shape of which might compare with an umbrella whose ribs were broken; some had a taste for the Western fashions, some had French caps, others the British naval style. Amongst them were also to be seen the Australian digger's felt slouch, and some had a fancy for the lion's mane, or the skin of the grizzly bear. There were ponderous iron helmets, and light bamboo or straw. It may be imagined, with such a variety of headdress, how varied their nether costume was." (Cortazzi 2002: 135–136)

Takashima Shuhan was finally released in 1853 and his name cleared. He was appointed instructor of the new Shogunate army. This turn of events had been prompted by the appearance of Commodore Matthew Perry's American naval squadron in Edo Bay in the same year. The Shogun had realised that both equipment and tactics of his own armed forces were hopelessly outdated. Takashima recommended the acquisition of 200 modern warships to meet the foreign threat. The Shogunate did not have the financial means for such a measure. Instead, in 1862 it issued permission for all domains to acquire ships and arms independently, while the government itself called in French assistance and embarked on its attempt to turn the Yokosuka arsenal into a production plant for modern steam-powered iron warships.

An infantryman equipped in the style devised by Takashima Shuhan.
Illustration by Sascha Lunyakov

Bakumatsu period military headgear

1-4: Variants of the *bajo-jingasa* which was flat and round, probably derived from the contemporary bowler hat. It was popular with mounted samurai and officers. A lacquered wooden bowl protected the wearer´s skull. It also sported a visor and provided increased protection for the neck.

5: *Tonkyo* helmet designed by Takashima Shuhan c. 1840 to facilitate operating in close formation.

6: *Eboshi* cap made from stiffened black gossamer. Typical for court dress, but also worn in more relaxed circumstances and under samurai helmets.

7: A simple helmet topped with dyed yak hair, popular with the wild shishi and later by officers especially in Western domains. Tosa used red yak hair, Choshu white, and Satsuma black.

8: An *ichimonji-jingasa* hat. Wide-brimmed and elegant, it was preferred by samurai on their journeys.

9: Classic samurai hairstyle, sometimes with shaved forehead as in fig. 14. The man´s long black hair is tied and fixed atop his skull. Handkerchiefs (*tenugui*) were worn wrapped around the head in various styles.

10-11: The classic cone-shaped, Ashigaru-style *jingasa* was still worn by some troops including Shogunate infantrymen, although often with a brim reduced in size which made handling a musket or a rifle easier. Satsuma forces were easily recognizable by their tapered version of the classic *jingasa* which was made from lacquered iron and came with a red *agemaki* decorative knot at the back.

12-13: Nirayama-style hats. These hats were among the most popular styles of headgear during the Boshin War. The were made from lacquered wicker and often painted with coats of arms, lines, or other patterns.

14: As samurai helmets proved ineffective against modern firearms, they were now often replaced by forehead, and sometimes cheek, protectors made from one or several pieces of very solid steel.

Illustrations by Sascha Lunyakov.

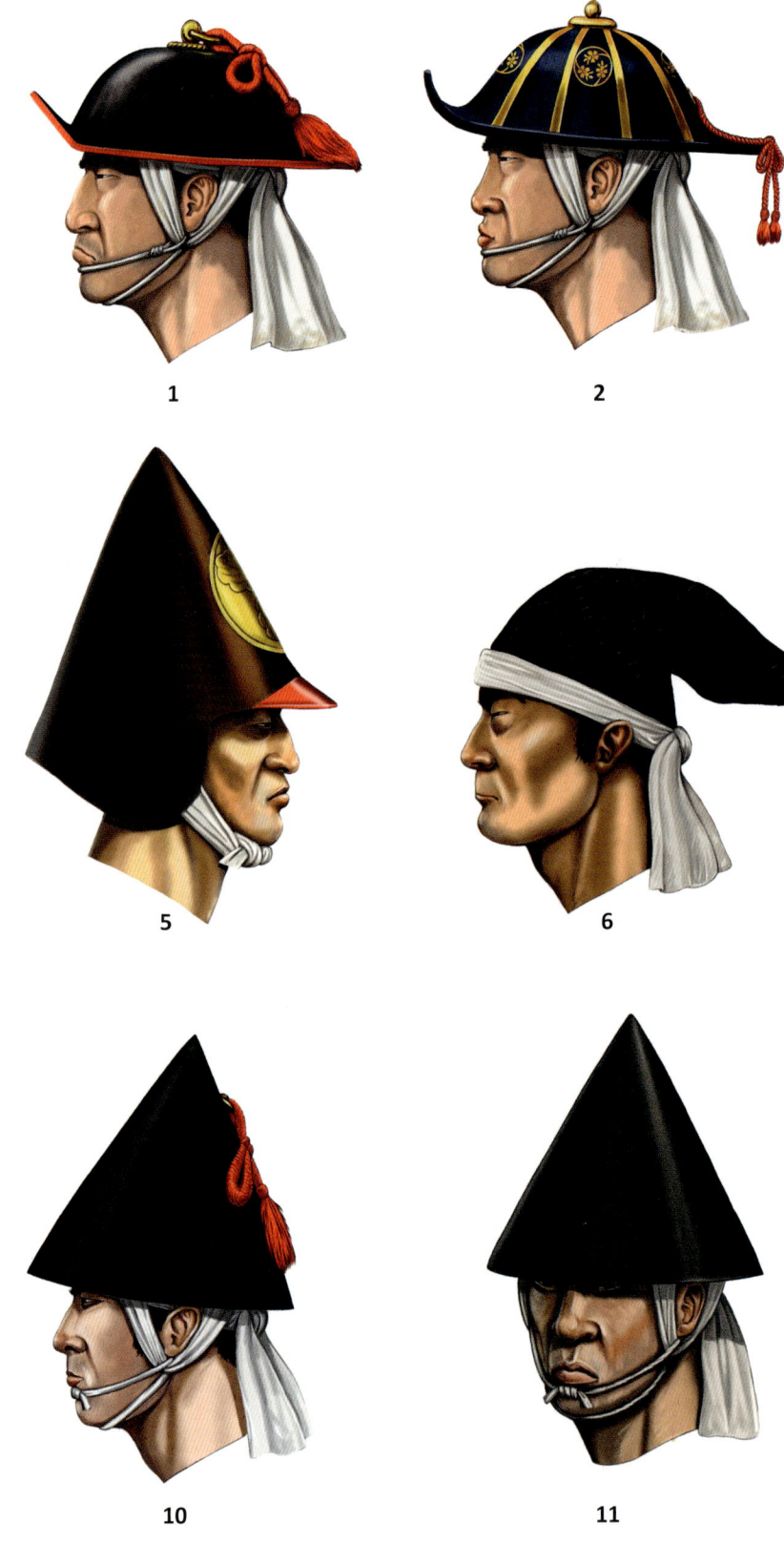

Unknown artist's impression of various troops of the Bakumatsu period now in the Colonel Bihin collection in Brussels. The samurai at top wear the ivy-leaf blazon of the Todo clan on the backs of their modern-style jackets. The Todo were lords of Tsu. One of the three soldiers of the Shogunate army conversing below is on fire watch duty but enjoys a puff from his Japanese pipe anyway! Note the bonnet-style headgear and the rich attire of the officer pictured at left. (Courtesy of Alfred Umhey, Lampertheim)

The first two attempts by the Shogunate to equip its newly raised infantry with modern uniforms. Garments are natural cotton colour or dyed in various shades of indigo. The patterns on the breeches served as unit distinctions. Sketch by an unknown artist after original garments in the collection of the Imperial Japanese War Museum at Tokyo, which existed until 1945. Now in the Colonel Bihin collection, Brussels. (Courtesy of Alfred Umhey, Lampertheim)

Tentative steps towards rearmament

The shock of Perry's expedition sparked first attempts at technological, administrative, and political reform of the delicate and complex structure which called itself the Japanese state. In 1855 a naval academy (*kaigun denshujo*) was founded with Dutch help at Nagasaki, as well as the famous war academy for Tokugawa vassals at Edo-Tsukiji (*kobusho*), where the employment of firearms was taught according to Takashima Shuhan's ideas. But the Shogunate's reforms remained haphazard and hesitant. The Japanese state and those who ran it were too deeply immersed in ancient tradition for measures to be more than half-hearted. Of course, many established samurai, who for all their lives had practised nothing but archery and swordsmanship, were aware that something was looming on the horizon which was apt to threaten their social privilege.

Since the 1840s, rifles with percussion caps had replaced those with the older flintlock mechanism in European armies. On Egawa's advice the Shogunate decided to produce these modern firearms, known by their Dutch name of *geweer*, at the Yushima arsenal. A total of 10, 000 was envisaged in 1855, of which a mere 8, 000 had been manufactured by 1861. The Japanese muskets were modelled on the Dutch 1845 model, which fired a calibre of 8 *monme* (1 *monme* = 3,75 g).

Unfortunately, even those muskets which had been produced were quickly becoming outdated in the face of new rifle technology. Springfield in the US and Enfield in the United Kingdom were now producing rifles which fired the latest Minié ammunition. These weapons were so powerful that they rendered Napoleonic mass tactics obsolete. Until the eve of the Boshin War Japanese arsenals were incapable of producing such weapons so that foreign imports once again became the key source. The military conflicts after 1866 clearly demonstrated the differences these new weapons had already made on the battlefields of the American Civil War. Instead of firing concentrated salvoes at massed bodies of troops at a range of 50 to 100 metres, the new generation of Enfield/Springfield/Minié rifles now permitted soldiers to engage the enemy already at a range of 200 or even 300 metres. This forced infantry to operate in loose formations and to fire from cover. Artillery also improved, while the role of cavalry steadily declined.

The political instability of the Shogunate itself eventually ruined all attempts at effective reform. This was due to the inadequacies of the men holding the office at a time when it would have required headstrong rulers to run the country, and the frequent change of the "strong men" heading the Shogun's government on his behalf. One exception was the rapid establishment of modern coastal batteries, which had been assigned to the local rulers as part of their feudal obligations in the wake of the Perry shock. These new batteries were gradually equipped with modern guns but were still no match for Western warships as battles at Kagoshima in 1863 and Shimonoseki in 1864 proved.

In 1862 conditions in the Shogunate improved to an extent that enabled a commission to draw up a plan which had realistic chances of success. It did not however recommend measures which would have brought about a radical breach in tradition, for instance the establishment of national armed forces (*zengoku osonae*). Military matters remained the prerogative of the nobility, of which the Tokugawa clan was still the most powerful by far. Instead, the feudal levy supplied by the Shogun's direct vassals was transformed into a Shogunal Guard (*shin'ei*). This guard was to comprise no less than altogether 12, 000 fighters divided into infantry, cavalry, and artillery.

The five *go-bankata* units, the core of the old standing army, were well-to-do Tokugawa vassals from the ranks of their samurai retainers, the *hatamoto* and *gokenin*. Many served on horseback, equipped with the traditional samurai panoply and arms. The commission had the good sense to ignore these old diehards and concentrated instead on the 3, 000 footsoldiers armed with *teppo* arquebuses, bows and lances. These were supplemented by recruits from the inactive reserves, the Hachioji and later also the Yokohama guards, and the samurai's retainers and servants (*hokonin*). In order to exploit new sources for recruitment independent of the traditional-minded noble élite, a five-year military service for members of the peasantry was introduced. These men, who were deemed easier to influence in favour of military reform than their masters, were to be chosen by the top vassals from the farmers working on their local estates. The samurai were required to pay for these men's rations and wages, while the Shogun undertook to equip and accomodate them. In 1863 these soldiers formed four infantry regiments each numbering 800 men, which were trained and stationed in barracks on the premises of Edo castle. Although it took a fair amount of time to turn these raw recruits into soldiers, these modern infantry represented the first military men raised by the Shogunate outside the samurai class after a period of 250 years. This was a feat nothing short of the sensational. One of the most important privileges of the samurai, exclusive military service, had fallen once and for all. The peasants and retainers were easier to form according to the new military concept, something that could certainly not be said of the samurai, who continued to resent the newly introduced Western military ranks and the British and Dutch military manuals which had come to replace the teachings of the Takashima academy. Even the duty roster at the Edo barracks, which followed the Western 24-hour system instead of observing the traditional Japanese system of twelve hours of varying length, met with disapproval.

The new non-samurai troops held the right to carry a sword as a sign of their improved social status (in real life, it was often a bayonet). They received their baptism of fire when they were called in to support the traditional and more prestigious samurai guard units in the suppression of the so-called Tengu revolt, a rising of xenophobic samurai (*shishi*) claiming to do the Emperor´s will, in the Mito domain 120 km to the north-east of Edo. Although the Shogunate troops greatly outnumbered the rebels, the fighting lasted for several months. The Shogun´s soldiers were defeated several times, but even in retreat the new troops proved to be more steadfast and better organized than the samurai of the guard, who in the course of time had obviously forgotten how to fight. In some situations, the infantry gave a decent account of themselves, and they learned from their mistakes. Nevertheless, there was criticism: they could not distinguish between long and short range, and pointlessly fired empty muskets. At the same time, they lack the skills to construct breastworks. They do not move with alacrity, and miss opportunities. Furthermore, because they do not evaluate the ground, they suffer from unexpected enemies." (Jaundrill 2016: 56)

Most of the problems addressed above reveal that the officers were still poorly trained, and that there was a lack of experienced NCOs. Attempts to solve these drawbacks were made by employing foreign military advisors and instructors. While the British remained unresponsive, the French stepped up to help in 1866. Help proved more than necessary, because in 1866 the Shogunate, supported by no less than 21 domains, disgraced itself utterly by failing to defeat the rebellious princedom of Choshu in 1866 despite its superiority of more than ten to one.[1]

The Shogun makes a clean sweep – the new army

In the summer of 1866, the first immediate measures were taken at Osaka, where the Shogunate permanently kept a large number of samurai under arms. Five new battalions on foot were raised, which were referred to as *yugekitai* (not to be confused with a unit of identical name at Choshu). The soldiers came from various smaller units which had been disbanded, some were minor samurai, others were *ronin*. All were equipped with modern firearms, and a rapid training programme was implemented. The *yugekitai* corps remained in existence until after the Battle of Toba-Fushimi, even though it did not greatly impress a British observer in 1868.[2] At any rate the Shogun gave orders for all his samurai to be equipped with rifles henceforth, and nominally being the Emperor´s military commander-in-chief, he also issued the same decree to all daimyo. Some complied, while others ignored the order, often simply because they lacked the means.

***Hohei* infantry unit numbers,** painted in red or yellow on black helmets and ammunition pouches. The units were named according to the location of their billets either in Edo castle or its surroundings: **1**. *Nishimaru-shita*, **2**. *Ote(mon)-mae*, **3**. *Sanban-cho*, **4**. *Ogawa-cho*.

These were only first steps. In January 1867 a group of French officers and NCOs arrived at Edo commanded by Capitaine Charles Chanoine.[3] Nearly all members of the delegation were veterans of the French campaigns in Mexico and China. They quickly drew up suggestions for the creation of a modern army based on the French model and immediately began to put their ideas into practice.

The most modern military unit in Japan, the *Denshutai*, were raised and trained by military scholar Otori Keisuke (1833–1911). These soldiers were armed with the new Enfield rifles, which fired Minié projectiles. The language of command was French. Their navy-blue uniforms with the white stripes that ran down sleeves and trouser seams decidedly resembled the design of the track suits produced by a well-known German sportswear company in the 1970s and 1980s.

Civil war was now brewing. In view of this threat, the Shogunate could not afford to be picky in its choice of recruits. Gamblers, thugs, gangsters, porters, grooms, and men from the lowly citizens´ fire brigades were all accepted into the ranks. Officers´ commissions, however, were only granted to Tokugawa samurai. It was only they to whom the Shogun appealed to undergo officers´ training at the military academy. But in 1867, fighting for the Shogun was beginning to be considered rather a liability than an asset by many.

All these new developments were late in coming. By December 1867, when the Denshutai was sent to western Japan to later take part in the Battle of Toba-Fushimi, only two battalions, a small artillery unit, and a squadron of rather French-looking cavalry had been raised. This force numbered altogether 1, 400 soldiers. However, these troops proved remarkably efficient, and only a few later changed sides. 1, 100 men fought on after Tokugawa Yoshinobu had surrendered, and some followed their commander Otori Keisuke to Hokkaido, where they continued to resist until 1869.[4]

In the years 1866 and 1867, it dawned on the Shogun that he would need a far greater amount of troops to

---

1 cf. *"The second punitive campaign against Choshu in 1866"*, p. 106

2 cf. *"'In this sign, conquer!' – the Battle of Toba-Fushimi (3rd – 6th January 1868"*, p. 111

3 cf. *"Jules Brunet, true 'Last Samurai'"*, p. 157

4 cf. *"Jules Brunet, true 'Last Samurai'"*, p. 157

Denshutai **troops of the Tokugawa infantry standing guard outside the British legation at Osaka, winter of 1867.** Short overcoats and balaclava-type hoods are worn to counteract the cold. Note the trumpeter and the drummer boy. The officer on the right has chosen to dress rather differently than his subordinates (Illustrated London News).

reestablish his own supremacy. The decision to scrap the feudal levy was finally made, but it came late. For years, as had become evident by 1866, this principle had merely created largely unmotivated and incapable samurai units of very limited military value. In future it was decided to rely forthwith only on taxpayers and soldiers from outside the samurai caste to maintain the armed forces. This move was a founding stone of the modern Japanese army. It failed to benefit the toppling Tokugawa but was to provide a firm basis for the new Meiji government.

Time was running out for the Tokugawa. Hastily raised platoons and companies of riflemen (*kumiai jutai*) numbering between 25 and 75 soldiers each were led by wealthy Tokugawa samurai whose income was 3, 000 *koku* or more. These units were now organised into battalions. Because the samurai and the rural population remained unenthusiastic, the ranks were filled with hired *ronin* and the inhabitants of the cheap mass accomodations which were a feature of Edo city life. The Shogun´s vassals serving as officers were worlds apart from their subordinates in social terms, and most were completely ignorant of contemporary military affairs. In October 1867, the experiment was ditched, and the units disbanded. The most useful men were transferred to other infantry units.

Vassals with a larger tenure were now taxed. Samurai serving in guard units (*go-bankata*) were literally forced to come off their high horse and dismount. They were given the option to either train as officers or serve as privates in the *okuzume jutai* infantry units. They grudgingly acknowledged that at least they were able to stay among themselves – since samurai resented being ordered about by someone socially inferior to themselves regardless of their military expertise, the military authorities took care to raise units composed of social equals. Samurai with a middle-sized income joined the *yugekitai*, the *yoriki* caste below were assigned to the *jutai*, while the *doshin* (the Tokugawa word for the old *ashigaru* foot soldiers) joined either the artillery or the *sappei-gumi*. The latter are best referred to as artillery guards, being infantrymen whose duty it was to protect the gunners and their pieces in battle, and to provide transport. Thus, the artillery was given its own infantry units, a most unusual measure at the time. Later the attempt was made to organize these troops along the same lines as the regular infantry but tribal mentality prevented such an improvement. Ironically, the battalions of regular foot soldiers (*hohei*) which had proved their worth in 1866 were lowest on the social scale, even though their military value was probably the highest in the army.[5]

These infantrymen, who were not members of the samurai caste, formed the backbone of the new Shogunate army. They were organized into companies of 50 men, ten of which formed a battalion. Battalions were trained to operate in half-battalions so that one could relieve each other in the firing line. Nearly all officers were now trained at Edo's military academy and were promoted according to personal merit not social rank. The two French-trained *Denshutai* infantry battalions were the élite corps of the *hohei* in 1867/68.

The level of command was also reorganized, but the result was not a happy one. The seeds for the perpetual competition between army and navy was sown, which until 1945 would lead to interminable bickering over resources and influence.

Command structure under the Tokugawa (after Totman 1980: 285)

	Army	Navy
High command	*rikugun sosai* (Army Minister)	*kaigun sosai* (Navy Minister)
Generals/Admirals	*rikugun bugyo, rikugun bugyo-nami* (commander-in-chief and second-in-command)	*kaigun-bugyo, kaigun bugyo-nami* (supreme naval commander and second-in-command)
Colonels/Commodores	*rikugun* and *rikugun bugyo-nami* as regimental commanders	*rikugun* and *rikugun bugyo-nami* commanding naval squadrons of several ships
Lieutenant-colonels and Majors/Captains	*kashira* (battalion commanders)	*kashira* (ships' captains)

In the provinces, peasant militia were raised to counteract local unrest. Regular Tokugawa troops, whose garrisons were concentrated in a few larger towns, were only supposed to deal with major military conflicts. It is believed that at the end of 1867, prior to the outbreak of the Boshin War, around 24, 000 soldiers served in the Tokugawa army. They were organized into 48 battalions, or units of similar composition (Hoya 2020: 158). Many were stationed in Edo and Osaka, the Tokugawa stronghold in the West; others patrolled the streets of Kyoto and guarded the port of Nagasaki.

When viewed as an individual force, the Tokugawa army in early 1868 was easily the largest of its kind in all Japan. It was however burdened with several serious problems: while manpower was not one of them, obsolete rifles and artillery pieces, the inexperience of its commanders, and the short amount of time in which the new army had been raised were all to prove serious shortcomings.

The military reforms had ushered in the end to the old feudal system of daimyo and their samurai. Taxes levied by a Shogunal bureaucracy now paid for a new army whose core was composed of professional soldiers of lowly provenance. At the end of 1867, the eve of its ultimate downfall, the Shogunate had shown itself capable of reform. Unfortunately, the new army lacked the training and experience to make it a truly effective fighting force. All the Shogun could hope for was that his army would crush the rebellious Satsuma and Choshu with its superior numbers.

---

5   cf. "The second punitive campaign against Choshu in 1866", p. 106

Tokugawa infantry on parade in 1867.
The private *mon* of a Tokugawa samurai emblazoned on his platoon´s standard indicates that the unit concerned is part of the experimental infantry companies (*kumiai jutai*) which were disbanded in October of the same year. The soldiers are uniformly well-equipped. Officers and NCOs are shown wearing jackets of hybrid Japanese-Western fashion with family crests on their backs. *Bajo* hats are worn by officers, *nirayama* hats by NCOs. All carry their pair of samurai swords. The image rather depicts the ideal than actual reality – equipment, training and discipline were still fairly deficient at the time (woodblock print by Utagawa Yoshifuji, public domain).

Corps of Drums of a musketeer unit from the same woodcut.

In imitation of contemporary Western armies, the Japanese introduced colourfully uniformed military bandsmen. Already while training with Dutch instructors at Deshima, it became apparent that recruits liked the beating of military drums the best. In the 1870s however, the drum was replaced by the trumpet or bugle as the most important signalling instrument. This was in keeping with the French practice of using the *clairon* to transmit orders acoustically.

The French military mission photographed by Emile Gsell (1838-1879) prior to its departure for Japan in 1867. The mission´s head, Captain Charles Chanoine is standing upright in the centre. Lieutenant, later Captain Jules Brunet is seated second from the right in the front row. Brunet was to become the "true last samurai", see p. 156. (Wiki)

Denshutai **infantryman, 1867/68.**

This soldier from one of the Shogun´s best infantry units is armed with a brand-new French Chassepot rifle. Nevertheless, he seems to comtemplate whether he should use the proper bayonet that came with the rifle or rather trust in his traditional *katana*-style sword. Illustration by Sascha Lunyakov.

THE ANTAGONISTS – SATSUMA AND CHOSHU

Satsuma

For a time, developments in Satsuma, a princedom on the southern main island of Kyushu, were no different from those at the remote headquarters of the Shogun at Edo. Things took a turn when in 1837 an American merchant ship dropped anchor in Kagoshima Bay in the naive hope of persuading the Japanese to commence commercial relationships. Kagoshima was the seat of the daimyo of Satsuma. His coastal defence consisted of artillery pieces outdated by 200 years, which were unable to score even a single hit on the American vessel. Unnerved by this poor showing, Satsuma followed the Shogun's example and turned its attention to the new Dutch firearms and the ideas of the Takashima school. Daimyos Shimazu Narioki (r. 1809–1851) and Shimazu Nariakira (r. 1851–1858), the latter a charismatic reformer, tried to include their entire samurai population. Satsuma was unusual in that its population was particularly numerous with the samurai forming a larger proportion than anywhere else in Japan – while in other parts of the country samurai formed between 6 and 7% of the populace, they made up no less than 25% of Satsuma's population. There was hardly enough arable land for the local peasants to feed an extra quarter of the overall population. While around 3, 500 adult male samurai and their families led well-to-do lives in fortified towns, the remaining 35, 000 men and their families lived in rural communities. These samurai were mostly quite poor and required to grow part of their own food. The small livelihood of the family of the great Satsuma general Saigo Takamori (1828–1877)[6] is a fine example of such marginal forms of existence. It is not surprising that the great Satsuma reformers, generals, and statesmen nearly all stemmed from these lower castes – the new ideas which had begun to take shape offered them prospects unheard of in a country virtually paralysed by hereditary privilege and feudal convention.

Another aspect which gave Satsuma armies an edge over their Tokugawa enemies was simply the large number of samurai, which made the recruitment of peasants obsolete. Recruits had already received some form of basic military training because they were rural samurai, they were used to living ascetic lives and considered fighting for their lords the very essence of their existence.

Satsuma reformers abolished local military doctrine, which hailed back to the 16th century tactics of the great Takeda Shingen. They attempted to include all rural samurai, thus taking reforms a step further than the Tokugawa had done. The samurai of the castle town of Kagoshima were organized into two battalions of musketeers consisting of altogether 18 platoons or 48-man companies. The artillery too was reformed, and together with British engineers Lord Shimazu Nariakira laid the foundations for a heavy industry which could produce the heavy barrels required for the artillery which was later to prove the showpiece of Satsuma armies. Dutch residents of Nagasaki were asked to translate French cavalry manuals into their own language, which in turn was translated into Japanese.

Although the establishment of the new cavalry arm ostentatiously offered a face-saving compromise to high-ranking conservative Satsuma samurai, reactionaries struck back after Nariakira's death in 1858 (possibly by poison) – all military reforms were stopped. Some measures were even revoked – bayonets were withdrawn and replaced with traditional swords; the central military academy was turned into a fencing school, and thousands of imported muskets were sold to other domains. Even 16th century military doctrine was reintroduced. In the early 1860s the idea of Satsuma's military power being capable of catching up with and finally overthrowing the mighty Shogunate would have been inconceivable.

Once again it was foreign ships which eventually brought about change in Satsuma. Conflict with Britain caused the bombardment of Kagoshima in 1863 by seven British ironclads, which literally pulverized three Japanese vessels and part of the city. The ten coastal batteries consisting of altogether 83 guns were operated by the artillery instructors which had previously been ostracized, and they succeeded in inflicting at least a token amount of damage on the British ships. It was realized that the defeat had not been caused by the reformers who had heretofore been so unpopular; on the contrary, the proud samurai had been forced to look on helplessly as the British ships laid their city in ruins. Even the most skilful warrior was powerless with sword and lance when it came to taking on an enemy armed with modern artillery. Everybody finally understood that for an ambitious political entity like Satsuma the only choice was either to modernize or perish. In the next three years the entire army was transformed into rifle-armed infantry. The rural samurai were the first to give up their old military life. The feudal cavalry was abolished. On the eve of the Boshin War, Satsuma had 3, 000 fully trained infantrymen under arms and was able to maintain a constant flow of reinforcements to units in the field, while back at home new recruits were constantly being trained. A navy, whose function was mainly to provide the necessary logistics for the land forces, was created, and several field artillery units were also raised. The soldiers' appearance also changed profoundly: Satsuma infantry and artillerymen were clad in austere uniforms of very dark blue cotton. They were easily recognisable by a narrow white brassard on their right upper arm and their distinctive high conical helmet adorned with a red *agemaki* (a

---

6 cf. *"Katsu Kaishu and Saigo Takamori"*, p. 153

Detail of a Satsuma battery at the Battle of Toba-Fushimi in January 1868. Uniforms a were identical for both infantry and artillery. They were made from dark blue cotton and sported a white band around the right upper arm for ease of recognition. The other Satsuma mark was the tall conical helmet with a red knot at the back. Since all Satsuma soldiers were born as samurai, they brought their own swords, whereas firearms and equipment were partly provided by the domain. (*Nishiki no mihata* 1907, plate XII)

knotted silk rope) at the back. Satsuma officers probably followed the example of their British colleagues in being allowed a great deal more freedom in their choice of dress. Some, like Saigo Takamori, wore uniforms similar to those of the men with a silken *jimbaori* (war surcoat) inofficially marking rank. More flamboyant individuals preferred high-topped boots, frock coats, winged collars, and lumberjack shirts. But for their revolvers and swords such officers would have resembled civilians in slightly unorthodox garb.

The massive expenses caused by the army reforms were met by Satsuma no longer asking its samurai vassals to turn out men according to individual wealth but to finance weapons instead. Simple country samurai had to pay for their own rifles if possible, more affluent vassals had to supply equipment for three fully equipped men, while the wealthiest had to purchase an artillery piece. Because samurai were required to provide their own weapons, their professional pride required them to operate and take care of them to the best of their abilities. Instructors travelled overland preparing the young rural samurai for their call-up. Any leftover anti-British resentment was duly swallowed, and relationships were improved. The Satsuma purchased British ships, Armstrong guns, and Enfield rifles, and British military drill was adopted in place of the Dutch. This enabled the Japanese to adopt the loose formations and skirmishing tactics which were more suitable to Japanese topograhy than the rigid battalion masses still favoured by many contemporary European armies.

In the case of Satsuma, a sensible-acting political leadership after a violent shock brought about from outside induced military reforms which due to their truly revolutionary nature outclassed those of its Tokugawa enemies. It created, indeed, an army which together with the troops of its Choshu allies was to prove the mose effective of the ensuing Boshin War. The peculiar social structure of the Satsuma state with its many rural samurai was able to provide a large pool of trained, military-minded men from which could be drawn highly motivated and hardy recruits. In number, Satsuma´s army exceeded that of Choshu. It stood out from other contemporary Japanese armies in that it was equipped throughout with Armstrong cannon and Enfield rifles, arms which were superior to those employed by most opponents. The muzzle-loading Enfield rifles were only capable of firing two rounds per minute, but repeating rifles were yet rare even in the Choshu army and would have caused a potentially harmful lack of uniformity. The Satsuma army´s main drawback was its structure: in contrast to its Choshu allies, the Satsuma army was not organised into battalions or half-battalions but relied on independent companies usually numbering around 90 soldiers each. This allowed for tactical flexibility but limited large-scale coordinated action on the battlefield.

One of the main differences between Japanese and European military doctrine in the 1860s was that in Japanese armies any form of military organisation beyond regimental and battalion level was non-existent. There were neither brigades, nor divisions, or corps. In spite of all modernisation here the old samurai obsession with individuality prevailed; more importantly, after such a brief period of furious reforming, there were as yet no experienced staff officers who would have been able to wield such a sophisticated weapon effectively.

Choshu

In contrast to its rival and future ally Satsuma, the princedom of Choshu with its two provinces in the west of the Japanese main island of Honshu, Nagato and Suo, made no pretence of its heart-felt enmity towards the Shogunate. The Imperial capital of Kyoto provided the stage for the conflict which occasionally flared into open fighting. Here the Choshu battled the Tokugawa and their Aizu and Satsuma allies for influence at the Emperor´s court.[7]

A samurai from Yonezawa[8] described the nature of the Choshu troops on the eve of modernization. Here is his account of one of the confrontations in the streets of Kyoto, written in 1863:

"The two lines were facing each other, poised with rifles and cannon [...] Squads were formed, the lines were drawn, both sides wore armor, and hiding themselves in readiness, each glared at the other [...] Choshu did not falter in the least [...] Among the Choshu forces were youths of fifteen or sixteen wearing headbands of white silk and carrying Western rifles; their eyes betrayed no fear of the huge armny confronting them." (Craig 1961: 207).

We are presented with the picture of a force of samurai which despite their ancient armour was at least in part equipped with modern firearms and determined to get to grips with the enemy regardless of their strength.

In 1864 fighting at Kyoto broke out once more, and Choshu was soundly beaten.[9] In Choshu reformers, moderates and traditionalists had held power in rapid succession, and military reforms had been slow and hesitant in coming. The most modern weapons were the five 20cm Dahlgren guns, a gift from the Americans which now served to secure the strategically vital Shimonoseki straits between Honshu and Kyushu.

Like Satsuma, the Mori daimyo of Choshu commanded a large number of samurai. There were altogether 5, 675 samurai families divided into 18 social sub-ranks from the blood relations of the Mori (six families) to the simple *ashigaru* and their batsmen (2, 598) (Craig 1961: 261). Of altogether 47, 000 members of Choshu´s samurai caste, 12, 000 carried arms. This number however was only valid on paper – many high-ranking samurai had long since turned their backs on the art of war. Class-consciousness and outright snobbery had produced a pronounced contempt for firearms since these were commonly associated with the lowly *ashigaru* caste whose members were armed with the classic *teppo* arquebus. Many samurai considered themselves above such menial tasks as arms drill and fighting in formation. Most were unwilling to give up their traditional form of armament, or their loyal sub-retainers. So where would the authorities find the manpower necessary to raise the new infantry which the princedom so urgently needed?

Choshu eventually possessed the wisdom to establish a new kind of of military organisation without immediately stripping the traditionalists of their time-honoured privileges. Instead, the new infantry units were raised from volunteers mostly from outside the groups traditionally called upon to provide the *daimyo´s* armed forces. One new group were the various locally based peasant militia (*noheitai*), whose soldiers only served part-time. The other group, the *shotai*, consisted of standing units of full-time soldiers. Takasugi Shinsaku, a middle-ranking samurai, is credited with being the father of this new basic military structure. Alluding to Sun Tzu, he wrote: "What we want is to organize [a unit] that will penetrate the gaps in the enemy masses, harassing them by disappearing and reappearing as if by magic. Because they will

---

7   cf. "The second punitive campaign against Choshu in 1866", p. 106

8   cf. "Firearms – from matchlock to Gatling Gun", p. 37

9   cf. "Shishi – men of high ideals, or unmitigated lunatics?", p. 75

use unorthodox methods to secure victory, they will be called the Irregulars (*kiheitai*)." (Jaundrill 2016: 61). The word *kiheitai* translates as "irregular troops" or "militia". Underprivileged samurai discontent with their position in Japan's inflexible class system proved willing recruits. In Choshu lived 1, 300 of these poor samurai whom high living costs in the castle towns had forced to move to the countryside. However, Choshu's militia, commonly referred to as *shotai*, were also open to non-samurai such as peasants, townspeople, and clerics. Only half of the 292 men of the famous First Kiheitai consisted of samurai. In the Second Kiheitai, only 25% of the 137 men were samurai. In the Yochotai, another prominent *shotai*, a mere 33% of the 227 soldiers belonged to the samurai caste.

These samurai however managed to infest the militia with their radical ideas. Their watchword was *Sonno joi* ("Honour the Emperor, drive out the barbarians!"), and they pushed Choshu into a number of military confrontations with the Western powers which they certainly had not wanted, let alone permitted. Two of these rash undertakings ended in utter defeat at Shimonoseki Straits in 1863/64, when Western battleships destroyed the local coastal batteries and landing parties routed the samurai sent against them. These disasters prompted the radicals to reconsider their aims and change their slogan to *Kinno tobaku*, meaning "Loyalty to the Emperor, and down with the Shogun!" It was now clear that for better or worse, the Western powers had to be put up with.

The *shotai* also differed from regular Choshu units in the fanciful names conceived by their commanders. These names were supposed to reflect the unit's character. The 500-strong *yugekitai* ("independent unit", not to be confused with the identically named Shogunate units) comprised sub-units called *Vajra* or alternatively *kongotai* (composed of Buddhist monks), the *shintai* "Divine force" platoon (Shintoist priests), the *sogekitai* sharpshooters (composed of hunters), and the "Brave wrestlers"; needles to say, the soldiers serving in this unit were Sumo wrestlers. This new military system thus succeeded in integrating men from the fringes of Japanese society into its armed forces, but this method also caused friction with the men of the *senpotai* ("advance guard") unit, which consisted of the long-established samurai who represented Choshu's conservative military élite.

Most militia did not wear uniform, and at first each man brought with him the Western firearm he wished to fight with. However, Choshu made up for this outward lack of uniformity with strict discipline. A system of ranks modelled on Western armies was introduced, the hierarchy featuring both officers' and NCOs' ranks: *sokan, gunkan, shoki, sekko, taicho,* and *oshigo*. After 1863, there were even three companies of social outcasts named *toyu* ("Brave butchers"), named after one of the few professions open to these outsiders. Being soldiers, it was no longer permitted to refer to them as *eta* (unclean). They were allowed to carry a single sword and wear a *dofuku* war jerkin, but they received black uniforms to set them apart from the blue uniforms and private attire worn by other units. As it was customary for lower castes, they were not permitted to acquire family names. The arm insignia (*sode-jirushi*) which were introduced for the *shotai* after 1864 also served to denote social rank. The patch displayed a soldier's name and unit; those who lacked family names were not permitted to write down even their first names. Higher-ranking samurai sported patches of white silk; all others made do with bleached cotton. Even military discipline was administered according to the offender's social rank: samurai were punished more severely than non-samurai soldiers.

Twice, in 1864 and 1866, the Shogunate tried to bring rebellious Choshu to heel.[10] In 1864 Choshu was saved by both the Shogunate army's unwillingness to fight, and the insight of a Satsuma staff officer named Saigo Takamori. Saigo understood that Choshu's defeat would only benefit the Shogunate, but certainly not his own princedom of Satsuma. Choshu's punishment was comparatively lenient, but it was ordered to disband all *shotai* militia except the traditionalist *senpotai*. Takasugi Shinsaku and his fellow reformers refused to accept this and in 1865 after a brief civil war forced the ruling élite in the capital of Hagi to resign. Now the *shotai* commanders themselves took over, and their militia served as a model for the radical measures undertaken to reform the regular clan army. The first units to be remodelled were those of the 3, 000 *ashigaru*, who were already familiar with discipline, firearms, and fighting in close formation. At the beginning of the Boshin War in 1868, Choshu had at its disposal the most experienced and efficient troops in Japan, by far outclassing the Shogun's army.

Little by little, the feudal samurai units were transformed into rifle companies despite a lack of modern firearms. The troops could not be uniformly armed due to Choshu's official outlaw status. It was not allowed to purchase rifles at Nagasaki but former rival Satsuma eventually proved to be a benevolent intermediary that was prepared to help. This discreet support was the first step towards the so-called Satcho alliance between Satsuma and Choshu. With Satsuma's help, Choshu managed to buy a modern warship and 7, 300 rifles. 4, 000 of them were modern Miniés which cost a combined 77, 400 *ryo* (gold coins). The remaining 3, 000 guns were conventional muskets of the older type which cost 15, 000 *ryo*. Sakamoto Ryoma, a high-ranking observer originally from Tosa, commented on Choshu's activities: "Choshu is putting everything into the training of its troops. Since April they have been drilling from around six to ten every morning. It's the same all over Choshu. Each of their battalions is made up of between three and four

---

10 cf. "The second punitive campaign against Choshu in 1866", p. 106

A photograph showing members of the Choshu *Kiheitai* in 1864 or 1865. Privately acquired Western dress and firearms probably mark these men as officers. They carry no muskets, which at the time were also mostly privately owned, resulting in a large variety within units. The men have retained their traditional swords. Takasugi Shinsaku is pictured seated wearing a white scarf and holding a riding crop. Not all of his comrades have yet parted with their *chonmage* hairknots, traditional symbol of the samurai caste. (public domain)

Choshu troops during a lull in the fighting at Toba-Fushimi, January 1868.
These soldiers, who are either regulars or militiamen, are clothed very uniformly in a close-fitting dark blue cotton uniforms, but wear *tabi* socks and *warabi* straw sandals on their feet. Their allegiance is recognizable by the single white line around their lower arm sleeves. Headdress consists of simple *nirayama* hats worn over cotton headbands. The *katana* sword is worn suspended from the belt in a leather frog, which was becoming common practice at the time. The traditional way of carrying the sword tucked under the *obi* belt did not go well with Western-style military garb, even though some continued to wear their sidearms in this manner. These men are lucky enough to also be equipped with bayonets, which were were by no means available for all. (*Nishiko no mihata* 1907: plate X)

Choshu militiaman.
This man probably provides a more authentic impression of ordinary campaign dress than the neat and uniformly-equipped soldiers depicted in the *Nishiki no mihata* (see opposite page). A sufficient supply of modern arms and ammunition was clearly more important than high levels of standardized military dress and equipment. The depicted militiaman wears privately purchased Western dress consisting of a jacket, waistcoat, and trousers. The golden buttons betray a certain individual wealth. The checkered shirt is of non-Japanese manufacture and has been imported from abroad. The man is armed with a Spencer repeating rifle whose distinctive black leather-covered ammunition box he carries with him. The Spencer repeater, which possessed a high rate of fire and was accordingly pricey, only reached the troops in larger numbers well after the outbreak of hostilities. The *kingire* field sign attached to the left upper sleeve dates this figure to March 1868, or a later date. It consisted of a small strip of brocade fabric from the Kyoto workshops and became the field sign of the new Imperial army. Illustration: Sascha Lunyakov

Battery at Maeda-mura covering the Straits of Shimonoseki after capture by British sailors and marines in 1864. This shocking defeat contributed to Choshu's setting a new course.

hundred men, with a general staff officer in command. The battalions in every district and every village drill each morning. There is nothing like it anywhere else in Japan. No matter where you go in Choshu – the mountains, the rivers, the valleys – you are bound to come across fortifications; and there are land mines planted on most of the main roads. [In addition,] Choshu is certainly at the forefront of Western artillery." (Hillsborough 2011: 139). Feudal samurai were obliged to dispatch their vassals to duty while themselves no longer were required to show up for mounted service in their ancient armour surrounded by their retainers on foot. The latter were henceforth trained and commanded by *shotai* officers of the domain's army and were thus removed from their masters' influence.

All these moves were part of Choshu's attempts to ward off the Shogunate's second punitive expedition in 1866. In contrast to the campaign of 1864, this was to end in a resounding Choshu victory, and a humiliating defeat for the Tokugawa forces.[11] These years also saw the complete reequipment as well as a comprehensive reorganisation of the Choshu army. Drill regulations were also revised.

Already by the end of 1865 the *ashigaru* and military servants (grooms, drivers, craftsmen, etc.) were serving in rifle battalions numbering 400 men (*daitai*), each battalion organised into companies or sections of 40 men (*shotai*). On a tactical level, half-battalions were capable of operating as *chutai*. From mid-1866, a force of 4,500 soldiers and modern artillery were available and ready for action. While in 1866 the *shotai* militia had been forced to bear the brunt of the fighting against the Tokugawa and their allies, the Boshin War of 1868/9 saw Choshu field the most modern regular forces in all Japan. These troops were highly motivated and eager to settle the old scores of the early 1860s.

---

11   cf. "The second punitive campaign against Choshu in 1866", p. 106

FIREARMS – FROM MATCHLOCK TO GATLING GUN

The example of Yonezawa

Most samurai were still reluctant to accept the fact that by the 1850s it was no longer individual fighting spirit or swordsmanship that determined the outcome of a battle, but which side was equipped with the best firearms and the most skilled in modern infantry tactics and functioning logistics. After 1830, the development of muskets, rifles, cannon and ammunition gathered an unprecendented momentum which in the Bakumatsu era also began to affect Japan.

To understand the technological developments and transitions involved in this process, it appears worthwhile to look at the medium-sized princedom of Yonezawa with its 130, 000 inhabitants in the north of Honshu, which may serve as a typical example.

With pride the Uesugi daimyo dynasty looked back on their legendary ancestor Uesugi Kenshin (1530–1578), who had commanded one of the most powerful feudal samurai armies of the day. The recipe to produce the black powder necessary for the operation of the Japanese *teppo* arquebus had been acquired comparatively early, but only under Uesugi Kagekatsu (1556–1623) and his right-hand man Naoe Kanetsugu (1560–1620) were larger units of arquebusiers raised. After the Shogunate had decreed their removal from Echigo to Yonezawa which meant a significant drop in income, the Uesugi nevertheless decided against dismissing many of their samurai vassals. They chose instead to share the economic hardships which had arisen with their retainers rather than diminish their military power. A large number of samurai served in the military and the civilian administration, but even samurai of elevated social status were forced to take over comparatively menial duties in Yonezawa´s feudal levy. The *teppo* arquebus, formerly the preserve of the *ashigaru*, became the standard infantry weapon. Already in 1604 production facilities for *teppo* and black powder were built in the mountainous forest region north of the castle town. Later, the gunsmiths lived in their own quarter inside the town. Neither trouble nor expense was spared to come by the necessary expertise, often with the help of specialists from abroad. In fairly short time a local variant of the *teppo* was developed (*Yonezawa-zutsu*), instantly recognizable by its short, stubby barrel and curved butt. Its other peculiarity was its fairly large calibre of 10 *monme* (19 mm), while in other regions much lighter calibres of 3 or 5 *monme* were the norm. According to Uesugi retainer Amakasu Tsugushige however, these sounded "like farts" when fired. Other Yonezawa calibres included 20 (23 mm), 30 (27 mm), 50 (33 mm), 100 (40 mm) or even 200 *monme* (50 mm), the largest calibers serving as veritable hip guns or on wheels which as late as the Boshin War in 1868 caused terror among the enemy.

These weapons enabled the Uesugi to recover lost prestige in the campaigns against Osaka in 1614/15. In the two centuries that followed and despite mounting economic hardships, Yonezawa never neglected its *teppo* production, and the training of its arquebusiers was continuously kept at a high standard. Local shooting academies instructed the vassal samurai who served in the *teppo* units in the handling of their weapons. Even the prince´s mounted household troops (*o-umawari-gumi*) were not above drilling with the *teppo* and engaging in competitions with rival units. Altogether there were nine samurai arquebusier units, and several additional units of *ashigaru* armed with the *teppo*. Inspections and competitions in the presence of the prince were held at regular intervals. 2, 177 samurai alone took part in a competition in the year 1867, firing at a square target with a side length of 51.5 cm at a range of 109 metres. At 35 per cent the strike rate was surprisingly high, the marksmen armed with the lighter 10 *monme* calibre actually achieving a remarkable 45 per cent. Heavier calibres fired either with musket rests or at hip level tended to be less accurate but could be fired from a range as large as one and a half kilometres.

During the Bakumatsu period Western firearms were purchased, and from 1859 specialist units were issued with these weapons. The remaining arquebusier units were equipped with the heavier *teppo*, preferably the 30 *monme* calibre. These investments in its military power placed Yonezawa among the upper third of all Japanese domains, as became apparent during a demonstration together with forces from five different domains at the Imperial Palace at Kyoto in 1863. 450 samurai from Yonezawa fired twenty 30-*monme* arquebuses and 140 muskets of Western manufacture. The noise and powder smoke so impressed the assembled court that the Yonezawa men were obliged to fire an extra round, which was considered somewhat eccentric in view of the high cost of gunpowder. Nakayama Tadayasu, a courtier present at the time, was clearly overwhelmed by this show of military prowess. He wrote that the marksmanship of the Uesugi troops was unsurpassable. It is noteworthy that the daimyo commanded his troops in person, and his well-drilled troops had no trouble swiftly changing between loose formation and closed ranks. Both old and new firearms had been effectively integrated to form a functioning and already partly modernized Japanese provincial army.

During the Boshin War, Yonezawa formed part of the Northern Alliance which remained loyal to the Tokugawa.[12] A shipment of weapons was commissioned from the brothers Edward and Henry Schnell, who were of Prussian origin.[13] The samurai and *ashigaru* received different weapons, the value and quality of the weapons varying according to the recipients' social rank.

Type and distribution of Western firearms in Yonezawa c. 1868

Type	Country of origin	Characteristics	Issued to
Geweer	Netherlands	Muzzle-loading, smooth-bore musket; 8 *monme* calibre (17 mm)	*Ashigaru*
Sanjosen-ju	unknown	Muzzle-loading rifle, barrel with three grooves; slender projectiles	Low-ranking samurai with an income up to 3 *koku*
Gojosen-ju	France (?)	Breech-loading rifle. Barrel with five grooves. Fired innovative ammunition with increased exit velocity	Samurai with higher income
Ippatsu-motogome-ju	US or Great Britain	Single-shot breech-loader. Copper jacket bullets. Metal cartridge	Company and platoon commanders, and higher-ranking officers
Spencer repeating rifle (*shichihatsu-motgome-ju*)	US	Seven rounds; copper jacket bullets	Officers and élite independent companies (*Yonezawa no motogome-tai*)

(data gathered from Jan Petterson: *The Yonezawa Matchlock. Mighty Gun of the Uesugi Samurai*, 2017)

Some samurai purchased Western firearms privately. The small units armed with Spencer rifles decimated enemy formations on several occasions.

Despite the attempt to distribute five different types of firearm among the troops and do justice to both tactical requirements and social convention, some Yonezawa units were armed with several types of rifle, and the authorities had problems supplying the soldiers with the correct ammunition. Yet due to its large amount of experience with military firearms, Yonezawa was still comparatively well off. Other domains, especially members of the Northern Alliance, were only able to field forces whose efficiency was quite low due to the fact that no sufficient attempt had been made to standardize the troops' armament and training. And if quartermasters supplied the wrong ammunition in the middle of an engagement, the units concerned would run into serious trouble.

In the first phase of the Boshin War, which began with the Battle of Toba-Fushimi in January 1868 and lasted until the occupation of Edo by the new Imperial army in April, Yonezawa chose to remain neutral. It later joined forces with 30 other domains to form the *Ouetsu Reppan Domei* League, the Northern Alliance, and fought against the new central powers. Yonezawa dispatched more than 1,000 troops to assist Nagaoka, which controlled the port of Niigata vital for the Northern Alliance's arms supply. Nagaoka castle had been lost to Imperial troops, but together with units from Nagaoka and Aizu the Yonezawa troops succeeded in retaking it, inflicting the first defeat on Imperial troops for a long time[14]. Four small Yonezawa units armed with 30-*monme teppo* (27 mm) were instrumental in the storming of the castle. This "mobile light artillery" was often called in to deal with critical situations on the battlefield. Several accounts relate episodes of soldiers' bodies "flying through the air" when a 30-*monme* bullet found its mark. The Imperial battle line was hit at least once from a distance of more than two kilometres by balls fired from these weapons.

In 1869, a defeated Yonezawa was ordered by the new Meiji government to provide a detailed list of all its firearms. According to this inventory, both the domain's arsenals and individual samurai had at their disposal 5,950 modern (i. e. Western) firearms. 3,150 of these weapons were of the latest manufacture and capable of firing Minié projectiles. Alongside these arms there were 2,300 *teppo* of the traditional type. 1,551 were of

---

12 cf. "The Hokuetsu War in Nagaoka", p. 130, "The bloody siege of Aizu-Wakamatsu", p. 138, and "Sendai, Yonezawa and Shonai in the Boshin War", p. 142

13 cf. "The influence of foreign arms dealers", p. 48

14 cf. "The Hokuetsu War in Nagaoka", p. 130

Yonezawa arquebusiers

This rare historic photograph dating from 1906 shows the former Uesugi daimyo family's arquebusier corps (*Uesugi teppo-tai*) firing its weapons during a public display. The unit's loose formation and the samurai officer with his distinctive commander's baton are both clearly recognizable. To this day, Yonezawa celebrates its military heritage with a traditional arquebusier society. (*Uesugihon Rakuchu Rakugai Zu* - Folding screen, private collection. With kind permission of Yonezawa City Uesugi Museum)

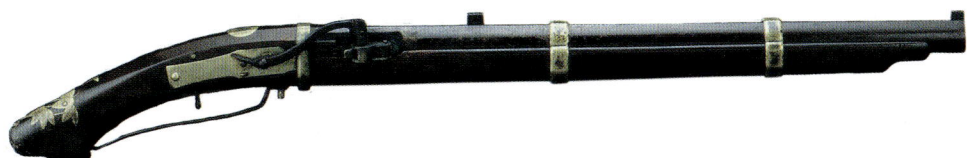

Yonezawa 10 *monme* arquebus (length: 93.8 cm; weight: 7.5 kg).

Yonezawa 20 *monme* arquebus (length: 93.2 cm; weight: 10 kg).

Yonezawa 30 *monme* arquebus (length: 94.3 cm; weight: 12.5 kg).

(Courtesy of the Miyasaka Kuokokan Collection, Yonezawa)

10-*monme*, 48 of 15-*monme*, 377 of 20-*monme*, 156 of 30-*monme*, 31 of 50-*monme*, and 52 of 100-*monme* calibre. Yonezawa also owned 18 artillery pieces, presumably twelve-pounders.

All of this constituted an impressive arsenal compared to the only 7,300 Western firearms which the far greater princedom of Choshu had managed to import in 1865. However, Choshu and its allies would achieve a much bigger and lasting success: the fall of ancient Japan and its resulting entry into the modern world.

Foreign arms and Japanese armies

Takashima and his pupils were the first to employ imported flintlock muskets with smooth-bore barrels around 1840. These weapons were marginally different from the models with which Napoleonic armies had been equipped. Even Bavarian muskets reached the Japanese market, but the majority of modern firearms were Dutch, or were delivered to Nagasaki by the VOC, giving rise to the Dutch loanword *geweer*. This word was also used for the newer models which operated with percussion caps and were produced in Edo at the orders of the Shogunate. The limited degree of Japanese industrialization however only allowed for an amount of altogether 8,000 muskets to be produced. A significant amount of the funds available to the individual domains was used to purchase imported foreign weapons. According to Kito Heishiro's autobiography, a "top quality" musket cost 42 *ryo* (gold coins) in 1868 (Meissner 1941: 85). Conservative estimates place the contemporary value of one *ryo* at c. € 200 in modern currency. Historian Arima Nariuri has calculated a price of 36 Mexican silver dollars in Japanese money for a Minié rifle (as opposed to 20 dollars in Great Britain), 68 dollars for an Enfield rifle, 104 dollars for a Snider, and 120 dollars for a Sharps breech loader (Arima 1958: 7, 8, 12). A French Chassepot fetched 80 dollars in 1868. One silver dollar was worth three Japanese silver *bu* (ca. 25 grammes of silver). Thus, a single Enfield rifle cost a handsome 1,7 kilogrammes of silver! In 1865, Choshu paid an astronomical 77,400 *ryo* for 4,300 Enfields, which would correspond to no less than € 330 million in modern European currency. At the time, the population of Choshu numbered around 800,000.

The firearms of the next generation had rifled barrels with an increasing number of grooves. This enabled the projectile to develop a spin while adhering to the inside of the barrel, thereby significantly improving both range and accuracy. Such weapons were imported, the most popular models being the the British Enfield rifle (available both as a long version, and as a carbine), and the American Springfield. The French 1866 Chassepot, a breech-loading needle lock rifle, constituted a further improvement. More than a million of these arms were produced in France in only a few years, and the Shogun Tokugawa Yoshinobu received no less than 2,000 of these rifles from Emperor Napoleon III. The French also sent 12 artillery pieces along with a personal gift for the Shogun. This consisted of a French cuirassier's panoply with Tokugawa arms emblazoned on the breastplate. It is now on display at the Yushukan Museum in Tokyo. Yoshinobu ordered another 40,000 Chassepots in 1867, but like the 30,000 Prussian Dreyse needle guns he had ordered in the previous year, these rifles were never dispatched. In the Boshin War, the majority of Shogunate troops remained armed with obsolete muskets of the older type and were thus no match for the Satsuma and Choshu armies.

Firepower was further improved by the development of Minié ammunition in France in 1847. This new type of ammunition was easier to load, and the projectile acquired a spin before leaving the barrel. This ammunition type could not only be fired from the Minié rifles produced by the same company, but also from the 1853 Enfield and the 1861 Springfield models. These muzzle-loading rifles were only capable of firing two rounds per minute; nevertheless, they became the standard firearm of West Japanese (later Imperial) armies.

Technology and firepower improved yet again with the introduction of breech-loading carbines such as the Sharps (1848), Starr (1858), and Spencer (1860). Repeating carbines were capable of firing up to ten rounds per minute, but they were much more expensive and inferior in range. However, troops armed with muzzle-loading rifles were at a serious disadvantage when pitted against repeater-armed troops, since the latter were able to operate in loose formation and fire their weapons from a prone position. In May 1868 Imperial troops encountered Tokugawa loyalists in Ueno; some Choshu troops were already equipped with repeating carbines and had no trouble routing the *shogitai* sent against them. The armies of Tosa, Aizu, and Yonezawa also included a few units armed with Spencers.

Historians have calculated that at least 569,844 muskets and rifles were imported to Japan between 1863 and 1869, the port of Yokohama admitting twice as many as Nagasaki. The peak of Japanese demand for foreign firearms was reached in 1867 as the country prepared for civil war. There was definitely a sufficient number of firearms available in Japan, the only remaining question was who would purchase how many, and in which quality (Fuess 2020: 89). Most high-quality rifles were breech-loaders of the Minié type, among which were the Enfields preferred by Satsuma and other domains. After the Boshin War, in the early 1870s, the new government ordered inventories made of all the firearms available in Japan. According to official records, this sum amounted to 370,000 rifles, muskets and handguns, and 6,600 artillery pieces. Of the rifles, 80 per cent were one-shot muzzle-loaders, less than 8 per cent were breech-loaders,

Yonezawa samurai arquebusier.
This samurai might have stepped from the photograph on a preceding page. His attire is typical of the Boshin War. Since the events of 1866 had proved that traditional samurai panoply had become useless against modern firearms, most traditional armour elements like resplendent crested helmets, tassets, arm and leg armour have been discarded. Only a sturdy breastplate is worn beneath the *jimbaori* surcoat. Oversleeves and leggings protect the man's arms and legs from the elements. A headcloth was commonly worn underneath the lacquered wooden *bajo-jingasa* helmet. Despite his concessions to the realities of contemporary warfare, this Yonezawa samurai is unwilling to part with his traditional pair of swords. Illustration: Sascha Lunyakov

Leftover arms and equipment from the Boshin War at the Byakko-tai Museum at Aizu-Wakamatsu.
Among the items shown are short-barreled muskets, *teppo* arquebuses, powder flasks and ammunition pouches.

and of these only a small proportion were repeating carbines, most of which had been imported only after the Battle of Toba-Fushimi.

The distribution of these arms across the country has also been the object of historical research. The Tokugawa arsenals contained altogether 75,000 firearms. Most were not of the most modern type, and there was a pronounced lack of trained and well-led infantry who would have been capable of operating these weapons effectively. Satsuma and Choshu each possessed about 20,000 guns, a number which was sufficient to equip their own troops. Including the most important allies, e. g. Saga (Hizen) and Tosa, the South-Western Alliance had more than 60,000 firearms at its disposal. The ten leading princedoms owned 90 per cent of all firearms, the rest being divided among 250 other domains. This may serve as an explanation for the profound differences in individual armies´ combat efficiency.

Apart from the muskets and rifles discussed above, tens of thousands of various French, American and British revolvers were imported to serve as officers´ weapons as well as for the samurai personal use. For instance, Satsuma purchased a large number of Smith & Wesson Army No. 2 revolvers from Thomas Glover at Nagasaki. Other models included Colt (1860), Savage (1861), and Starr revolvers (1863).

It is remarkable how swiftly Japanese customers were able to access the international arms market. The Bakumatsu era was a time of incessant technological innovation, and governments were constantly forced to purchase new arms to keep their armies´ equipment up to date. Japanese customers often had sufficient means to buy the latest innovations available. Immediately after the end of the Boshin War, the princedom of Kii was the first domain in Japan to buy the Krupp guns which had proved so deadly efficient in the Franco-Prussian War of 1870/71. Kii also owned 14,000 German Dreyse needle guns and employed an arms instructor by the name of Carl Köppen (Fuess 2020: 98 f.). The spiral of Japanese military modernization continued uninterrupted after the Boshin War. The artillery arm was also dependent on imports. As the artillery duels between the Choshu and Satsuma coastal batteries and Western warships had painfully made clear, the bronze-barrelled cannon which had been manufactured in Japan since the 16th century were by now hopelessly outdated. When due to increased demand prizes for copper soared in the mid-19th century, it became apparent to everyone concerned that the future belonged to iron and steel.

Limited funds often led to local improvisation. For example, guns with wooden barrels were constructed, and all the gunners could hope for was a decent amount of shots before the barrels burst. The large-calibred *teppo* arquebuses, so-called *o-zutsu*, in which the Yonezawa domain specialized[15], certainly inspired a little more confidence. Such a heavy handgun could be mounted on a gun car-

---

15 cf. *"The example of Yonezawa"*, p. 37

A Satsuma battery at Toba-Fushimi, January 1868.
Uniforms were identical both for infantry and artillery. (*Nishiki no mihata* 1907: plate XII)

riage with spoked wheels. The Boshin War also saw the use of modern Western mortars with calibres of 13 or 20 cm.

Modern field guns were particularly sought-after. Especially Satsuma and Saga favoured models supplied by the the British Armstrong foundry, which they purchased at Nagasaki until they finally felt capable of producing pieces of similar quality themselves. In 1865 Nagasaki arms dealer Thomas Glover called the sum of 183, 847 silver dollars for 35 Armstrong field guns of the latest manufacture; in other words, these guns were sold at 5 250 dollars apiece. The field guns had been developed in England by Sir William Armstrong, and production lasted from 1855 to 1864. That year, economic constraints forced the British government to return to the older muzzle-loading models, which is why many Armstrong guns found their way to Japan via the international market. The Armstrong gun´s construction represented a complete novelty: the rifled barrel consisted of several layers of steel and wrought iron, and as a breech-loader its rate of fire was high. The lead-jacketed shells followed the Minié principle. Although Armstrong initially believed that his system would only work with light field and mountain guns, he later succeeded in constructing larger pieces applying the same principle, with calibres up to 300 mm for some garrison and naval guns. All guns worked with the patented Armstrong breech-loading mechanism.

Eventually the arms factories in the western Japanese domains of Satsuma and Saga managed to produce artillery pieces which were effectively simplified versions of the original British model. This of course significantly reduced expenses, and the *daimyo* were able to augment their artillery accordingly. The renegade princedoms thus outclassed the Shogunate forces, which still used imported French pieces of 4- to 12-pound calibre with ranges of merely up to one kilometre. These weapons had been designed in accordance with Napoleonic performance parameters and were by now clearly outdated. In the early 1850s, Satsuma and Saga had established experimental industrial plants called *seirenjo* whose job it was to overcome the metalworking problems which had initially been encountered. Already in 1850 Saga had commissioned the country´s first open-hearth furnace and from 1853 was able to produce steel gun barrels. In 1857 Saga was able to deliver a shipment of 200 barrels to the Shogunate to equip mainly the coastal batteries. Of these altogether up to 1, 000 pieces of different sizes were counted in 1868, which shows that fears of a "barbarian invasion" ran deep. In 1858 the Shogunate and the Tokugawa domain of Mito possessed their own open hearth and blast furnaces. Nirayama, seat of the Egawa academy, also produced gun barrels. The Shogunate later shifted almost its entire industrial focus to ship building, which proved fortunate for its enemies, since it was land battles which ultimately decided the conflict. Ironically, the new government was then able to take over the former Shogunate´s precious naval arsenal at Yokosuka and turn it into one of the headquarters of the new Imperial

Wooden gun barrel at the Shinsengumi Museum at Aizu-Wakamatsu.
For its artillery pieces, Japanese commanders were mostly forced to rely on imported weapons, since the bronze cannon which had been manufactured in Japan since the 16th century had proved obsolete in the duels between the Choshu and Satsuma coastal batteries and Western warships. When as a consequence of increasing demand prices for copper went through the roof in the mid-19th century, iron and steel became the only alternatives, unless one wished to resort to wood. (Aizu Shinsengumi Museum, Aizu-Wakamatsu)

Ancient Japanese bronze cannon, outdated by the 1860s. This piece is on display facing the Straits of Shimonoseki, where Choshu domain kept several batteries.

Another local alternative to expensive cannon imports: extra heavy *teppo* (*o-zutsu*) mounted on a modern gun carriage. Precision would have required somewhat firmer attachment than shown. (Byakko-tai Museum, Aizu-Wakamatsu)

Choshu 24-pounders in action in 1864. The gunners are still equipped in the manner of late 16th century feudal infantry (*ashigaru*). The eleven Shimonoseki batteries comprised no less than 14 different types of gun, reaching from ship and field artillery pieces to howitzers and even a few mortars.
(Diorama at Moji Museum)

Six-pounder breech-loading Armstrong gun on display at Fukushima Prefecture Museum at Aizu-Wakamatsu.
The 1.34 m long barrel (63.5 mm calibre) fired shells 13.58 cm in length weighing 2.53 kg. Range was up to three kilometres. Their performance made Armstrong guns the most effective artillery pieces of the Boshin War. Their comparatively small weight and size also made them highly adaptable to the limitations of Japanese logistics. Armstrong guns formed the backbone of the victorious southern and western domains' modern artillery in the Boshin War.

navy. According to the sources, the hub of Satsuma's armament industry, the *Shuseikan*, had employed 1,200 workers by 1858. Similar projects in Choshu and Tosa failed. While Tosa's finances did not permit the establishment of an arms factory, it was decided in Choshu that the Saga barrels simply did not meet the standards set by imported Western products. In 1865, Satsuma engineers succeeded in developing a device powerful enough to bore out gun barrels, thus enhancing the quality of arms *made in Japan*.

Japan's mountainous topography (the first railway was opened in 1872) was the reason why – apart from fortresses and coastal defences – field and mountain guns with calibres between 4 and 12 pounds remained the norm. Heavier weapons presented almost insurmountable logistical obstacles; long distance transport being practically limited to shipping. And so, the obsolete French four-pounder with a range of 600 metres (called *yonkin-sanpo* in Japanese) remained the backbone of the Shogun's field artillery. Often the carriages were done away with and only the barrel dragged along by a lone horse, which would be assisted by the gun crews and baggage attendants when negotiating particularly steep stretches. Often the complete gun was simply dismantled and transported on horseback.

Along with all other modern weapons, the Gatling Gun made its appearance in Japan at this time. Satsuma possessed one, the princedom of Nagaoka two of these rapidfire weapons which had been developed in the US after 1861.[16] Gatlings were capable of inflicting heavy losses, but the dense black smoke which invariably developed above the gun before the invention of smokeless powder normally swiftly gave its position away to enemy artillery or snipers. Early models were also prone to jamming.

---

16 cf. *"The Hokuetsu War in Nagaoka"*, p. 130

Choshu coastal battery at Dannoura guarding the Shimonoseki Straits.
These 24-pounders are modern reconstructions, the original pieces having been destroyed by landing parties from Western warships in 1864.

At the beginning of the Boshin War in early 1868 the following types of artillery pieces formed part of Japanese arsenals:

Name of domain	Income (*koku*)	Total guns	Total Breech-loaders
Tokugawa	4m to 7m	1500	394
Satsuma	770, 000	290	50
Tokushima (Awa)	256, 000	259	39
Choshu	370, 000	220	109
Kaga	1, 025, 000	205	146
Saga (Hizen)	360, 000	201	45
Owari	620, 000	124	5
Akita	206, 000	111	11
Kii (Kishu)	550, 000	105	40
Fukuoka	470, 000	104	0
Matsue	186, 000	101	32
Tosa	242, 000	100	0

(Table after Aoki 2014. Only domains with 100 or more pieces are covered. All domains fighting against the Tokugawa after February 1868 are given in red, the Tokugawa in blue).

It is conspicuous that ample financial resources (cf. the *koku* figures provided) did not necessarily result in a numerous or modern artillery. The armies of the great Tokugawa domains Owari and Kii were not equipped in the latest fashion and quickly surrendered after the Shogun´s defeat at Toba-Fushimi. The leading renegade domains in the west (Satsuma, Choshu, Tosa, Saga) had taken great pains to modernize their forces ahead of others, even though the notoriously hard-up Tosa was outdone by its neighbour Awa. The most important allies of the Shogun, Aizu, Shonai and Kuwana, do not even feature in the above table. Regarding the large number of Shogunate pieces, it must be said that the majority were deployed in coastal defences and fortresses and were irrelevant to either conduct or outcome of the war.

The influence of foreign arms dealers

Official arms deals of the Shogunate or other *daimyo* with foreign governments like the one between Emperor Napoleon III and Tokugawa Yoshinobu in 1867 were the exception rather than the rule. The ambassadors of most foreign governments, especially the Americans, were under strict orders not to interfere with inner-Japanese squabbles and to remain politically neutral – at least, officially. It was an open secret that Britain favoured the rebellious West, while France´s support for the Shogunate established a certain equilibrium in this respect. After the shogunal reforms of 1862 all domains had unrestricted access to the international armament trade. The Shogunate had taken this step under pressure in order to improve national defence capacities against foreign intervention. Of course, it proved a double-edged sword – the Tokugawa soon found themselves looking down the barrels of the guns they had allowed their peers to purchase.

Weapons and ships which could not be built in Japan had to be imported with the help of foreign arms dealers. Interestingly enough, this was a time when trade restrictions in order to prevent or at least contain foreign military conflicts were as yet inconceivable. Few were unduly troubled by the idea of troops having to face enemy weapons produced in their own country. Governments and industrial companies of leading global arms producers Great Britain, the US, France, the Netherlands, and Germany/Prussia all embraced the notion of lining their pockets by selling the latest technological innovations to warring factions.

Initially, the most important port for the Japanese armaments market was Nagasaki in western Japan. It had been the Dutch merchants of the *Vereenigde Oostindische Compagnie* (United East India Company, VOC) who were the first to supply Japanese customers like Takashima Shuhan with firearms from their trade post at Deshima in the 1840s.[17] From 1862 the Dutch and Germans supplied artillery pieces and muskets to the Shogun and anyone else who happened to be interested and willing to pay. Since the other daimyo formed part of the Shogun´s feudal army and the 1862 agreements officially sanctioned individual armament purchases, the ensuing deals ran

---

17 cf. "Refom of the Shogunate – The new Takashima academy", p. 14

Shogunal artillery, 1867/68.

Artillerymen serving a newly-imported French four-pounder La Hitte gun. Dubbed *yon-pyon* by the Japanese, these light field pieces were the most common type used by the shogunal forces; their comparative mobility and manageability (the four-pounder's mountain version could be dismantled to facilitate transport) at least partly made up for their deficiency in range in comparison to the enemy's Armstrong guns. The French-style uniform worn by the gunner in the foreground was introduced in 1867. Combinations of Western jackets and Japanese dress were also common. Basically, the artillerymen differed very little from the infantry in their outward appearance. The officer is the proud owner of an imported telescope and wears tailor-made clothing according to individual taste. His wooden helmet is painted in an elegant blue and lacquered with golden decorations. Illustration: Sascha Lunyakov

Japanese awe of foreign military prowess cast in stone.
In the 1850s and 1860s the Shogunate ordered the building of numerous modern coastal batteries. Many of these were built by local *daimyo* at the Shogun's request. The picture above shows the remains of the Maiko battery in Kaji Bay outside Kobe, which was completed by Katsu Kaishu in 1865. The 70 metres long and 10 metres high granite emplacement supported up to fifteen pieces.

The Nishinomiya artillery tower situated between Osaka and Kobe, measures 12 metres in height and has a perimeter of 53 metres. Likewise designed by Katsu Kaishu, it was completed in 1866, a time in which it was no longer of any military significance.

smoothly and without serious opposition. As more and more ports were opened, private arms traders flocked to Japan. Among the ten most successful arms dealers based at Nagasaki could be found three Britons, three Germans, and one Portuguese, Dutchman, Frenchman and American respectively. Especially Satsuma drew most of its arms from the port of Nagasaki. In order to repair the Kagoshima coastal defences destroyed by the Royal Navy in 1863, Satsuma purchased 80 Armstrong guns with rifled barrels from a Russian dealer, thus buying weapons from a country whose navy had been the cause of the original predicament. Satsuma bought altogether several tens of thousands of small arms at Nagasaki, purchasing 1, 800 rifles, 3, 000 muskets and 6, 300 pistols in June and July 1865 alone. Many of these arms were sold to the Japanese by Thomas Glover (1838–1911), a local businessman of Scottish origin whose mansion perching on the heights above Nagasaki´s port can still be visited today. Glover not only sold weapons but offered to his eager customers any commodity he could lay his hands on abroad. Most of these goods were acquired in Shanghai and shipped to Japan. Although trading with outlawed rebels was a criminal offence, Glover also conducted business with Choshu after 1865. He later wrote that "Of all of those in rebellion against the Tokugawa government, I felt that I was the greatest rebel." (Craig 1961: 316). In 1866 Glover suggested selling his arms at Shanghai, where they were received by Satsuma agents and subsequently delivered to Choshu. Glover also assisted in sending young samurai to Britain where they were to undergo Western military training and imported the first steam railway engine to Japan. After the end of the Boshin War, having equipped several Japanese warships at the new government´s behest, his business finally dried up, and in 1870 he went bankrupt. He gained employment as a manager in Kyushu´s coal mining industry and spent the rest of his life in Japan.

In eastern and northern Japan the situation was an entirely different one, and even hard-nosed businessmen like Glover shied away from doing business with both parties at the same time. Importers, many of them Frenchmen or Germans, had their headquarters at Yokohama and provided the Shogunate with weapons. All in all, Yokohama´s trade volume doubled the size of Nagasaki´s. One important, if not the *most* important source for the acquisition of Western arms for Aizu, Nagaoka, Yonezawa and other domains faithful to the Tokugawa cause was the business of the Prussian-born brothers Henry and Edward (or Heinrich and Eduard) Schnell. Between the autumn of 1867 and spring 1868 Yonezawa alone purchased 6, 790 firearms, of which French Miniés formed the majority, but also a number of older Dutch *geweers* and 250 very expensive seven-shot Spencer repeating carbines. Another time, the Schnell brothers received 6, 000 or 10, 000 silver dollars from Nagaoka for two Gatlings. The weapons were delivered via the Sea of Japan to the officially neutral port of Niigata. In the second phase of the Boshin War, the capture of this port was one of the prime objectives of the Imperial forces, which led to heavy fighting around Nagaoka.[18]

Like France, Prussia and Italy tended to favour the Shogunate. Max von Brandt, the Prussian envoy (after 1867 of the North German Confederation), secretly employed the Schnells´ services in Echigo province, of which both Nagaoka and Niigata formed parts. Henry, the older of the two brothers, had ceased his work for the Prussian consulate at Osaka in January 1868, then secretly conferred with Brandt at Yokohama and taken an American steamer to Niigata.

Henry Schnell was a flamboyant character. He employed a French cook, a Chinese valet, and generally preferred a life of luxury. He was appointed military advisor at Aizu-Wakamatsu castle, the Northern Alliance´s military headquarters. His masters´ appreciation was reflected in his Japanese name, Hiramitsu Buhei. "Hiramitsu" is an inversion of the two kanji characters forming the family name of Matsudaira (Katamori), prince of Aizu. To others, he was simply known as "the Prussian general".

On their father´s side, the Schnells had Dutch roots and probably grew up in Batavia (modern Jakarta). Edward, the younger of the two brothers, was also called "the Dutch merchant". He was in Japan from at least 1862, and his Japanese was fluent. He also possessed a certain degree of military experience. He arrived in Niigata in 1868 on board a ship together with Nagaoka´s top retainer, the *karo* Kawai Tsugiunosuke. On board the same ship were 150 Nagaoka and 60 Kuwana samurai together with more than 100 troops from Aizu, as well as artillery pieces, muskets, and ample supplies of rice. Kawai had sold off the furniture of Nagaoka´s residence at Edo and used the money to buy military equipment before embarking to Niigata. Like Nagasaki, Yokohama was a place where everything was available in abundance.

The Schnells even managed to rustle up an ironclad and were able to supply two Gatlings to Nagaoka. Japanese orders for powder, ammunition or priming caps were usually shipped from Yokohama within 40 days, or from San Francisco, reaching their destination within 100 days. In only three months, the Schnell brothers received goods worth altogether 144, 000 dollars from their company headquarters at Yokohama, all of which were intended for sale in the North. They also negotiated deals for other companies based at Yokohama, for instance 56, 000 dollars´ worth of ammunition for the German trading company of E. Wyttenbach.

All of this occurred at a time in which a multitude of fairly uncensored newspapers has just started to appear in Japan. The press noted that the domain of Aizu employed two Prussians and two Frenchmen whose job it was to drill the prince´s troops and instruct them in the use of

---

18 cf. *"The Hokuetsu War in Nagaoka"*, p. 130

modern artillery. According to an article published in the *Chugai Shinbun* newspaper, the Schnell brothers trained "three types of military units". The sources do not always clearly distinguish between Henry and Edward, and various newspapers also refer to them as Dutch, Italian or even Ottoman – possibly the result of a contrived undercover business strategy!

In October 1868 the troops of the new government were able to defeat their enemies, and fighting in northern Japan came to an end. About one of the Schnell brothers, the authorities wrote in their official report:

"The Italian [*sic!*] Schnell went back and forth to Okuetsu [the north-eastern part of present-day Niigata prefecture], and was instrumental in securing equipment and ammunition for the traitors. He also commanded various troops and acted as if he knew all the military secrets of the world. However, with our troops´ victory, his course of action came to an end and at the risk of being arrested, he bowed his head and begged for mercy. Being a foreigner, he was released and returned by ship."

(Hakaoshi 2017: 129)

The notorious "unequal treaties" between the Japanese and the Western powers signed years previously granted foreigners exterritorial status and immunity. Thus, the Schnells were not only able to save their skins but also received financial indemnity from the Meiji government for four confiscated Niigata storehouses. These buildings had housed pistols, powder, wool, paper, glass bottles, saddlery, stockings, wine, ammunition, dyes, and 300 pairs of boots. A Dutch citizen, Schnell was unsurprisingly acquitted in his trial before the Dutch consul.

Henry Schnell left Japan in 1869 together with his Japanese wife and around two dozen samurai (possibly his old companions from Aizu) and emigrated to the US. His skills at tea farming did not match his business talents, and so we lose track of this remarkable pair of brothers. Like their final places of rest, their biographical data are not reliably known.

Prussian arms dealer Henry Schnell at Aizu in c. 1868.

This impression of Schnell (reconstructed by the present author and the artist Sascha Lunyakov) is based on a photograph showing him in Japanese clothing, and an article in the June 1868 edition of *The Japan Punch*, where he is referred to as "Aizu's general" (Hakoishi 2017: 118, 123). Henry Schnell was followed around the fortress city of Aizu by his own personal entourage; passers-by fell to their knees at his approach. Like many of his contemporaries, he wore a mixture of Japanese and Western clothing and weapons. The outer garments and his pair of swords are Japanese, while the sash around his waist shows French influence. He wears riding breeches and long riding boots. Schnell must have been very proud of his voluminous *haori* jacket emblazoned with the Tokugawa badge, which also served as the arms of the lord of Aizu, Matsudaira Katamori. To be presented with such a garment was a sign of the *daimyo*'s high favour and appreciation, and constituted a huge honour to the person on whom it was bestowed. This explains the veneration of the people who met up with the wearer in the streets. Some sources state that he occasionally wore a cavalry sabre instead of the *katana* and *wakizashi* – we choose to show both variants. Illustration: Sascha Lunyakov

THE SHOGUNATE, IMPERIAL FORCES, AND ALLIES – AN OVERVIEW OF THE MOST IMPORTANT DOMAINS AND THEIR BANNERS AND INSIGNIA

Of the more than 250 Japanese domains, over 190 mobilized forces in aid of the former renegade armies of Satsuma and Choshu, which in the course of the Battle of Toba-Fushimi had become the Imperial army.[19] Between 1862 and 1869 the Shogunate or its remnants also succeeded in appealing to more than 100 domains to raise troops for its increasingly lost cause. The obvious inconsistency in the above numbers is a result of the numerous turncoats who did not hesitate to change sides even while the Battle of Toba-Fushimi was still raging. In a brief amount of time, all of western and central Japan had joined the Imperial side.

In this chapter, the names of the ruling daimyo will be given as well as the economic resources available to them im *koku*. Wealth however did not always result in the willingness or ability either to modernize one´s troops or to commit them in case of a military conflict. The wealth of some domains was in reality larger than stated in official records since modern sources of income such as import duties were not normally included.

This chapter will also feature the various troop and naval flags as well as the daimyo´s personal insignia (coat of arms: *mon*) or badges (*aijirushi*) used in the standards of their domains. The middle of the 19th century saw the introduction of Western-type rectangular flags flying from a single staff. Flag designs were either universal for all units of a domain, or differentiated with the help of colours, stripes, waves, characters, or other graphic elements. Flags were assigned either to platoons or companies. In contrast to European custom, these standards were not the sacred objects presented to individual regiments by the ruling prince. In Japan, only the supreme commander´s personal standard (*uma-jirushi*) and a small number of heirlooms within a clan received a comparable degree of veneration. The majority of ancient Japanese flags (most of which were the rectangular *nobori no hata* or *sashimmo* banners attached to two staffs, cf. Weber 2022) were used for signalling and not considered particularly valuable. During the Bakumatsu period platoon and company flags were likewise considered primarily functional, while signalling devices survived in the form of small command pennons carried by the unit commanders and NCOs. These flags had succeeded the traditional war fans and batons wielded by samurai commanders (*gunbai*, *saihai*). Since no great material or emotional significance was attached to these objects, only very few original examples survive.

The design of the new standards did not necessarily adopt a daimyo family *mon* or the simplyfied *aijirushi* badges. Since modern armies increasingly consisted of different contingents and troop types, and because tactics required units to operate in looser formations it was important to recognize individual units from a distance. Thus, simple motives and geometrical patterns like bars, bands, and especially stars and planets became typical design elements for the new flags. The Shogunate chose the red sun disc on a white background, the *hinomaru* (not yet the official national flag at the time), as its flag motive.

Often, though by no means always, western Japanese domains favoured white and red as their identification colours, while those loyal to the Tokugawa tended to choose white and black.

The military flags of the period have been reconstructed from the available sources. Further information can be gained from the English-speaking website https://www.fotw.info/flagsjp_bosh.html, and Hugo Ströhl´s indespensible work *Japanisches Wappenbuch. Nihon Mondo*, first published in 1906. Occasionally, it is easier to research naval flags, since sources are rich with depictions of contemporary ships, and naval flag identification manuals also survive in fairly large numbers. For reasons of space, only the most important domains mentioned previously can be considered.

Small signalling flag (fanion) carried by a file-closing Satsuma NCO. Individual platoons and companies also carried larger flags emblazoned with the Satsuma arms. (Nishiki no mihata 1907, plate XVI, detail)

---

19 cf. "'In this sign, conquer!' – the Battle of Toba-Fushimi", p. 111

The Tokugawa and their allies[20]

1 – Aizu

Daimyo: Matsudaira Katamori, 1862–1867, Protector of Kyoto
Income: between 230, 000 and 280, 000 *koku*
Notes: Standing army of 4, 500 troops. Highly efficient force frequently employed by the Shogunate

Troop flag 1: *ai* character from "Aizu" | Troop flag 2: daimyo´s mon (Tokugawa hollyhock) | (nach Ströhl) | *sashimono* (back flag for armoured samurai) | *sode-jirushi* (shoulder insignia) with unit distinction.[21]

2 – Fukui

Daimyo: Matsudaira Mochiaki
Income: 320, 000 *koku*

 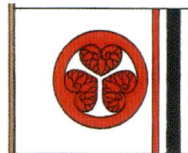

Troop flag | Naval flag was also red-white-red, without Tokugawa/Matsudaira *mon*. (after Ströhl)

3 – Fukushima

Daimyo: Itakura Katsumi
Income: 30, 000 *koku*
Notes: Changed sides twice; half-heartedly joined Northern Alliance. Surrendered after the capture of Nihonmatsu castle.

Itakura family *mon*

4 – Hikone

Daimyo: Ii Naonori
Income: 350, 000 *koku*
Notes: At Kyoto in 1863/64; campaigned against Choshu with 1, 900 samurai in 1866, among them 900 mounted in red armour. At Toba-Fushimi: retainer Okamoto Hansuke was at Osaka castle with Shogun, but majority of troops dispatched to Otsu and Yotsuka to guard against Tokugawa. Changed sides.

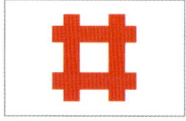  

Troop flag: well motif (also in white on red) | *Mon* of Ii clan (also in white on yellow) | (after Ströhl)

---

20 The number of the domain corresponds with the numbering on the previous page's map.
21 cf. pp. 70–72

5 – Himeji

Daimyo: Sakai Tadakuni
Income: 150, 000 *koku*
Notes: Forced into Imperial army after Toba-Fushimi

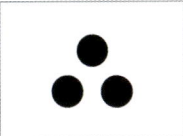

Troop flag: 3 black planets on white background

6 – Kuwana

Daimyo: Matsudaira Sadaaki
Income: 113, 000 *koku*
Notes: A hard-fighting and loyal Tokugawa veteran: Although Kuwana domain surrendered to the Emperor after Toba-Fushimi, the prince himself fought on until 1869.

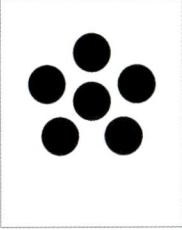  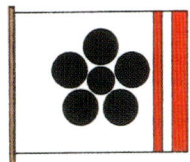

Troop flag: 6 black planets on white background

(both flags after Ströhl)

7 – Morioka

Daimyo: Nambu Toshihisa
Income: 200, 000 *koku*
Notes: Fought against Imperial supporters Akita and Tsugaru in the North.

9 white planets on blue background

8 – Nagaoka

Daimyo: Makino Tadakuni
Income: between 74, 000 and 140, 000 *koku*
Notes: Offered heavy resistance to Imperial forces in the Hokuetsu War; led by generals Kawai Tsuginosuke and Yamamoto Tatewaki

Troop flag with ladder motif (see also pp.???)

Family *mon* Makino (also in white on yellow)

(after Ströhl)

9 – Ogaki

Daimyo: Toda Ujihide
Income: 100, 000 *koku*
Notes: Fought against Choshu in 1866. Abandoned Tokugawa on third day at Toba-Fushimi and changed sides. Distrusted by the Emperor, the troops were deployed in the front ranks in the campaign against Edo.

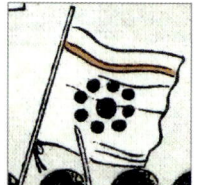

Troop flag at Toba-Fushimi

10 – Ohu Reppan Domei (Northern Alliance)

31 domains in the Tohoku region north of Edo/Tokyo.
Notes: Not a federal force in the literal sense, but mutual military assistance.

Flags of the Alliance [22]

11 – Republic of Ezo/Yezo

Daimyo: President Enomoto Takeaki, ruled January–June 1869
Notes: Last pocket of resistance against Imperialists on the northern island of Hokkaido.

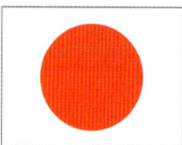 

Hinomaru (troop and naval flag)   Identification flag for ships of Shogunate navy

12 – Sendai

Daimyo: Date Munemoto
Income: 625, 000 *koku*
Notes: Fourth largest domain after Tokugawa, Kaga, and Satsuma, with 33, 000 samurai. Financial difficulties prevented rapid military modernization. Suffered several defeats before surrendering.

Naval flag; size proportions ca. 3:4   Prince´s *mon* (also white on red flag colour)   (after Ströhl)

---

22 Now at Yonezawa, see also p. 134

13 – Shingu

Daimyo: Mizuno Tadamoto
Income: 35, 000 *koku*
Notes: 300 modernized samurai troops distinguishing themselves against Choshu in 1866. A charismatic leader and stout fighter, the daimyo was nicknamed *Oni-Mizuno* ("Mizuno the Devil") by the enemy.

Family *mon*

14 – Shinsengumi (police unit)

Commanders: Kondo Isami, Serizawa Kamo, Hijikata Toshizo
Notes: Around 250 samurai at Kyoto. Remaining troops fought on before finally surrendering on Hokkaido in 1869.

Character *makoto* = "sincerity", "honesty"

15 – Shogitai (militia)

Commanders: Shibusawa Seiichiro, Amano Hachiro
Notes: Samurai militia; defeated at Ueno on 15th May 1868. Survivors fought on until surrendering on Hokkaido in 1869.

Original flag at the Yushukan Museum, Tokyo (white has yellowed)

16 – Shonai

Daimyo: Sakai Tadazumi
Income: 167, 000 *koku*
Notes: Energetic modernized fighting force. Surrendered only after fall of Aizu.

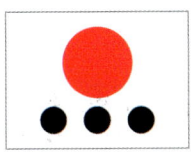 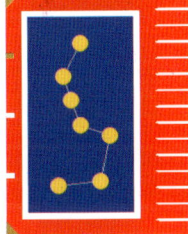

Three planets surmounted by sun disc

Flag of the 2nd battalion under Sakai Genba: "To defeat the enemy with the stars", following the ancient Chinese belief that the army with the top star would be victorious.

17 – Takada

Daimyo: Sakakibara Masataka
Income: 150, 000 *koku*
Notes: Fought against Choshu in 1866. Some Takada samurai supported the Shogitai at Ueno. Forced to change sides in 1868, Takada troops were deployed against their Nagaoka neighbours.

Sakakibara family *mon*

18 – Tokugawa/Shogunat

Daimyo: Tokugawa Iemochi (1858–1866), Yoshinobu (1866–1867)
Income: 7 million *koku*, 4 of which were personally owned by the family
Notes: Government army composed of feudal vassals and modern infantry regiments.

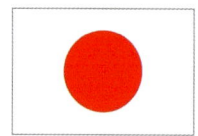

Hinomaru troop flag

Family *mon* (trifoliate hollyhock), black or dark blue on white

19 – Yonezawa

Daimyo: Uesugi Narinori
Income: 300, 000 *koku*, later reduced to 147, 000 *koku*
Notes: Powerful samurai army with famous arquebusier units and long-standing firearm tradition. Partly modernized; fought in the North.

Uesugi family *mon* (also white on blue background)

(after Ströhl)

Satsuma, Choshu and their allies

1 – Aki (Hiroshima/Geishu)

Daimyo: Asano Nagamichi
Income: 430, 000 *koku*
Notes: Having faced the power of Choshu in 1866, Aki was one of the five victors at Toba-Fushimi. Its contingent was comparatively small however.

Troop flag | Naval flag with Asano family *mon* (falcon´s feathers) | Various other flags | | (after Ströhl)

2 – Choshu

Daimyo: Mori Motonori
Income: 370, 000 *koku*
Notes: Greatest military power in the West besides Satsuma. Driving force of the rebellion, openly fighting the Shogunate since 1864.

 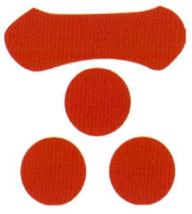

Troop flag: size proportion 5:4 on flagstaff | Prince Mori's *mon* (also red on white background)

3 – Fukuoka

Daimyo: Kuroda Nagatomo
Income: 470, 000 *koku*
Notes: Both internal dissent and disagreement with the Shogunate became apparent at an early stage. Refused to follow its feudal obligation to levy troops in 1866; present at Ueno in 1868.

 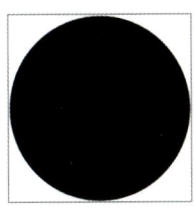   

Kuroda *mon* | Allusive arms: Kuroda (= black field) | Naval flag. Size proportions: 3:4 | | (both flags after Ströhl)

4 – Fukuyama

Daimyo: Abe Masatake
Income: 110, 000 *koku*
Notes: A massive gunpowder explosion in Fukuyama castle severely weakened this domain's military capacities, making it easy for Choshu to defeat it. Changed sides in 1868 when faced with an Imperial besieging force. Fought numerous engagements in the Boshin War despite financial hardships, 500 men took part in the Hokkaido campaign.

daimyo's *mon*

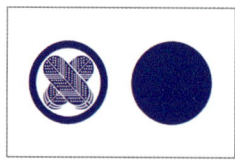

Naval flag: prince's *mon* and sphere; size proportions 5:8 (very dark blue)

5 – Hirosaki

Daimyo: Tsugaru Tsuguakira
Income: 100, 000 *koku*
Notes: Sided with Emperor almost immediately and attacked its neighbour Shonai. Briefly changed sides and joined Northern Alliance, but soon back with Imperialists. Fought at Hakodate in 1869.

Prince's *mon*

Naval flag: black *manji* (Buddhist swastika)

6 – Kaga (Kanazawa)

Daimyo: Maeda Yoshiyasu
Income: 1, 025, 000 *koku*
Notes: Wealthiest domain after Tokugawa, but militarily backward. 7000 men fought in the Boshin War.

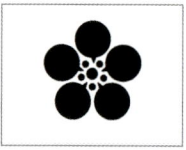

Troop flag: black Maeda plum blossom on white background

Naval flag

(after Ströhl)

7 – Imperial Flags (see p. 121)

8 – Kii (Kishu)

Daimyo: Tokugawa Mochitsugu
Income: 555, 000 *koku*
Notes: Quarreled with Shogunate in 1866. Despite Kii being the second of three main Tokugawa branches, the domain held back in early stages of campaign and swiftly changed its allegiance at Toba-Fushimi. Later highly successful military reforms.

Troop flag: "Ki" character (from "Kishu")

Naval flag

Flag carried in Emperor's entourage

9 – Kokura

Daimyo: Ogasawara Tadanobu
Income: 150, 000 *koku*
Notes: Frustrated by the Shogunate's lack of support in 1866, Kokura joined the Imperial cause despite its lasting misgivings about Choshu.

Ogasawara *mon* (also white on blue background)

"Ko" character (after Ströhl)

10 – Kubota

Daimyo: Satake Yoshitaka
Income: 225, 000 *koku*
Notes: Left Northern Alliance after internal disagreements. Suffered heavily from Morioka and Ichinoseki attacks until fighting in Tohoku ceased.

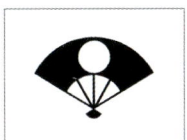

Daimyo's *mon*: fan adorned with *hinomaru* sun disc (Satake)

11 – Kumamoto (Higo)

Daimyo: Hosokawa Yoshikuni
Income: 540, 000 *koku*
Notes: Only provided scant help to Kokura in 1866. Reforms slow in coming due to the domain's notorious financial difficulties. Present at Battle of Ueno.

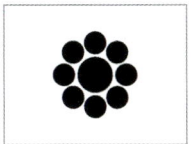

Troop flag: Nine planets (Hosokawa *mon*)

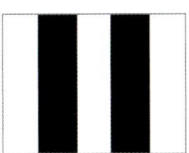

Naval flag

(after Ströhl)

12 – Kurume

Daimyo: Arima Yorishige
Income: 21, 000 *koku*
Notes: Ardent supporters of isolationist policy.

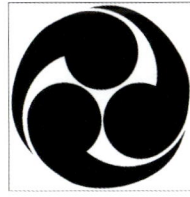

Daimyo's *mon* (also in red on white background)

Naval flag

(after Ströhl)

13 – Matsue

Daimyo: Matsudaira Sadayasu
Income: 186, 000 *koku*
Notes: Fought against Choshu in 1866. Distrusted by Imperialists in spite of its changing sides.

Twin mountain motif; alternatively twin mountains and Tokugawa / Matsudaira hollyhock.
Size proportions: 3:4

14 – Ogi

Daimyo: Nabeshima Naotora
Income: 73, 000 *koku*
Notes: A branch line of the Nabeshima of Saga, this domain fought for the Emperor in the North.

Nabeshima *mon*   Naval flag

15 – Okayama (Bizen)

Daimyoen: Ikeda Mochimasa, Ikeda Akimasa
Income: 315, 000 *koku*
Notes: Involved in the Kobe incident (firefight with Western forces); troops present at Ueno.

Ikeda of Bizen butterfly (also in white on yellow background)   (after Ströhl)

16 – Omura

Daimyo: Omura Sumihiro
Income: 27, 000 *koku*
Notes: Omura´s Shinsetai unit was commanded by Watanabe Kiyoshi. In 1868, it operated in Aizu, Akita, and at Ueno.

Daimyo´s *mon*   (after Ströhl)

17 – Owari

Daimyo: Tokugawa Yoshinori, Tokugawa Yoshikatsu
Income: 620, 000 *koku*
Notes: The first of the Tokugawa family tree´s three main branches, supplied many shoguns. Changed sides anyway after Toba-Fushimi.

Tokugawa *mon*   Naval flag   Flag carried in Emperor´s entourage.   "O" character (after Ströhl)

18 – Ozu

Daimyo: Kato Yasuaki
Income: 60, 000 *koku*
Notes: Modernized its army after 1866. Fought for Tokugawa at Toba-Fushimi, changed sides afterwards.

Kato snake eye (naval and troop flag)

19 – Sadowara

Daimyo: Shimazu Tadahiro
Income: 27, 000 *koku*
Notes: Branchline of the Shimazu of Satsuma; fought at Ueno in 1868.

Satsuma *mon* variant

20 – Saga (Hizen)

Daimyo: Nabeshima Naohiro
Income: 360, 000 *koku*
Notes: Leading producer of artillery, and a loyal supporter of the Emperor.

  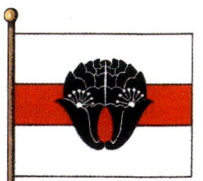

Army flag
(displaying Nabeshima *mon*)   Naval flag   (after Ströhl)

21 – Satsuma

Daimyo: Shimazu Tadayoshi
Income: 770, 000 *koku*
Notes: Most powerful domain alongside Choshu. Driving force of the rebellion.

Troop flag   Variation: Shimazu family *mon* (horse bit enclosed by ring), variants in black on white background, and white on blue.

22 – Tokushima (Awa)

Daimyo: Hachisuka Narihiro, Hachisuka Mochiaki
Income: 256, 000 *koku*
Notes: The sun wheel (swastika) is a Buddhist motive. It served as the Hachisuka clan´s family mon.

Daimyo´s *mon*   Naval flag   (after Ströhl)

23 – Tosa

Daimyo: Yamauchi Toyonori; preceded by Yamauchi Yodo (Toyoshige, (1827–1872), one of the "Four remarkable lords of the Bakumatsu period".
Income: 242, 000 *koku*
Notes: Home of Sakamoto Ryoma. After considerable delaying, finally one of the five victors of Toba-Fushimi.

Army flag. Size proportions 5:4   Naval flag. Size proportions: 3:4   Flag with prince´s mon (after Ströhl)

24 – Tottori (Inshu)

Daimyo: Ikeda Yoshikatsu
Income: 325, 000 *koku*
Notes: One of the five victors at Toba-Fushimi, but present only with a small contingent of artillery.

Ikeda *mon* (butterfly and ring); also in white on black background.   (after Ströhl)

25 – Tsu

Daimyo: Todo Takayuki
Income: 280, 000 *koku*
Notes: Spectacularly changed sides on fourth day of Battle of Toba-Fushimi. Its artillery took the Shogunate forces in the flank. Took part in the campaign against Edo.

   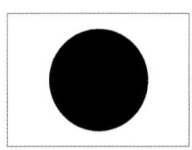 

Army flag; size proportions 5:4   Naval flags   Todo *mon* on maku at Toba-Fushimi (also as a flag blazon)

26 – Uwajima

Daimyo: Date Munenari
Income: 70, 000 *koku*
Notes: The infantry also wore red insignia.

Troop flag   Naval flag; (variants in black on white background, or white on black)

Samurai with main battle standard of the Ii clan of Hikone (line drawings by Sascha Lunyakov for KLIO-AG *SHOGUN*).

Other *mon* and standards

A young samurai from Nagaoka.
This historic photograph from the 1860s clearly shows on his large sleeve tag the ladder motif common to many Nagaoka standards. His personal *mon* worn on his breastplate shows from under his open jacket.

Although many troops fighting in the Boshin War looked much alike, there were hardly any official uniforms which could have served to distinguish between different contingents. The distinctive white stripes and helmets worn by the Tokugawa *denshutai*, and certain helmet forms and brassards worn by forces from the West were certainly an exception. Most modernized infantry wore dark blue cotton dress (which could occasionally be white in summer), more or less modelled on Western fashion. Many samurai wore their own kimono, jackets, trousers and waistcoats, all of them privately owned and thus lacking uniformity. Basically, officers wore what suited them. Even before the Bakumatsu period only a few *ashigaru* and lifeguards had been uniformly equipped and dressed. Most troops were recognizable by the *sashimono* attached to the back of their armour. These flags showed either the wearer's individual *mon*, or a symbol identifying his unit. When armour was gradually discarded, this method of identification became obsolete, one of the reasons being that in a fight with modern firearms the *sashimono* would have given away the wearer's position.

These tactical changes brought about a much older form of identification, which had been abandoned when suits of armour painted with *mon* or other badges had become the norm in the 16th century. In the Japanese Middle Ages, samurai had relied on cloth patches painted with their names or simple badges for identification. They were attached to the helmet and termed *kasa-jirushi*; if they were worn on the armour's shoulder plates, they were called *sode-jirushi*. These cloth patches were now again attached to the upper sleeves of uniforms, thus providing a by no means new but nevertheless very simple and effective way of signifying the wearer's loyalty or even unit. This method was as flexible as it was cheap – soldiers took a rectangular patch of cloth mostly white in colour (materials could be either hemp, cotton or silk), and attached a small crossbar at the top. The wearer's individual *mon* or unit badge was then either dyed or painted on. The tag was then hung from the left sleeve just as similar badges had been attached to shoulder armour in previous centuries. Some photographs also show *sode-jirushi* worn on the right shoulder or the chest. Some *sode-jirushi* were also sewn to the wearer's sleeve. Some men wore more than one cloth tag simultaneously. From March 1868, Imperial troops wore their own clan's badge supplemented by the piece of brocade cloth (*king-ire*) which served as the Imperial field sign. Some armies used cloth tags to mark individual units, but research in this area is scarce as yet, and not much reliable information available. Not many *sode-jirushi* from the Bakumatsu period have survived, and often the badges of domains and units displayed on those that still exist are difficult to identify.

Another method of signifying the wearer's domain, unit and rank which was especially popular in the western theatre were stripes or symbols attached to the lower sleeves. This method had obviously been adopted from European armies.

A report published in the *Japan Gazette* on 6th June 1868 provides a good impression of how the units of various *daimyo* serving in the Imperial army appeared on parade: "Almost all of the Daimyo's samurai were dressed alike, in black camlet suits with brass buttons, and their distinguishing badges. These latter consisted of stripes, crosses, diamond-shaped patches, triangles, etc.; or in the case of some, calico marked with a "mon" or device, fastened to the shoulder by a piece of paper string."

(Cortazzi 2012: 136)

The troops from Satsuma wore a narrow white brassard on their right upper arms, while troops from Saga (Hizen) wore a red one.

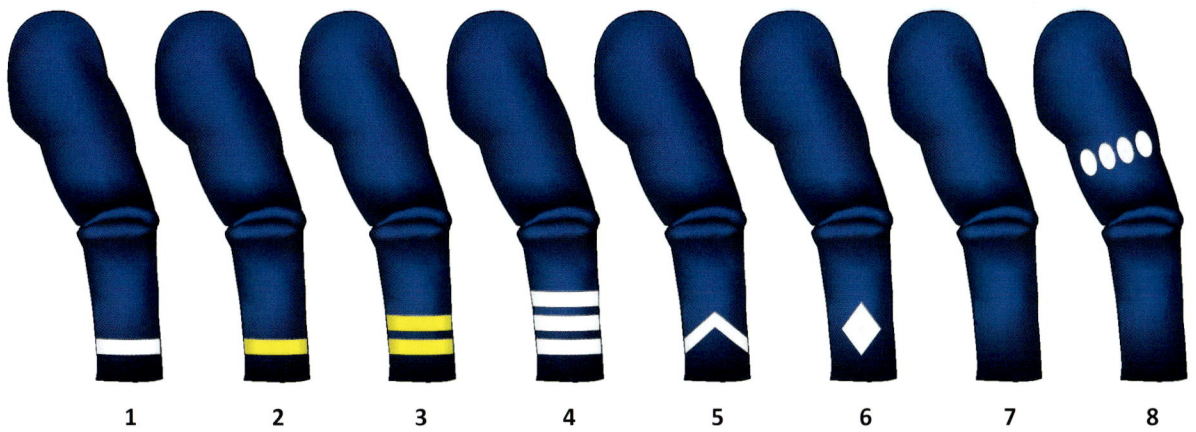

Sleeve-mounted insignia
1 Choshu: white ring **2** Ogaki: yellow rings **3** Ogaki officers: two yellow rings **4** Aki, Fukuyama: 3 white rings,
5 Kurume: white chevron, **6** Okayama (Bizen): white lozenge, or diamond, **7** Satsuma: no insignia worn,
8 Echizen: four white dots
All mounted on black or blue uniform backgrounds.

Nishihara Tanetoshi, an Imperial infantryman from Yanagawa domain.
He wears a pair of broad and narrow rings around the bottom of his sleeves, marking him a soldier from Yanagawa in Kyushu. He is armed with the 1858 Enfield 2 Band pattern rifle. This model had an extended barrel, making it suitable for use in marine warfare. (Archive Rod Johnson)

Ueda Jingoemon from Tokushima (Awa) wearing two *sode-jirushi* on his right shoulder. He carries a pocket watch, his sword, and a French model Lefaucheux pinfire revolver. He also seems to have attached another badge to his lower sleeve. (Photograph presumably from 1869; https//mag.japaaancom/archives/154925)

Aizu standard bearers in 1868.
The left flag shows the princely *mon* (identical with that of the Tokugawa), the right flag features a stylized character from the name "Aizu".
(Detail from *Nishiki no mihata* 1907, plate II)

Aizu

Aizu troops' shoulder tags worn after the beginning of modernization in 1868 can be reconstructed to a certain degree, although only few examples survived the catastrophe. Both the stylized kanji of "Aizu"[23] and a hand-painted red sun disk with five, eight or ten rays or points was used.[24] These emblems were supplemented by kanji characters and numbers for specific units.

Aizu samurai were organized in units ("companies") of c. 100 men. Units were structured according to age (four classes) and social rank (three classes), which added up to twelve large groups subdivided into companies.[25] The 16- and 17-year-old *byakko-tai* were the youngest warriors. These were recognizable by their shoulder-tags incorporating a five-pointed star and the stylized kanji for 会津 "Aizu" (second illustration on p. 72). The *seiryu* warrior category comprised men aged between 37 and 49 years. Their unit name incorporated the kanji for "blue", which is why badge 3 with its blue stripe may be attributed to this group. The employed kanji 大 "dai" signifies "big" or "upper". Most agree that it served to designate the *shichu*, the highest-ranking group of Aizu samurai. The Sino-Japanese character 三 or "three" was also employed, marking the third company of the socially supreme members of this age group.

The *suzaku* age group (18 to 35 years) bore the brunt of the fighting. Unfortunately none of the lesser-known shoulder tags can be attributed to them, but their unit designation incorporates the Japanese word for "purple", so it can be reasonably supposed that this colour featured in the unit's badge. Members of the middle and lower classes (*yoriai* and *ashigaru*) may have been distinguished by the 中 "chu" ("middle") and 小 "sho" ("small" or "lower") kanji characters respectively, supplemented by unit markings for 1, 2, 3, and so on. Improvisation seems to have been the rule rather than the exception in this respect, and decisions were rarely entirely based on rational considerations. This explains the fourth tag illustrated, which refuses to fit into the scheme described above. Both the red, mountain-shaped triangles at top and bottom and the name "(lightning) strike" are entirely new elements – only the kanji for "second unit" appears to confirm one of the principles of this admittedly speculative reconstruction.

---

23 cf. *"The Tokugawa and their allies"*, p. 54
24 First illustration on p. 72
25 cf. *"Samurai – the last battlecry of the old feudal élite"*, p. 82

These modern reproductions of banners of Nagaoka´s Makino clan are on display at the Kawai Tsuginosuke Museum at Nagaoka.

The Makino were among the most loyal followers of the Tokugawa and offered stiff resistance to Imperial forces in the Hokuetsu War in summer 1868. The ensign on the left with the five-step ladder motive is an army flag, some of the smaller banners are the classic *sashimono*, which since the 16th century were attached to the back of the armour of individual warriors within the same unit. *Sashimono* became obsolete when most samurai discarded their armour before or during the Boshin War. The floral *mon* is the *maru-ni-mitsu-kashiwa* (three oak leaves surrounded by a ring) of the Makino clan.

Sode-jirushi (shoulder tags)

  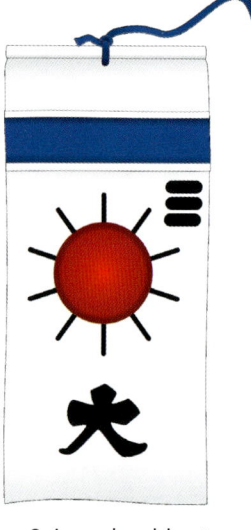 

Aizu shoulder tag with eight-rayed sun emblem

Byakko-tai shoulder tag (warriors aged between sixteen and seventeen years)

Seiryu shoulder tag (37–49 years); Shichu upper class, 3rd company

Shoulder tag incorporating the the "Aizu" kanji and characters meaning "two" and "lightning (strike)", identifiying the wearer as a member of the lightning troop´s second company

Shoulder tags

All Aki (Hiroshima) (black, blue, or red stripes)

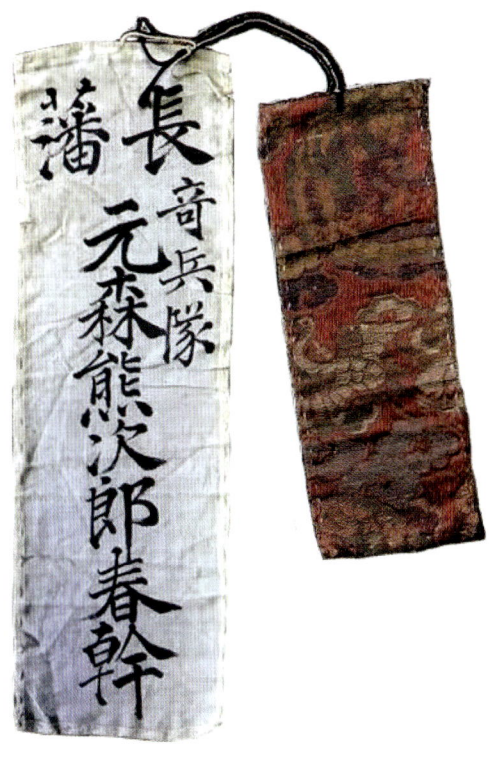

Choshu, *Kiheitai* militia. Tag of the platoon leader Motomori Kumajiro (1845-1868). The tag features the wearer's name, rank, and unit; the Imperial *kingire* is visible on the right. (Imperial Nikishi brocade verified by a seal)

Imperial retainers

Hirado or Himeji

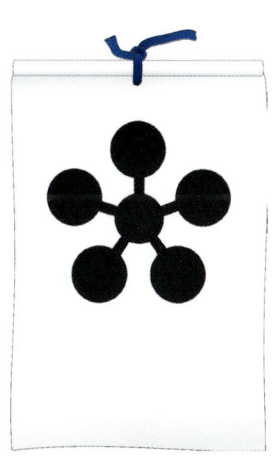

Kaga (possibly a simplified depiction of the Maeda's plum blossom *mon*)

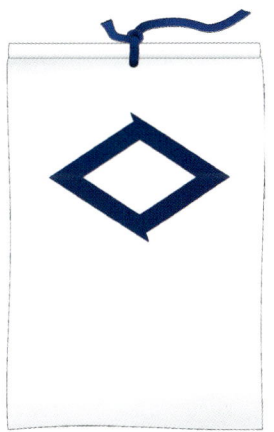

Kaga domain, Yanagisawa vassal family (to be displayed on the wearer's chest)

Kurume

Okayama (Bizen)

Owari domain; with *mon* belonging to one family of vassals on the right

Saga (Hizen)

Shinsengumi

(Sources: various Japanese collections, www.touken-world.jp, and Nakanishi 2006: 14–19)

Tokushima (Awa), displayed on the wearer's chest

Tsu, displayed on the wearer's chest

  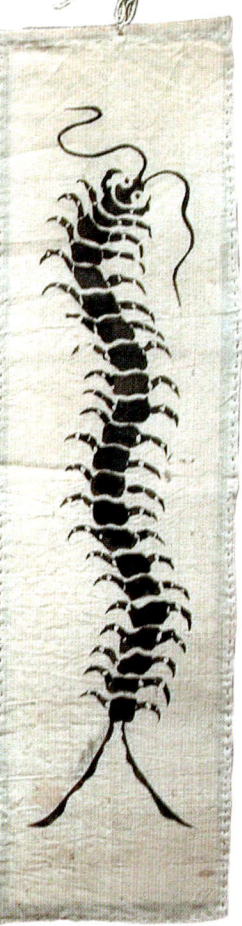

Stylized "Yamamoto" kanji characters

Lines, wave, and kanji character *kyu* ("nine")

Family *mon* and geometric forms

Centipede

THE COMBATANTS

Shishi – men of high ideals, or unmitigated lunatics?

As the year 1867 drew to its close, British diplomats Ernest Sato and Algernon Bertram Mitford witnessed the arrival of the resigned Shogun´s entourage at Osaka on the eve of the Battle of Toba-Fushimi. Satow wrote:
"Small bodies of drilled troops were marching about headed by drummers, and field-pieces were placed so as to sweep the narrow streets. We saw men in all sorts of military costumes with their heads muffled up to protect them from the cold, not presenting a very martial appearance [...] There were wonderful groups of men in armour, wearing surcoats of various gay colours, armed with spears and helmets. Here we found Kubota Sentaro, the commander of the Tycoon´s drilled troops, with a couple of colleagues [...] the bugles sounded to arms and we saw a long train of drilled troops advancing [...] On they went, followed by a herd of men in fantastic costumes (*yu-geki-tai*, "brave fighting men"), some wearing helmets with long wigs of black or white hair reaching half-down their backs, others in ordinary helmets, basin-shaped warhats (*jin-gasa*), flat hats, armed, some with long spears, short spears, Spencer rifles, Swiss rifles, muskets, or the plain two swords. Then a silence came over the scene. Every Japanese knelt down as a group of horsemen approached. It was Keiki [i. e. Tokugawa Yoshinobu] and his train. We took off our hats to fallen greatness. He was muffled in a black hood, and wore an ordinary war-hat. What could be seen of his countenance looked worn and sad."
(Cortazzi 1983: 298 f.)

Satow´s colleague Mitford chose a more elaborate style in his description of the Tokugawa troops:
"A more extravagantly weird picture it would be difficult to imagine. There were some infantry armed with European rifles, but there were also warriors clad in the old armour of the country carrying spears, bows and arrows, falchions, curiously shaped, with sword and dirk, who looked as if they had stepped out of some old picture of the Gempei wars in the Middle Ages. Their jimbaoris, not unlike heralds´ tabards, were as many-coloured as Joseph´s coat. Hideous masks of lacquer and iron, fringed with portentous whiskers and moustachios, crested helmets with wigs from which long streamers of horsehair floated to their waists, might strike terror into any enemy. They looked like the hobgoblins of a nightmare."
(Cortazzi 2002: 66 f.)

Of interest are the descriptions of the men of the Yugekitai, a unit formed in 1866, comprising five irregular infantry battalions. These were a conglomeration of assorted samurai warriors. Despite their picturesque appearance in the ranks of the Tokugawa army, Satow dismisses them as a "herd" of ragtag samurai in a colourful, curious, and partly rather frightening mixture of clothing and equipment.

The description conveys a graphic image of the appearance of the famous *shishi*, "men of high purpose", as they liked to refer to themselves with the aid of a borrowed Confucian phrase. Others preferred to call them a band of crackpots, or outright terrorists. They were also denounced as cantankerous braggarts, *sake*-swilling womanizers, and imperial lickspittles. Such men were not only to be found in the Tokugawa forces (often hailing from the princedom of Mito), but even more frequently among the Western rebels, especially in Tosa and Choshu. The shishi movement emanated from a combination of several trends in the 1850s. On the one hand, many samurai practised *katana* swordfighting at one of the country´s many academies *(dojo)* in order to be prepared for the fight against the "Western barbarians". The most famous of these schools in eastern Japan were Chiba-dojo, Saito-dojo, and Momonoi-dojo. Thus, samurai from many different fiefs met up at Edo and established friendly relationships, hereby creating a network brimming with testosterone that reached far beyond the traditional borders of individual domains. On a social level, discontent among the samurai from lower and medium income groups was rife, since they were denied any prospect of social advancement or political influence due to the received and strictly enforced hereditary laws which condemned them to a life of poverty. For example, in Sendai domain which was huge with its 33, 000 vassals and sub-vassals, samurai were categorized into eleven rigid classes which allowed for only few chances of advancement. In Choshu there were no less than eighteen classes. Personal talent was immaterial, it was merely the paternal position that determined a young man´s career. Military functions, e. g. commissioner of firearms, were also hereditary, barring any young man from pursuing a career of his own choosing.

Samurai ranks in the princedom of Sendai

Position	Rank	Position and duties
1	*Ichimon*	Blood relatives of Lord Date
2	*Ikka*	High-ranking domain officials
3	*Jun-ikka*	Retired Ikka
4	*Ichizoku*	Long-time followers of the Date
5	*Shukuro*	Hereditary *bugyo* (officials in charge of specific administrative fields)
6	*Chakuza*	Vassals with access to the lord´s castle (1st class)
7	*Tachi-jo*	Vassals with access to the lord´s castle (2nd class)
8	*Meshidashi*	Vassals with access to the lord´s castle (3rd class)
9	*Heishi* and *Obanshi*	Majority of samurai (organized into 10 military units, each numbering 360 men)
10	*Kumi-shi*	Common followers, paymasters, falconers´ assistants, tea teachers etc.
11	*Sotsu*	Foot soldiers, porters, footmen

Source: http://st.cat-v.ne.jp/sasho/kasin.html

Many a discontent young samurai left the badly-paid service of low or medium vassal´s rank and became a freelance *ronin* instead. Shishi samurai were marked by their love of individualism, which, among other things, caused them to despise the collective drill-based fighting technique of uniformed infantry. Sakamoto Ryoma (1836–1867), arguably the most famous shishi whose death was as typical as it was exemplary (he was assassinated in a guesthouse by a group of young samurai), hated his Tosa home, calling it a place "where you can´t have any ambition and you spend your time in stupid ways like an idiot." (Orbach 2017: 12)
Holding the office of Shogun, the Tokugawa were obliged to organize and lead the country´s defence; it was nevertheless perfectly clear to the more insightful that an armed conflict with the Western powers would unfailingly end in defeat and colonisation. The Shogunate was unable to rid itself of this dilemma even in the face of mounting unrest among the shishi, who were eager to prove their mettle in combat. The shishi demanded that the Shogun fight and underscored their determination with violence: numerous foreigners and officials of the Shogunate were murdered by armed swordsmen, contributing to an atmosphere increasingly charged with insecurity and agitation. When in 1858 the Shogunate actually negotiated treaties with the hated Westerners, the shishi began to place their hopes in the person of the Emperor himself (*sonno joi* movement). After centuries of insignificance, Kyoto once again became the focal point of Japanese politics. The Imperial court could be controlled by exercising pressure on the court nobility, thereby inducing the Imperial administration to issue decrees in the Emperor´s name either in the interest of the Shogun or against him. From the year 1862, samurai flocked to the ancient capital. The Shogunate sought to keep the young and aggressive shishi in check by pitting the ferocious veteran samurai of Aizu against them. 27-year-old Matsudaira Katamori, Lord of Aizu, was pronounced "Protector of Kyoto" (*Kyoto shogoshoku*). Matsudaira´s troops were reinforced by Satsuma forces (before this domain changed sides and allied itself with Choshu in 1866), and by the Shinsengumi, an altogether rather flamboyant police force from eastern Japan.[26] The Shinsengumi proceeded to engage the anti-shogunal shishi in a series of bloody skirmishes. Four of the five "young blades" from Choshu introduced in a separate chapter[27] can also be reasonably counted among the latter. In contrast to many other shishi however, these Choshu men succeeded in successfully developing from a gang of ruffians into responsible leaders capable of ruling both their domain and later the entire state.

The fighting reached its peak on 20th August 1864, when during the so-called Kinmon Incident Choshu troops clashed with warriors from Aizu, Satsuma and Shogunal forces in a running battle in the streets of Kyoto, in the course of which much of the capital burned down. Influential shishi samurai from Choshu, who no longer felt any obligation to obey their lords if they thought differently, had hatched the reckless plan to abduct the Emperor to make him a figurehead in the struggle against foreigners and the Shogun. Satsuma artillery and traditional Aizu warcraft killed 400 Choshu samurai in the area surrounding the Imperial palace. Tokugawa Yoshinobu himself, mounted on horseback and in the thick of the fighting, cut a good figure, his party suffering only 60 losses.

---

26 Whom some preferred to call a bunch of cutthroats, cf. *"Shinsengumi – shining heroes, or gang of thugs?"*, p. 77

27 cf. *"Choshu's Young Blades"*, p. 151

This military incident triggered two unsuccessful Imperial punitive expeditions against Choshu.[28] The Kyoto defeat resulted in implacable hatred between the warriors from Choshu and their Aizu opponents, and when Aizu fell in 1868, the new rulers had considerable difficulty containing Choshu's lust for revenge.

It was characteristic of the shishi to make their moves without rational planning and careful consideration. This attitude was encouraged and praised as indicative of a "pure heart". Actions were often devised during drinking bouts at local taverns, with huge amounts of *sake* and *shoshu* (a strong spirit brewed from rice, barley, or other ingredients), often causing sufficiently inebriated participants to act spontaneously and immediately put their ideas into action. Hesitation and deliberation were deemed acts of cowardice. The revolutionary and criminal became increasingly indistinguishable. Formal hierarchy was considered unnecessary, those who had killed the most enemies commanding the highest reverence. So quick were the shishi to use their swords that even police units were reluctant to put a stop to their antics unless markedly superior in numbers. One outward subcultural element of this radical movement was the shishi's refusal to comply with formal convention – many declined tying up their hair in the traditional topknot and made a point of dressing sloppily. In other words, the shishi were something very much akin to an ancient Japanese Punk movement, only these punks carried swords as sharp as razors. To the shishis' delight, contemporaries used the *kyo* ("mad") kanji character when referring to them, so that some samurai, among them Yamagata Aritomo and Kido Takayoshi[29], even added it to their nicknames.

After their defeat at the hands of the Satsuma and Aizu at the palace gates of Kyoto in 1864, a large number of these angry young men were finally prepared to integrate themselves into their domains' regular troops. Some chose foreign service, especially in Choshu, where they joined the famous Kiheitai or other militia. These troops fought for the same cause, but in contrast to the shishi believed in discipline and military efficiency as the best means to pursue their aims. Some samurai, including former shishi not native to Choshu, even became officers in the new infantry formations there. Their vigour and experience were to prove a valuable asset to the Choshu forces in the conflicts to come.

The Tokugawa's Yugekitai troops, although also composed of samurai, were comparatively undisciplined and badly armed, so that apart from those shishi who had joined Choshu units this radical military movement was ultimately only of minimal significance in the Boshin War, which started in January 1868. Pragmatism became an increasingly important principle as even the shishi realized that far-reaching military reforms were unavoidable. Some rose not only to prominent military commands but also became political leaders holding the highest offices. They eventually succeeded in two of their key aims, namely deposing the Shogunate and abolishing the domains and the samurai caste itself. Thus from the 1870s, ambitious and talented young men, though no longer carrying the double swords, finally were able to seize the opportunities offered to them by a new Japan – something the shishi had fought for for so long.

Shinsengumi – shining heroes, or gang of thugs?

Since 1863, the key opponents of the anti-shogunal *ronin* in Kyoto had been the mostly young samurai of the Shinsengumi, a word that simply translates as "newly raised troop". Like their opponents, these men were basically shishi and expert swordsmen who had first been recruited in Tokugawa territory in the vicinity of Edo. What is to be made of these men? Were they heroes or assassins, or simply the most feared police force in all of Japanese history? Or were they actually a complete failure on the battlefield?

The Shinsengumi were led by Kondo Isami from Musashi province (b. 1834) and Serizawa Kamo from Mito (b. 1830). Both men had been chief sword fighting instructors at academies in eastern Japan and brought along their best pupils. The rank and file were stocked up with particularly aggressive *ronin*, some freshly released from gaol. The third prominent leader was Hijikata Toshizo (b. 1835 in the same province as Kondo). He shared the office of second-in-command with Serizawa. Officers down to the rank of *kumi-gashira* (leader of individual units, which could number up to ten in the total force) were entitled to ride. *Gocho* (corporals) and *hirataishi* (privates) went on foot.

Shinsengumi strength varied between 100 and 300 men. The corps was supplemented by the slightly more respectable Kyoto Mimawarigumi ("patrol corps", in existence 1864–1868). This unit consisted of up to 400 young samurai from noble families. The Kyoto Mimawarigumi, though allied with the Shinsengumi, remained a less well-known unit.

Even today, depictions of Shinsengumi would be instantly recognizable to most Japanese people. They were distinguished by their conspicuous loose-fitting jackets (*haori*) decorated with white triangular patterns (*yamagata*, "mountain tops") around the sleeves. This fashion was probably introduced by Serizawa in 1863, when he donned a light-yellow jacket with white *yamagata*. Light yellow was commonly associated with *seppuku*, signifying that the wearer was prepared to fight to the death. Other colour combinations including white, red, and black were also worn, but the light blue Shinsengumi jacket with white triangles becoming the most widely known

---

28 cf. *"The second punitive campaign against Choshu in 1866"*, p. 106

29 cf. *"Choshu's Young Blades"*, p. 151

Painted folding screen with scenes from the Kinmon Incident depicting warring factions fighting in the streets of Kyoto in 1864. Choshu troops fighting under the banner of Prince Mori are shown suffering heavy losses. The men carry mixed equipment and are only lightly armoured. They are armed with muskets or *teppo* arquebuses and carry swords, which presumably makes them Shishi or early militiamen. They are depicted using obsolete Japanese bronze cannon.

variant. No authentic example has survived however, and later black breeches (*hakama*) and jackets (*haori*) were introduced. Many Shinsengumi wore chainmail under their jackets. Sometimes even breastplates and iron forehead protectors and gauntlets were worn. The red-and-white Shinsengumi banner measured 5 x 4 feet and was emblazoned with the *makoto* ("sincerity") character signifying sworn allegiance to the Tokugawa. All carried the twin swords, occasionally supplemented by short lances. Rifles and light field cannon also formed part of the Shinsengumi arsenal. Their self confidence bordering on the arrogant, the men tied their hair in luxuriant topknots. Commander Kondo Isami had the swagger of a feudal lord, which belied his humble origins (he was a peasant's son) – he wore a black silk jacket with his family's *mon* of three bars enclosed by a ring, wide grey silk hakama with thin black stripes, and a pair of swords with black handguards in wax-coloured sheaths.

At first the Shinsengumi patrolled Kyoto, its members wearing their uniforms and carrying the corps' ensign. Suspicious persons, mostly ronin venturing from abroad, were checked and questioned, and, if necessary, detained. At this early stage, no "licence to kill" existed as yet. But the atmosphere in Kyoto was becoming increasingly violent, prompting Protector Matsudaira Katamori to order a constant presence of the Shinsengumi "by day and night". The main difference between the impetuous and unruly shishi roaming the streets and the sake shops and the Shinsengumi force was the latter's strict code of honour. It was forbidden to resign or desert the corps. Other forbidden activities included the acceptance of bribes, uttering accusations, and settling personal grievances violently. Leaving a guesthouse or tavern without paying, committing adultery, and voicing radical political ideas were likewise prohibited. Killing an enemy however was not forbidden but positively encouraged, in contrast to giving quarter: "In the case of a fight the opponent must

Shogunate troops defending the Imperial palace at Kyoto in 1864. The standards shown are those of Aizu feudal units. Most of the soldiers are regular *ashigaru* equipped in the traditional way, carrying arquebuses, *naginata*, and swords. They too are shown using bronze guns, whose size is slightly exaggerated.

be killed. If this proves impossible, one must commit *seppuku* just as if one had been wounded in the back". Offenders were condemned to ritual suicide or dishonourable beheading. The number of Shinsengumi warriors who perished in this manner is unknown but was considerable, one unfortunate member dying for having got the unit's accounts wrong! Only three of the most famous 22 officers survived the Boshin War. Serizawa and his retinue fell victims to an internal power struggle in 1863. Despite the severity of its rules, the corps was never short of recruits.

The killing of enemies frequently developed into a frenzy. While shishi from the western provinces had been the first to call a *chimatsuri* ("blood festival") – between August 1862 and July 1864, a political murder in Kyoto occurred at least every fortnight – the Shinsengumi eventually killed almost daily. Commander Kondo Isami became the most proficient killer, having already killed between 50 and 60 opponents when merely half of the time of the Shinsengumi's existence had passed. Due to the Shogun's official commission, which incidentally was well-paid, the Shinsengumi have come to be considered a "legal terrorist organization" (Hillsborough 2011: 151). In June 1867 its leading members were promoted to hatamoto status, which made them high-ranking Tokugawa retainers instead of the simple ronin they had once been. Henceforth Kondo took part in the meetings of the daimyo loyal to the Tokugawa faction.

In spite of the violence, the tables were turning against the Tokugawa cause. In July 1867 Shogun Iemochi died suddenly at Osaka Castle. Emperor Komei, who had supported him to the last, followed him to the grave in December. The new Emperor Mutsuhito (Meiji) was only 14 years old. His youth benefited the rise of Iwakura

Tomomi, the leader of the anti-Tokugawa faction at court. To this added the profound loss of face the Tokugawa suffered unsuccessfully trying to defeat Choshu.[30]

Satsuma had now joined forces with Choshu. When the new Shogun Yoshinobu stepped down on 14th October 1867, the situation for the Shinsengumi became increasingly precarious. Although the Tokugawa government stayed in power (it had previously proved capable of functioning without a Shogun at its head), the Tokugawa´s enemies procured an Imperial decree banning the former Shogun and his protector from Kyoto along with the Shinsengumi. Stripped of their former duties, the Shinsengumi gathered in the western Tokugawa stronghold of Osaka, where they were gradually transformed into a field unit. Partly rifle-armed, they were assigned to a contingent charged with defending the town of Fushimi outside Kyoto against the anticipated enemy advance. Chaos and desertion ensued: on 18th December 1867, a mere 50 veterans and an unknown number of recruits could be found in the headquarters of the local magistrate at Fushimi. Their formerly flamboyant attire had long since become a thing of the past – the remaining Shinsengumi were dressed in whatever clothes they were able to lay their hands on.

Kondo Isami, who had been wounded in the shoulder in an ambush, was absent at the Battle of Toba-Fushimi, which was fought in early January 1868.[31] The Shinsengumi, which had been assigned to the troops based at headquarters, was led by Hijikata Toshizo. Although the corps had a cannon at its disposal and some men carried rifles, they lacked the necessary training to employ them effectively. When Satsuma artillery fired on them from slightly elevated positions, the Shinsengumi responded with a series of pointless and ineffective attacks with sword and lance, losing over 30 men dead and many wounded. The survivors joined Kondo at Osaka. Not even 20 veterans were left in the ranks. As a military unit, the "legal terrorist organization" had proved worthless. The remainder of the corps formed part of the core of Tokugawa supporters and continued to fight, but its former glory had been irrevocably tarnished.

After some replenishment, 117 survivors and wounded were transported to Edo on warships. It was there that Hijikata concluded: "Swords and lances no longer hold any value on the battlefield. They are incapable of holding their own against firearms." He purchased modern breech-loading rifles for the Shinsengumi and reinforced the corps by 200 new recruits. Hijikata had cut his hair and now dressed in Western style, encouraging his men to follow his example. Kondo recovered from his wounds and returned to duty in February.

The unit was renamed *Koyochinbutai* ("Pacifiers") and was ordered westwards to Kofu, but before their arrival the castle fell to 3,000 Imperial troops under Itagaki Taisuke from Tosa. Straining for a fight, Kondo led his men to believe that reinforcements were on the way and sent Hijikata to Edo to ask for them. Some of the new recruits however soon realized what their commander was about and deserted. Only 121 men of the Shinsengumi reached Katsunama along with other Tokugawa loyalists. There were no trained artillery crews to man the two guns accompanying the detachment. On 29th March 1868 an enemy force of 1,200 men attacked barricades manned by the Shinsengumi, who suffered 38 losses to the

---

30 cf. *"The second punitive campaign against Choshu in 1866"*, p. 106
31 cf. *"'In this sign, conquer!' – the Battle of Toba-Fushimi"*, p. 111

Samurai of the Shinsengumi, 1863–1867 and 1868–1869.

To this day, the members of the Shinsengumi are famous for the flamboyant attire in which they fought the Shogun's enemies in the streets of Kyoto in the 1860s. The upper figure has managed to catch an enemy off guard inside a house. The man is only clad in a light house *kimono*. From the beginning of 1868, the appearance of the Shinsengumi underwent a number of changes: its members now also employed firearms and began to wear more practical clothing. The Shinsengumi banner (above left) was reduced to a small patch worn on the sleeve. The Boshin War did not go well for these proud samurai, and this exhausted fighter resting on a barrel of *sake* in the foreground seems to be thinking back on a more glorious past. Iillustration: Sascha Lunyakov

enemy´s single casualty. Defeated, it retreated to Edo. Again, the Shinsengumi had proved itself of little value on the battlefield, but Kondo and Hijikata refused to surrender. To them it was literally a matter of life and death. Together with 100 men and equipped with 118 rifles and three cannon they moved north-east. Kondo met his end when his force was surprised by a 300-strong enemy force under staff officer Kagawa Keizo from Mito. The recruits took to their heels, and Kondo was captured and quickly recognized. His trial began on 8th April. His conduct had made Kondo many enemies, who considered him nothing else but a murderer. He was executed on 25th April 15 kilometres away from his home, where only a month previously he had been given a glorious welcome.

Hijikata Toshizo fought on until the end came in Hokkaido in 1869. Promoted to staff officer rank, he became the commander of an independent force. His troops were repeatedly beaten, and he was wounded in the foot by a bullet. Together with Enomoto Takeaki and a varying number of companions Hijikata retired to Hokkaido, the last pocket of Tokugawa resistance.[32] He was appointed vice-commander of land forces, but his strategic position was untenable. In his death poem Hijikata, a prolific writer of *haiku*, referred to the powerful founder of his lord´s dynasty, Tokugawa Ieyasu: "Though my body may perish on the island of Ezo, my spirit will protect my lord in the East". Commanding on horseback, he was shot in the stomach in June 1869. The wound proved fatal. One week later, the last fortress, Goryokaku, fell.

A new era in Japanese history began, and the ephemeral Shinsengumi corps ought quickly to have passed into oblivion, but curiously this did not happen. The adventures and misdeeds of the Shinsengumi have been depicted countless times in the Japanese popular media of the 20th and 21st centuries. In every new generation, especially young people are fascinated by this flawed band of heroes. Why is this so?

Romantic idealization has presented these young samurai as men of pure heart, brave patriots who were devoid of petty squabbling and deliberations. They are often presented as having led free, self-determined lives following their own personal convictions. This is a particularly appealing idea since it rejects the omnipresent urge to conform with social convention which remains prominent in Japanese society to this very day. These men seemed to have abjured such social constraints and were prepared to pay the price. Although this perceived attitude is certainly not valid for the vast majority of young Japanese people today, it certainly appeals to hidden desires. Especially young Japanese continue to be intrigued by the proud men of the Shinsengumi.

Samurai –
the last battlecry of the old feudal élite

The zest of the young men in the ranks of the Shishi and Shinsengumi stood in stark opposition to the lack of motivation displayed by so many members of the established samurai caste in middle and higher hereditary positions and offices. Kondo Isami of the Shinsengumi witnessed the performance of government faction samurai during the second Choshu expedition[33] and remarked: "Although the *hatamoto* [high-ranking vassals of the Tokugawa] have gradually reached Geishu province [aka Hiroshima/Aki] they display no fighting spirit whatsoever." They spent their time "getting souvenirs together" and "grew weary just waiting to return to the east. [...] we cannot expect victory if war should break out." (Hillsborough 2011: 138). Incidentally, their peers among the old Choshu vassals were not much better, seeing themselves exposed to the biting criticism of Takasugi Shinsaku.

How had the old warrior élite become so degenerate? The feudal structure of Tokugawa-ruled Japan with the Shogun at its head had been in existence for 250 years. It demanded that in the case of war every samurai, depending on his income, was to provide his lord with a specific number of warriors accompanied by a larger number of unarmed retainers and servants. The lords of the domains (*daimyo*) were required to serve the Shogun, something they were less and less prepared to do. A daimyo had to have a minimum annual income of 10,000 *koku*. Apart from the feudal levy, the Shogun had at his disposal 17,000 hereditary samurai retainers (some sources give an even higher number) with an annual income less than 10,000 *koku*. 5,000 of these served in the higher *hatamoto* class. The remainder were classified as *gokenin*. These samurai and their sons were expected to educate themselves in two particular fields, namely *bu* (martial arts comprising fighting with sword, lance and handgun, archery, riding, swimming, strategy and tactics), and *bun* (cultural arts, e. g. calligraphy, poetry, tea ceremony, flower arrangement, ink painting). Since armed conflict became rare after the middle of the 17th century, the Shogun´s vassals turned from warriors to administrators serving in offices as county bailiffs (*daikan*), at court, or maybe for an occasional bout of ceremonial duty as guards of honour or escorts. More menial duties such as policing, sentry duties, etc. were left to the lower ranks serving as *ashigaru / doshin*. This meant that many *hatamoto* and *gokenin* no longer possessed any real military experience or proficiency, and naturally led to these men becoming more and more inclined towards *bun* than *bu*. The latter was mostly practiced by men of lower rank, or by those of medium rank who had become bored and frustrated by their military inactivity. Some of these men

---

32 cf. *"Last stand of the Shogunate party in Hokkaido – the surrender of Hakodate on 27th June 1869"*, p. 142

33 cf. *"The second punitive campaign against Choshu in 1866"*, p. 106

One of the old Imperial Palace gates in Kyoto (Kyoto Gosho). Even though still occasionally in use by the Imperial Family, the Palace is now mostly uninhabited. During the Bakumatsu period, it was essential for the political stakeholders of the day to exercise their influence on the Emperor via the court nobility, thereby legitimizing their own actions and ostracizing enemies.

Street scene in modern Fushimi, today a district located in southern Kyoto. The two-storey wooden houses form a typical part of the local scenery of the Imperial capital. These houses have remained virtually unchanged since the close of the Edo period.

drifted towards the shishi or became renegade ronin[34] who in the course of time came to heartily despise not only the hereditary privileges of those samurai "gone soft", but also the Tokugawa system as a whole.

Another problem was the high number of non-combatants in samurai units, or rather, the small number of effective fighting men. Sources mention the example of a "modern" battalion from the Tokugawa domain of Kii, which paraded through Osaka with 507 men and a small artillery contingent in 1865. Of these, 65 were samurai sword fighters, 104 were infantry with firearms, and 302 were porters or servants (figures quoted after Totman 1980: 188). Less than half of the unit was actually composed of fighting troops. In rural areas things could be even worse. Suzuki Zanzaemon, owner of a large farming estate, described a contingent despatched against the Mito rebels by the Prince of Katsuyama (22, 000 *koku*) on the coast of the Sea of Japan in 1865:

"Later the Lord of Katsuyama sent out more than 600 men, but these were not samurai but provisional fighters such as townsmen armed with swords, and peasants had been recruited to act as porters. The number of genuine samurai cannot have been higher than 50. Rumour has it that they even brought ashigaru and minor civil servants with them; these people are a laughing stock."

(Ehlers 2020: 132)

The number of fighting men in mounted samurai units was even smaller since every cavalryman was accompanied by several grooms and servants.

Another reason why the above-mentioned battalion from Kii possessed such little value as a fighting force was that it was a mixed arms unit composed of too many small and incompatible contingents. Small groups (*gumi*) of ten, twenty or thirty men armed in the same manner were typical and could be combined with other units similarly equipped. This however did not mean that they were capable of manoeuvering in an effective manner, even though many were already armed with rifles. Lacking training as a unit, they were incapable of delivering volleys on company or battalion level or delivering coordinated attacks.

In spite of their limited combat value, the samurai units of the Tokugawa forces gobbled up a considerable amount of available funds. This is why the later Shogunate reforms preferred to turn the samurai into taxpayers and providers of recruits rather than attempt to arm them with rifles and turn these arrogant snobs into modern infantry. Sons of peasants, ronin and townsfolk were easier to train and might eventually have made a fine fighting force, if there had been more time and higher-quality armament – after all, Satsuma and Choshu had shown what was possible.

There were nevertheless also a few domains whose samurai had managed to avoid decadence. Among these was Yonezawa, which had a long tradition of firearms and marksmanship[35] and the larger domain of Aizu. Both domains were situated to the north of Edo.

In Aizu samurai were not only part of the military establishment in theory but were still expected to practice the use of arms. Of a population of 230, 000, 23, 000 inhabitants of Aizu were members of samurai families, of which 4, 500 were immediate male vassals of the prince. This provided the *daimyo* with a standing army of this number, which made Aizu something of a superpower among the Shogunate's allies. When the Shogun needed help in keeping the shishi and Choshu at bay in Kyoto, Aizu responded to the call in 1862. In 1863 a standard Aizu unit still consisted of around 150 men of different arms and social rank: 50 samurai on foot equipped with sword and lance, 60 *ashigaru* armed with Japanese *teppo*

---

34 cf. *"Shishi – men of high ideals, or unmitigated lunatics?"*, p. 75

35 cf. *"The example of Yonezawa"*, p. 37

Traditionally-equipped samurai from Aizu, 1860s.
Like his predecessors who roamed the battlefields three centuries previously, this samurai is armed with the traditional yari lance. It is supplemented by the hallmark of his caste, a pair of swords tucked into his belt. Those elements of armour not yet discarded are now worn mostly beneath the clothing. This man has also donned a steel skullcap with a mail aventail. Right up to the battle of Toba-Fushimi, most Aizu warriors (and those of many other domains) would have fought similarly equipped. After the battle's disastrous outcome, Aizu also began modernizing its armed forces by raising regular rifle-armed infantry. Illustration by Sascha Lunyakov

Composite armour consisting of mail and folding elements.

Although modern firearms had made complete samurai armour obsolete – during the Edo campaign in 1868 the commander-in-chief, Prince Komatsu Akihito, is said to have been the only officer in the entire new Imperial Army to have worn a full set of armour. However, body protection through armour was not completely abandoned. Some samurai wore coats of mail underneath their clothing. Forehead and cheek protectors of anatomically-shaped steel plates, and iron gauntlets were widely used. Complete sets of armour composed of mail and foldable light pieces of armour like the two splendid examples shown could not be afforded by everyone however. (Photographs courtesy of Samurai Museum, Berlin – Peter Janssen collection)

Aizu troops arriving at Fushimi bridge on 2nd January 1868.

Only the two standard bearers are shown wearing Western-style cotton uniforms. The samurai are armed according to century-old tradition with lances and swords. Only one carries a musket. Their equipment is carried by porters. The samurai have acknowledged the penetrative power of modern firearms and have done away with armour, although a few might still wear individual elements under their dress. They wear light hats instead of helmets, and individually worn kimono, billowing *hakama* trousers and *jimbaori* or *haori* surcoats make this troop very colourful to behold. (*Nishiki no mihata* 1907: plate II)

Aizu samurai in January 1868 (detail).

Original forehead protector consisting of several lacquered segments with a faded painted-on heraldic device. It was attached to the wearer´s head with a coarse cotton headband. (Shinsengumi Museum Aizu, Wakamatsu)

What remained of samurai armour on a 19th-century battlefield?
If armour was still worn in the campaigns of 1868/1869, it was mostly elements like these – a breastplate for the upper torso, a heavy cloth or mail bonnet, and an iron forehead protector. The armour shown here bears the device of Shinsengumi commander Kondo Isami. (Modern reconstruction, Samurai Museum Shinjuku)

arquebuses, 20 *yoriki* (high-ranking samurai, presumably mounted), and 18 officers and specialists. This composition only changed in 1868.

A member of the multitudinous Matsudaira dynasty, Lord Katamori was related to the Shogun, and his family sported the Tokugawa arms with the three hollyhocks surrounded by a ring. Although Aizu was comparatively slow in the adoption of modern firearms, Aizu troops had no trouble keeping the wild shishi in check when it came to close-quarter fighting with sword and lance, as the great battle outside the gates of the palace at Kyoto in 1864 had shown.

Aizu´s military law was relatively new, having been codified in the 1790s. It contained a number of very modern rules. For example, the code explicitly forbade the destruction of rice fields and the mistreatment of the civilian population through rape, pillaging, or theft.

Troop maintenance in Kyoto cost the huge sum of 300, 000 *ryo* (gold coins) *per annum*, and Aizu was only partly reimbursed by the increasingly hard-up Shogunate. Aizu farmers were forced to pay crushing taxes, and after the defeat of the samurai the first thing to go were the widely-loathed instruments of Aizu´s inland revenue – in 1868, villagers gleefully watched the houses of their local administrators burn down, and the tax lists along with them. In spite of the ruthless taxation, there was at first no money to equip Aizu troops with modern firearms. From March 1867, and all the more so after the experience of battle at Toba-Fushimi in January 1868, serious attempts at military reform were undertaken. The acquisition of sufficient numbers of modern firearms and ammunition proved difficult, because the large ports were far away. Only 800 rifles were supplied by Henry Schnell via Niigata[36], which is why mixed units of riflemen and soldiers armed with lances remained in being. Schnell also functioned as an instructor. Large stocks of rifles, guns and ammunition were taken over from the disintegrating Shogunate in 1868, but these arms were not always compatible. On the other hand, motivation among Aizu´s samurai remained high, so that they did not have to be replaced by commoners. In the end, even women, children and old men fought alongside peasants and ronin to defend Aizu´s ancient fortress city of Aizu-Wakamatsu.[37]

In 1868, Aizu samurai were organized into modern companies and platoons according to a rational yet not altogether too progressive system. Samurai and ashigaru were grouped into different companies according to age and rank. Each company numbered 100 men. Veterans aged 50 years or older were referred to as *gembu*, men between 36 and 49 were called *seiryu* (these were entrusted with border defence). Young men between 18 and 35 years of age, the *suzaku*, providded the mainstay of the fighting troops, while youngsters aged 16 or 17, the *byakko*, formed the reserves. All of these units were threefold, categorized according to social rank. The ranks of *shichu* ("full samurai"), *yoriai* ("common samurai") and *ashigaru* (foot soldiers) denoted the men´s social status. This principle successfully negated the problem of the samurai´s unwillingness to take orders from their social inferiors. Units were largely homogenous regarding social rank and age, which made things easier for everyone concerned, and it was possible to promote men to leading positions according to merit not rank. The altogether 343 adolescent *byakko* for example were organized into six units, two each of upper class, middle class and ashigaru category. So ardent was the will of these young people to defend their homeland that several 15-year-olds and even one 13-year-old joined the ranks with false papers.

Several obsolete types of rifle were used. These were superior to the ancient *teppo* arquebus but no real match for the modern weapons employed by the enemy. Probably the most famous of these formations was the 2nd upper class adolescent platoon, the *shichu-byakko-tai* ("Full Samurai White Tiger Platoon"), 19 warriors of which tragically took their own lives during the Battle of Aizu-Wakamatsu. From the top of Mount Imori they had seen the blazing castle in the valley, and assuming that the daimyo and his family were dead, and all was now lost, committed suicide. In fact, the prince was very much alive. The graves of these unfortunate young men continue to attract large numbers of visitors to this very day. Apart from the regular samurai units, the army of Aizu also fielded several units of *shogitai* militia, which had already been raised after 1865. In the summer of 1868, the levied peasants and townspeople suffered from low morale, while the scattered Tokugawa supporters who had rallied in Aizu had already seen battle and were keen to once again get to grips with the enemy. The number of irregular troops eventually rose to 8, 000. Historians know no less than 39 units by their often-picturesque names, which could hold any number between 25 and 250 men in their ranks. Most contingents, however, were of company size numbering between 80 and 100 men.

Aizu´s exploitation of the limited resources at its disposal can be called nothing short of masterful. Even though not very large or rich in income, it thus rose to become the most powerful of the Tokugawa´s allies. Most other domains in the north and east of Japan were much weaker and often managed to send only traditional samurai contingents to their lord´s aid. Many of these warriors were armed only with sword and lance, while a few carried a motley conglomeration of mismatched firearms. If Aizu had had more time and money to carry its military reforms further, with access to better-quality firearms, its samurai may have had the potential to stand up to and possibly beat even the most powerful of the Shogun´s enemies, the forces of Satsuma and Choshu.

---

36   cf. "The influence of foreign arms dealers", p. 48

37   cf. "The bloody siege of Aizu-Wakamatsu", p. 142

Modern Infantry

In 1867 British diplomats Ernest Satow and Algernon Bertram Mitford saw the daimyo of Awa's infantry on parade on the island of Shikoku:

"Some five hundred men, divided into five bodies of varying strength, were put through their drill. Their uniform was in imitation of European style, black trousers with red stripes down the side, and black coats; happy the soldier who could muster a pair of boots, the rest had only straw sandals. On their heads they had hats of papier-maché, either conical or of dish-cover shape, with two horizontal red bands. They used the English infantry drill, with the quaint addition of a shout to indicate the discharge of their firearms. In the opinion of those who were competent to judge, they acquitted themselves very creditably."

(Cortazzi 1983: 263)

"The next day there was a review of some five hundred men in a sort of tatterdemalion European dress, some with boots, some without. The drill was capital.

(Cortazzi 2002: 59)

Just over a year later, Satow witnessed the entrance of Emperor Meiji in Edo/Tokyo:

"The display could not be described as splendid, for the effect of what was oriental in the courtiers' costumes was marred by the horribly untidy soldiers with unkempt hair and clothing vilely imitated from the West."

(Cortazzi 1983: 391)

Both accounts provide an image of the infantry serving in the forces of those daimyo who had carried out military reforms before and during the Boshin War. The soldiers, both samurai and commoners, were organized into companies of about 100 men, and in most domains four or five companies made up a battalion. Only Satsuma continued to rely on independent rifle companies of between 90 and 120 soldiers, which helped to economise on both administration and staff. These small self-contained units were also particularly suitable for the often-difficult terrain of the many small battlefields of the Boshin War. Arms drill was performed according to current British or slightly outdated Dutch drill manuals. Shogunate forces betrayed strong French influence. The armour and colourful attire of individual samurai had given way to the uniforms of the regular infantry. The jackets and trousers more or less modelled on Western military fashion were made of cotton and dyed with indigo (both of which were in ample supply in Japan); the "black" of the Awa troops described above was in fact probably a very dark indigo blue as a result of repeated dying. One other traditional Japanese dye, that of the tea plant, which gave various shades of brown, had become decidedly unpopular, probably because so many of the Western soldiers and sailors present in Japan wore dark blue uniforms. If a lighter summer uniform existed, it was occasionally left undyed, so would have been off-white in colour.

Headdress consisted of hats or helmets of various types.[38] Choshu troops wore *nirayama* hats, while Satsuma favoured tall conical helmets. Other types or hybrid forms were also common. Because leather was a rare commodity in Japan at the time only few soldiers wore boots. Most favoured the traditional, dark-coloured *tabi* socks and straw sandals (*warabi*). This footwear was almost universally worn by the entire Japanese population. The scarcity of leather was also the reason why the rifle-armed troops' webbing necessary to support various items of equipment (belts, bandoliers, cartridge boxes) was of mixed manufacture and made of various materials such as lacquered textile or paper, the latter even being used for saddles! Apart from imported items, Japanese soldiers helped themselves with various locally produced equipment, e. g. fabric belts and especially the pouches, bullet bags and powder horns manufactured by Japanese craftsmen. Cartridge boxes were frequently made waterproof by applying several layers of lacquer. Cartridge boxes were usually painted with a samurai personal arms, or those of his lord.

In order to distinguish between individual units, various methods were used. As seen, Awa troops' uniforms sported red trouser stripes and two horizontal bars on the helmets. Tokugawa denshutai clothing was marked by broad stripes along the seams; the battalion number was worn painted on the wooden helmet.[39] Helmets frequently received markings to identify the wearer's unit and were also often painted with the samurai personal badge, or that of the daimyo. However, the most common place of unit identification was the upper sleeve. Markings varied from a simple white brassard tied around the right arm (Satsuma) to the different *sode-jirushi* sleeve badges worn on the left or right arm.[40] These consisted mostly of a rectangular piece of fabric sewn onto the sleeve or simply suspended from below the shoulder. The symbols and varying combinations of markings and characters permitted clear identification of the wearer's native princedom, and occasionally also his unit. The most important sleeve tags however were the small pieces of Nishiki silk brocade from Kyoto (*kingire*) which had been employed in the production of the Imperial standards at Toba-Fushimi.[41] These were distributed to the troops between the march on Edo and the Battle of Ueno. These conspicuous markers made each wearer a representative of the Emperor – resisting him meant resisting the Emperor himself, and

---

38 cf. *"Reform of the Shogunate – The new Takashima academy"*, p. 14
39 cf. *"The Shogun makes a clean sweep – the new army"*, p. 23
40 cf. *"Other mons and standards"*, p. 68
41 cf. *"'In this sign, conquer!' – the Battle of Toba-Fushimi"*, p. 111

Shichu-byakko-tai ("White tiger platoon") troop of adolescent high-ranking Aizu samurai in 1868.
These boys have become so famous both in regional and universal Japanese history that they have even made their way onto soft drink vending machines, as this example from Wakamatsu shows. (photographed by the author in 2018)

Satsuma and Aki (Geishu) troops, victorious at Toba-Fushimi, with the Imperial banners.

Satsuma soldiers wearing conical helmets are shown standing in the first rank (red over white banner), while the Aki troops, recognizable by their *nirayama* hats, stand in the foreground (banner with two red bars on white background). The Imperial standards comprise one large troop flag displaying the black chrysanthemum device on a white background, and the two Nishiki banners with sun and moon discs suspended from crossbars in the old-fashioned manner. These banners were invaluable psychological assets for the troops. The array is made complete by two staff flags with characters indicating the presence of members of the court nobility, who though hardly experienced soldiers served to legitimize the new Imperial army. It is worth comparing the modern equipment and clothing of the victors with the traditional attire of the Aizu samurai fighting in the same battle, as depicted above in the same pictorial source on p. 88.
(*Nishiki no mihata* 1907, plate XV)

Drum major and drummers from the domain of Ueda.

The "drum major" is in fact Prince Matsudaira Tadanari in person. His fief took part on the Imperial side in the Hokuetsu War and the siege of Aizu-Wakamatsu in 1868. Styles continued to vary from modern to the traditional, as a report from Kyoto in 1868 shows: "Among the drummers, one had his instrument slung on a pole, which gave it the appearance of a large-sized paper or skin warming-pan, which was carried before him, and he beat it behind his carrier's back with as many flourishes as any of our own regimental drummers."

(Cortazzi 2002: 136)

Head of a marching column of Satsuma infantry. The bearer of the Imperial banner is followed by a soldier carrying the banner of Satsuma. Behind them march the drummers and the rank-and-file. The NCO in the foreground carries a bayonet flag (*fanion*) in the French fashion, the mounted company commander wears a *jimbaori* surcoat over his dark blue uniform, and a shallow wooden *ichimon-jingasa* lacquered in black. (*Nishiki no mihata* 1907, XVI)

Column of infantrymen from Aki (Geishu/Hiroshima). The formation is preceded and followed by standard bearers carrying the princely banner. The men are marching in military step. One of the officers carries a small signalling flag. Two musket-armed irregulars follow the column. (*Nishiki no mihata* 1907, XVI)

this concept was used by the soldiers as a pretext for all kinds of coercive measures, often involving considerable violence.

European observers like Satow did not find these soldiers' appearance altogether convincing. Deficient equipment and supplies even among the victorious Imperial troops led to uncleanliness and deteriorating hygiene. The long campaign north of Edo/Tokyo which lasted until the end of 1868 was also marked by numerous privations. Only in the 1870s did the government manage to issue to all of its troops standardized and modern uniforms in Western (i. e. French) style.

In Choshu in 1859, modern-minded samurai officers still caused something of an outcry with their appearance, which consisted of an outrageous mixture of styles, one officer wearing a shirt with Western style buttons and tight-fitting sleeves, another wore a buttoned shirt and an "outlandish" hat, together with Japanese *hakama* trousers. Conservatives were shocked by this breach of clothing etiquette: "They are already aping the barbarian in their garb; their hearts must also be barbarian. Are we, the sons of the Divine Land, to imitate even the grimaces of the barbarians?" (Craig 1961: 136).

The answer to this rhetorical question was definitely yes. Western dress was not just a way of demonstrating to one's environment a personal desire for change, it was also so much more practical for troops handling mid-19th century firearms. These officers of the Choshu militia were among the first to adopt Western fashion and equipment, often mixing them with Japanese elements. Other domains followed suit. As was common in many contemporary Western armies (especially the British), officers were allowed a great deal of liberty in their choice of service dress. Items were purchased and worn according to personal taste. Appearances varied greatly, reaching from traditionalists attired in kimono, *haori* or *jimbaori*, billowing *hakama* and even the odd piece of armour to those dressed completely in Western clothing including upturned collars, frock coats, breeches, riding boots and golden watch-chains. All kinds of combinations of the two styles were seen. The traditional heavy suits of armour worn by the samurai of the past had largely vanished from the battlefields of the Boshin War, although some samurai were able to afford light armour consisting of folding plate armour or chainmail, both of which were usually worn under the top layer of clothing.

Some officers wore the same dark blue cotton uniforms as the men, together with a splendid-looking *jimbaori* surcoat and a form of exotic headdress peculiar to this period: a cap secured by a chinstrap which sported a huge shock of dyed yak hair.

A Dutch instructor drilling Japanese recruits, possibly at Nagasaki. These men provide a good impression of what most militia probably looked like before the Boshin War. (*Public domain*)

Outrage, 1859

For conservative samurai, the numerous changes in Japanese politics and society of the 1850s and 1860s represented the downfall of civilization. In Choshu, the sources mention a notorious flap which occurred when the two young samurai Kuruhara Ryuzo and Awaya Hikotaro, both freshly returned from training with their Dutch instructors at Nagasaki, appeared on parade clad in a manner that could only be described as unorthodox: one wore a jacket with "tight-fitting" sleeves, the other a buttoned shirt, and an "outlandish" hat together with *hakama* pants. The present author and his artist have attempted to reconstruct this garish attire, which shocked contemporary bystanders. The hat has been reconstructed as a bowler, a form of headdress which became universally popular worldwide after 1849. The musket is an 1845 Dutch muzzle-loader with priming cap mechanism. Conservative protests at this new fashion were mostly ignored, and so the mixture of Western and Japanese clothing was to remain popular for years to come.

Illustration: Sascha Lunyakov

Mounted Satsuma officer at the head of his troops in Kyoto during the Battle of Toba-Fushimi, January 1868.
(*Nishiki no mihata* 1907, plate XV)

Officer's tunic from Aizu. The large white stripes on the shoulders probably seek to imitate the tabs worn on the shoulders of American officers' tunics. (Byakko-tai Museum, Aizu-Wakamatsu)

Staff officer, 1868.
(*Nishiki no mihata* 1907, plate XXXVII)

Officers attend a briefing.
Apart from the Imperial *kingire* sleeve tag of brocade fabric, the right-hand man wears another tag, possibly identifying him as an officer from Hiroshima/Aki.
(two narrow red stripes on white background)

Yak hair wigs as part of officers´ or other samurai headdress

Princedom	Name	Hair colour
Satsuma	*koguma* ("Black bear")	black
Choshu	*haguma* ("White bear")	white
Tosa	*shaguma* ("Red bear")	red
Shogunate and allies (e. g. *yugekitai*)	*haguma, koguma*	white or black

Variations were not uncommon. In 1867 Dr. William Wills came across a group of Tosa samurai wearing yak hair wigs: "At Fushimi we were met by a perfect nightmare in the shape of a guard of Tosa men – wild-looking fellows, clad in armour with their faces hideously masked and long elf locks of black or white horsehair hanging down from their helmets over their shoulders. With this weird escort of pantomimic demons were marched into Kyoto [...]" (Cortazzi 2012: 107).
The source demonstrates the desired intimidating effect these shaggy-looking accoutrements possessed. The origins of this spectacular but ephemeral military headdress remain unclear. Possibly the long red hair of some Dutch traders at Deshima provided inspiration. At any rate, a bestial, barbaric appearance in battle designed to terrify the enemy was an inseparable part of samurai tradition.
The material itself, dyed yak hair as a means of decoration for helmets and weapons, had already been appreciated by Tokugawa Ieasu and his contemporaries and was also used in the Japanese theatre, and as part of Buddhist rites. In the 1860s, this type of headdress was often worn by company commanders, but the sources seem to imply that coloured yak hair caps were also worn by others, e. g. red ones by the élite Tosa *jinshotai* troops. Satow also spotted them among the Yugekitai militia fighting on the side of the Tokugawa: "A herd of men in fantastic costumes (*yu-geki-tai*, "brave fighting men"), some wearing helmets with long wigs of black or white hair reaching half-down their backs".[42]
Military signalling also underwent a series of reforms. It is hardly surprising that the Tokugawa under French influence employed buglers apart from the usual drummers and fifers, while Satsuma and Choshu equipped their bandsmen with flutes and snare drums. The bandsmen marched ahead of the columns beating time to the military step in accordance with the newly introduced drill.
Flags were also employed in a much more rational manner than had been the case in the old feudal armies, in which every samurai of rank had worn his own *sashimono* battle flag attached to the back of his armour. Many officers or NCOs of various domains now carried a small flag to signal to their men (e. g. when operating in loose formation in broken terrain), while companies, batteries and larger formations all had a standard bearer carrying an ensign with the same blazon. These blazons usually consisted of the domains´ respective symbols, either newly-devised simple geometric combinations, or patterns, lines, or some other easily recognizable motive – or the daimyo family´s traditional *mon*. Aizu made use of both. The respective motive was also to be found on the soldiers´ sleeve tags, making it easy to tell friend from foe. Due to the altogether confusing variety of uniforms and dress, this means of identification was certainly of vital importance. Generally speaking, we can say that while the western princedoms favoured combinations of red and white, the Shogunate forces preferred black and white.[43]

Bizarre and unappealing though these infantrymen may have appeared to the observer, they were nothing short of a revolution if we consider the state of Japanese military affairs which remained the norm well into the 1860s. A Japanese witness had noted with surprise and distress in 1853 that all of the one hundred sailors and soldiers landed by Commodore Perry´s squadron were armed and thus potential combatants. Even the crews of the jollyboats had carried weapons. This was unthinkable in Japan – to carry arms was the prerogative of the samurai caste, which constituted less than ten per cent of the entire population; samurai also did not row. The number of fighters among the troops turned out simultaneously by four daimyo to receive the foreign emissaries made up less than ten percent of the total. The traditional Shogunate army was based on the time-honoured and unchanged formula of one samurai with an annual income of 500 *koku* having to procure eleven men for war, only two of which were to be fighters: 2 samurai, 1 armour-bearer, 2 porters to carry the samurai lance and bow, 2 trunk porters, 2 grooms, the master´s sandal-bearer, and a further two porters for any other luggage. The higher a vassal´s income, the fewer the relative number of fighters.
It was soon recognized that feudal Japan had by far failed to exploit its full military potential. It was noted that if one succeeded in detaching the large number of retainers and servants from their masters´ retinue and turning them into infantry, the effective amount of troops would rise practically overnight in an unprecedented manner. The aim was to create combat units whose manpower consisted of one hundred per cent of soldiers armed uniformly with rifles. Especially Satsuma consistently implemented this objective.

---

42 cf. *"Shishi – men of high ideals, or unmitigated lunatics?"*, p. 75

43 cf. *"Other mons and standards"*, pp. 68–74 for illustrations

Satsuma and Choshu introduced firearms drill for all samurai in 1854 and 1857 respectively and abolished the old system of samurai being accompanied by several servants. Under pressure, Choshu completed its military reforms in 1865 by abolishing both traditional weapons and vassal units and raising new rifle-armed infantry from the old *ashigaru* and samurai servants. All were to be uniformly armed with rifles of Minié construction. The artillery arm was also created systematically. Former lords literally found themselves reduced to "lone riders" which were no longer needed. Many who could bear to do so sold off their chargers and armour, which served to considerably enlarge American and European collections. These painful social changes were gradually rewarded by success – some high-standing samurai quickly understood that it was of little use resisting change and preferred to encourage their sons to become officers in the new armies. Eventually no more cavalry formations were raised as they were considered militarily obsolete. Only officers remained mounted, and a number of horses were retained for scouts and dispatch riders.

In this area too the Shogunate got the short end of the deal since its reforms occurred too late and were not radical enough to have the desired military effect. Precious funds and manpower were wasted on the retention of expensive but obsolete cavalry formations.

The easiest units of all the vassal forces to transform into modern infantry were the *ashigaru*, which had already previously fought on foot in close formation under the command of a feudal lord or had at least been trained to do so. All that remained in theory was to re-equip these men with rifles instead of the old lances, bows and arquebuses, and to allow for a certain amount of time required to teach the men to operate their new weapons effectively. In Choshu, modernized *ashigaru* units along with militia carried the brunt of the defensive actions in 1866. The samurai rifle units were finally ready for action in 1868.

Satsuma and Choshu were not the only ones to outdo the Shogunate by a long shot. Kii (Kishu), one of the three main Tokugawa lines, based in Wakayama, took radical steps after the eye-opening disaster of 1866, even though these reforms only truly bore fruit after the Boshin War.[44] Kishu demanded that "...regardless of social rank every samurai should regard himself as an individual soldier". The disbandment of all feudal units was decreed and the duties of non-combatant retainers abolished. Only rifle-armed units were to be raised forthwith. All ancient military offices were scrapped and every samurai not fully employed in civilian administration was assigned to a rifle unit. Samurai with a 1, 000 *koku* income now found themselves drilling shoulder to shoulder with their 20 *koku* peers. This was of course problematic because the idea of equal pay for equal work was hardly reconcilable with the huge income differences which these men had inherited from their forefathers. This was one of the reasons why Kishu was unable to make any noteworthy impression in the Boshin War. Aizu managed to tackle the problem better by raising units according to the men's social rank.[45]

In 1868 Nagaoka drastically reduced the income gaps among the samurai serving in its rifle units. The prince himself appealed to the men's feeling of solidarity and apologized to them with the words: "I regret on behalf of my higher-ranking retainers who are being made to suffer that it has been decided to drastically reduce the income differences among our samurai." (Sonoda 1990: 95).

The notion of doing away with the samurai caste and its hereditary income altogether was no longer very far away. If lower-ranking samurai and even non-samurai were able to fulfil the new military requirements better than lavishly-paid feudal retainers, why bother to keep so many of the latter?

Shotai Militia

Our survey of the various troop types in existence around 1868 will be concluded by the militia, who were summarily referred to as *shotai*.

So far the Choshu militia, most prominently Takasugi Shinsaku's *kiheitai*, have been introduced, units which triggered a veritable revolution not only in the military but also in the social sense, since more than half of the men in their ranks were no longer from the samurai caste.[46] On the opposite side of the wide range of militias were to be found the *yugekitai* of limited efficiency, which had been raised by the Shogunate's arbitrary throwing together of samurai who hailed from entirely different backgrounds.

First-class militia like those of Choshu were thoroughly disciplined and capable of delivering two-rank volleys at a distance of 350–400 metres on an advancing enemy. Their training enabled them to surround an enemy or enfilade him by sniping at him from concealed positions on two sides of a sunken road. They operated in close and loose formation and thus became the model on which all of Choshu's samurai and *ashigaru* units were eventually based.

Choshu managed to gradually overcome the problems posed by mismatched and obsolete equipment and armament, something other militia fighting for the Tokugawa never succeeded in doing since they were often a rag-tag mixture of men of varying motivation and morale. Many came from entirely different backgrounds: stragglers from units that had been destroyed in battle, highly motivated *ronin*, peasants, discontents, and a sprinkling of Shishi fanatics. The lack of funding to equip these units adequately was endemic in the Shogunate forces,

---

44   cf. "The influence of foreign arms dealers", p. 48

45   cf. "Samurai – the last battlecry of the old feudal élite", p. 82

46   cf. "Satsuma, Choshu and their allies", p. 61

so many of these militia were poorly armed with obsolete muskets, lances and swords. In Choshu on the other hand, rich merchants were "encouraged" to make more or less voluntary donations in order to properly equip the domain's militia.

Arguably the most well-known of all these units were the *shogitai*, a corps of Tokugawa supporters dyed in the wool who were still bent on avenging their lord when he had already resigned and submitted to Japan's new political order.

After the Imperial army's victory at Toba-Fushimi in January 1868 the incompletely reformed Shogunate army was already beginning to disintegrate, and former Shogun Yoshinobu quickly decided to abandon all resistance. Yet the humiliation of having their lord declared an enemy of the Emperor's Court (*cho-teki*) and knowing him in a self-imposed exile patiently awaiting his fate at Edo was enough to raise the fighting spirit of thousands of Tokugawa followers and encourage them to continue the struggle. While a moderate Katsu Kaishu negotiated a peaceful surrender of Edo castle with the approaching victors and succeeded in handing over the Shogunate capital without further bloodshed, Admiral Enomoto Takeaki and General Otori Keisuke together with his land forces refused to surrender. Both retired north[47], while many supporters of the old order still remained at Edo. In February 1868 seventeen of Tokugawa Yoshinobu's former retainers founded the Shogitai militia. Although there were never enough modern firearms available and the militia was usually hard up, there was never a shortage of manpower. The militia, which lacked any form of political legitimisation, consisted of no less than 3, 000 furious and mostly young men (scholars have calculated the Shogitai militiaman's average age at 24 years). One of its first leaders, Honda Toshisaburo, explained: "When a lord is disgraced it is time for his retainers to die" (Steele 2005: 130). The militia was not about implementing any specific political alternative, let alone defeating the enemy and restoring the Tokugawa Shogunate. Instead, the Shogitai preferred to wallow in the highly romanticized, irrational and hopelessly outdated ideal of a samurai devotion to his lord. In this respect, many Shogitai fighters and hotheaded Shishi were kindred spirits.[48]

The Shogitai conspiracy was codified in form of a founding document signed in blood. It is telling that only a few of the militia's members hailed from the higher ranks of the samurai caste. Most of these had come to terms with the new order. The Shogitai attracted young samurai of humble background as well as townsfolk, Shinto priests, and a few disgruntled courtiers for good measure. The militia also became a refuge for young samurai from domains which had surrendered, and who had refused to accept defeat and deserted. The degree of military experience and the quality of equipment varied greatly within the unit since most professional soldiers had left Edo with Enomoto and Otori and taken their equipment along with them.

The Shogitai's headquarters were in the Ueno quarter of Edo in the huge complex of the Kan'ei-ji. This temple was Edo's protector against the demons from the northeast. It was governed by a young abbot of Imperial blood who was friendly with the Tokugawa. It was (and is) also the resting place of several Shoguns, and it was to this place that Tokugawa Yoshinobu had voluntarily confined himself.

Katsu Kaishu, the most important and influential Tokugawa partisan left at Edo, called upon the Shogitai to perform police duties around the capital. Although Edo had previously harboured a million people within its walls, its population had sunk, and the precarious political situation allowed criminals to roam freely, making life in the city increasingly dangerous and unpleasant.

On 11th April the castle of Edo was handed over to Imperial troops, which gradually set about dissolving the old régime's municipal administration. Part of the Shogitai under Shibuzawa Sei'ichiro departed Edo and reconstituted itself as the new Shinbutai militia, fighting at first north of Edo and subsequently in Hokkaido until 1869. The remaining Shogitai under Amano Hachiro meanwhile began to harass the occupying forces from the West by launching nocturnal attacks on small and isolated groups of Imperial soldiers. Thus, a part of the Shogitai had chosen to fight as a military force on the battlefield, while others resorted to partisan warfare using underground tactics. Perhaps it is not too much to say that the latter had become a contemporary terrorist organisation. The Shogitai were a thorn in the flesh of the Imperial troops based at Edo. Although their commander, Imperial Prince Komatsu Akihito, was firmly established in Edo castle, both money and troops were in short supply The Imperial high command was frequently forced to despatch troops to the north, where the enemy had to be fought simultaneously on several fronts. No treasury had been found inside the castle's walls, which gave rise to rumours (some still persistent today) that the Tokugawa's "immeasurable riches" had been buried somewhere in the grounds. What was to become of the former Shogun himself was another question urgently awaiting an answer. Meanwhile the number of Shogitai fighters continued to grow, Katsu Kaishu reckoned that there were about 4, 000 of them currently at large, which was probably an exaggeration. On May 3, 000 Shogitai were quartered at Ueno. The militia had been organized into two types of companies, 18 regular ones, and 16 companies of auxiliaries. The better-equipped men thus formed units which could not be interfered with by inexperienced and poorly equipped newcomers. The proposed unit size

---

47 cf. "Last stand of the Shogunate party in Hokkaido – the surrender of Hakodate on 27th June 1869", p. 142

48 cf. "Shishi – men of high ideals, or unmitigated lunatics?", p. 75

Seated in his litter carried by no less than fifty porters and accompanied by a military escort, Emperor Meiji makes his way to Tokyo in November 1868. This coloured woodcut by Utagawa Yoshitoshi was published in the same year.

was typical of contemporary militia – any acceptable volunteer was taken, but units should not to exceed a certain number since due to the men's poor discipline sheer size would have made them unmanageable.

After despatching troops to the northern theatre of war and the withdrawal of several domain's contingents from the army, Imperial troops at Edo numbered merely 2, 000 for the time being. They were thus outnumbered by the 3, 000 Shogitai. The new government at Kyoto began to feel uneasy, fearing that Edo might slip from its grasp. It sent Omura Masujiro from Choshu, a crafty tactician and strict disciplinarian. The problem was that extensive street fighting would massively increase the risk of fire. Since Edo consisted in large part of wooden buildings, the chance that the city might take harm in a similar way to Kyoto's burning in 1864 was very real. Eventually Omura received unexpected help from the government, which had sent an envoy with 250, 000 *ryo* to purchase the mighty ironclad *CSS Stonewall* anchored at Yokosuka from the Americans. Ironicaly, the vessel had originally been ordered by the Shogunate. The Americans at first insisted on observing strict neutralitiy and refused to sell, so that the money and 1, 000 men from the domain of Hizen (Saga) were sent to assist Omura at Edo.

On May 11 Omura was appointed the city's first Governor. On the same day, the decision was taken to assault the fortified Shogitai positions on Ueno hill. The civilian population and the Tokugawa family had been officially informed in advance, and on May 15, 1868 troops from Choshu, Satsuma and Hizen opened fire on the Shogitai positions. The battle was over at dusk.

The Battle of Ueno is described in detail in The Battle of Ueno (15th May 1868).[49] Effectively the Shogitai ceased to exist. The survivors scattered in all directions, went into hiding or joined other militia units. This practice repeated itself after each defeat suffered by the Tokugawa loyalists and only ceased after the final capitulation in Hokkaido in 1869.

The new government now saw itself in the position to send more troops north and to drive forward the transformation of the ancient city of Edo into the capital of the new Japan, Tokyo. On 26th November 1868 the Emperor Meiji was able to make his unhindered entrance into his new capital – what had once been the castle of the Shogun had become the Imperial residence.

---

49 p. 127–131

Historical map of the Battle of the River Oze. The Seto Inland Sea can be seen at the bottom to the south. Shogunate troops moved from East to West along the coastal road. They were ambushed from the far side of the River Oze while attempting to ford it, and put to a headless flight back East. Further Choshu troops lay in ambush on both sides of the road.

Following double spread (p. 104/105):
Battle of the River Oze, 1866.

In summer 1866, the fourth and largest contingent of the shogunal forces advanced on Choshu via the coastal road running from east to west. In accordance with ancient tradition, the famous "Red Devils", samurai from Hikone clad in their distinctive red suits of armour, formed the advance guard. 450 of these men, supported by 150 samurai from Takada were fording the River Oze, when they came under withering fire from Choshu militia stationed on the far bank. These infantrymen were armed with modern rifles and reinforced by a small contingent of artillery. The samurai were routed. The fleeing troops were fired upon by troops positioned on the hills lining the road. Many samurai were killed or wounded along with massive loss of equipment. Thus the shameful defeat of the glorious Red Devils of the House of Ii stood for the downfall of Japan´s once-proud samurai warrior élite. Far-sighted domains recognized a need for military reforms by 1866, and had begun to implement changes by 1868. Illustration: Sascha Lunyakov

CAMPAIGNS AND BATTLES OF THE 1860s

The second punitive campaign against Choshu in 1866

When the princedom of Choshu ignored the conditions of the peace treaty after the first punitive expedition sent against it in 1864 and continued to radically modernize its military[50], it became evident that the Shogunate would have to conduct another punitive campaign to demonstrate that it was still capable of bringing a renegade to heel.

Before the beginning of the 1866 campaign there had occurred a political turn of events which was to prove decisive – Sakamoto Ryoma, a well-connected and far-sighted *ronin* from Tosa, had negotiated an alliance between the old arch-enemies Satsuma and Tosa, both of which had finally come to recognize that if they wanted to topple the Tokugawa they would have to work together. This alliance was also called the Satcho Alliance. The new political situation came as a nasty surprise to the Shogunate since it had counted on Satsuma to establish a fifth front against the rebellious domain by invading from the sea and marching on the Choshu capital of Hagi. Satsuma simply cancelled its participation, thereby openly resisting the Shogun's summons to war. In the previous centuries, such an open act of defiance would have been inconceivable. It was a part of the realities of the year of 1866 that Satsuma not only refused to obey the Shogun but also bought British arms for Choshu in Shanghai, delivering the purchsed items with a ship from its own navy. For a long time, a lack of good firearms had been Choshu's biggest problem.

Despite these setbacks, the Shogunate was still capable of fielding around 150, 000 troops in 1866, just like it had done two years previously. Most of these forces were provided by the 21 domains in the region allied with the Tokugawa. The imprecise figures in this context show how indifferent some domains had become regarding their military obligations. Many did not send their best troops. Conrad Totman has succeeded in establishing reliable figures regarding the Shogunate main forces when they first set out on their march from Edo to Osaka. Here we have before our eyes the Shogunate's military state of affairs in 1866, after the start of military reforms but before the arrival of French military advisors. The troops were organized into 16 *ban* ("brigades"), each consisting of two sub-units of either *daitai* ("battalion") or *shotai* ("company") size – or even smaller. Traditional contingents were mostly referred to as *kumi (-gumi)*; their sizes could vary considerably. The following examples give an idea of the Shogunate army's organization:

1. 1st Brigade (very large): 1 field battery (8 guns, 64 gunners), 2 infantry battalions (*hohei daitai*, of 400 men each), 3 independent infantry companies (*shotai*), 9 officers and inspectors.
2. 6th Brigade: 2 companies of *sakite* (advance guard skirmishers), 2 companies of *shoinban* (high-ranking sword-armed samurai), 10 officers and inspectors.
3. 9th Brigade: Shogun's retinue, consisting of numerous non-combatants, various *kumi* units, several contingents from different domains with differing armament.
4. 15th Brigade: disbursing officer's men and equipment.

The army also comprised other troop types such as 70 cavalrymen with horses in Western harness organized into two *shotai*, 400 cadets of the Kobusho Academy, 250 (according to other sources, 400) *sennin* (*teppo* arquebusiers), 1, 500 artillery guards, 80 élite samurai of the Oban, 312 pikemen in 3 *kumi*, and around 800 swordsmen in about 25 units, each numbering between 20 and 239 men (Totman 1980: 187 & 503 f.). It was a huge conglomeration of different troop types: modernized and traditional samurai and infantry, artillery together with its own infantry contingents, specialist troops, small and even tiny units, along with numerous non-combatants. Of the 8, 000 combat troops, about 6, 000 carried some form of firearm, the others made do with bladed weapons. Though the sheer figures appeared impressive, the actual combat value of a bunch of 20 or 30 sword-armed fighters pitted against modern infantry was entirely a matter of conjecture.

Although Choshu had a mere 4, 000 or 4,500 soldiers at its disposal, it was able to swiftly move these companies and battalions about to wherever they were needed, effectively deploying them on several fronts. The brunt of the fighting was still borne by the *shotai* at this early stage, but regular troops were already in existence, supplemented by peasant militia (*noshohei* or *noheitai*) with high morale. Choshu's great tactical advantage lay in its greatly superior armament, which consisted of modern field guns and rifles, many of which were breech-loaders that suited the hit-and run guerilla tactics of the *shotai*. Loading the rifles no longer required standing up, and firing was possible lying prostrate from behind cover. Nevertheless, the threat to Choshu was substantial, with attacks coming from four sides:

From the north, samurai from the domains of Fukuyama and Hamada were to attack; from the south, troops from Tokushima and Iyo-Matsuyama (from Shikoku) were to take the island of Suo-Oshima with the aid of modern Shogunal troops and ships. A third army was raised at Kyushu from troops of the Kokura, Fukuoka and

---

50 cf. "Satsuma, Choshu and their allies", p. 61

Kumamoto domains. These forces were to cross the straits of Shimonoseki and attack Choshu from the west. The main thrust was to lead from the Shogunal headquarters at Hiroshima via the western Japanese coastal road into the heart of Choshu territory. The majority of Shogunal troops, consisting of most of the contingents listed above, were detailed for this attack. Troops from the eastern domains of Takada, Hikone and others also formed part of this force. Fifty field guns were ready for action.

To the Shogun's dismay, his allies failed to gain their objectives on the three remaining fronts. Although the island of Suo-Oshima was initially taken, it could not be held. A relief force consisting of the Second *kiheitai*, the *kobutai* (two modern Choshu rifle units) and the peasant militia landed on the island and with sheer momentum their attack crushed the Shikoku samurai along with two Shogunal infantry battalions. Of the 1, 300 men originally forming the Shogunal force, 700 became casualties, the remainder fleeing back to their ships. Sources even mention Choshu farmers' wives and children occasionally attacking Shogunal troops with bamboo spears – protecting one's homeland was clearly no longer regarded a samurai exclusive privilege.

In the north, things went even worse. In the Iwami area traditional samurai forces from Hamada and Fukuyama and troops from far-away Kii were unable to prevent Choshu troops under Omura Masujiro[51] penetrating deep into Hamada territory. Omura himself was later known to speak of a "hare hunt". To add insult to injury, Hamada was even forced to burn its own castle and abandon its capital after suffering a number of humiliating reverses. The Shogun's vassals were only saved by Choshu's reluctance to pursue the beaten enemy. Choshu preferred instead to dispatch its far from numerous troops to other theatres, where they were more urgently needed. Hamada domain had been lost along with several Shogunal estates in the area.

In the south Choshu took the initiative before the Shogun's cumbersome military machine was able to spring into action. Several *shotai* spearheaded by the First *kiheitai* crossed from Honshu to Kyushu and defeated the garrison of Mojiko, which itself belonged to Kokura. This was in fact an ironic reversal of the Shogun's intended strategy. Kokura was a medium-sized princedom allied with the Tokugawa which had shown little interest in any kind of military reform. Only about 100 of Kokura's samurai were armed with modern firearms. They had been reinforced by 700 samurai from the minor domain of Karatsu, which like Kokura was ruled by the Ogasawara clan and held overall command in the region. The auxiliary contingent which had been dispatched by the Shogunate was rather small, consisting merely of 250 *sen-nin-gumi* and 150 embassy guards, both units just about equalling a battalion in size. They were supplemented by two strong battalions from Kumamoto, which however proved reluctant to follow orders. This hotch-potch little army was of doubtful combat value, and it took Choshu a mere 1, 000 troops to destroy it: Kokura and its allies stood no chance against the verve, firepower and modern tactics of the *shotai*. Instead of crossing to attack Choshu as ordered, Kumamoto after a heated discussion opted for retreat while Fukuoka had made no appearance in the first place. Lord Ogasawara Tadanobu had no choice but to fire his castle, an action traditionally associated with the surrender of a Japanese feudal lord. Nevertheless, the Ogasawara clan remained loyal to the Shogunate to the last – even in Hokkaido in 1869 Ogasawara samurai were to be found fighting furiously against the despised Choshu, and the new order.

The Tokugawa had contributed to this defeat by clinging to the time-honoured custom (classically applied at Sekigahara in 1600 and elsewhere) of holding back their own contingents in order to present other daimyo with the opportunity to cover themselves with glory – and to preserve Tokugawa forces. This also occurred on the Aki front, where Hikone, Takada and Kii formed the Shogunate vanguard. Lord Ogasawara had himself originally intended, in best Tokugawa manner, to send ahead the Kumamoto contingent, but this had failed to follow orders.

A samurai from Kaga, one of the richest domains in all Japan which had already begun to abandon the Shogunate and was to fight on Satsuma's and Choshu's side in the Boshin War, witnessed the performance of the Choshu *shotai* at the Battle of Ogura in 1866, and related his experience with astonishing naivety:

"When the Choshu forces appeared, their rifle units were running forward together, and when the time came to fire, the beat of their drums stopped and they would come to a halt. They would then quickly disperse, quickly spying out individual cover and concealing themselves. They would only show their faces when they fired or crawled forward. [...] Their ranks would constantly be replaced by fresh troops, and even with the approach of nightfall they did not let up in their fighting. Wherever they sensed a weak point, they would drive forward. Their guns were all new and they did not use a muzzle ramrod but loaded the bullets through a hole at the back. And each soldier steadied the butt of his rifle on the ground when ready to fire. I could not help but admire the speed with which they loaded the ammunition and how the dispersed soldiers moved with such nimble efficiency. Their cannon meanwhile would alternate between firing pointed shells and round shells. Down to the platoon level they were equipped with small, short banners, but did not have a single spear. Their uniforms were narrowsleeved, either black or dark blue in color. And probably the majority of them did not even wear haori [short coats worn with kimono]. As for bamboo hats, even though they were

---

51 cf. "Choshu's Young Blades", p. 151

equipped with Nirayama-style hats, when fighting they would not bother to wear them even in the rain. (quoted after Hoya, n. d.)

The samurai utter amazement at his enemy's efficiency is palpable in this excerpt. The speaker came from a region hardly touched by military reform, and he marvels at the absence of lances and the new miracle weapons he encounters. Helmets and voluminous jackets were an encumbrance and thus no longer worn in battle. The Kaga samurai had witnessed a battle in which one side employed superior armament and skirmishing tactics against traditional samurai equipment and tactics and had denied the latter any chance of victory although at least some were armed with muzzle-loading rifles. It is entirely possible that here the *kiheitai* itself is described, since these soldiers had seized some large-sized drums from Ogura castle in the wake of their victory, which can still be seen at Shimonoseki today. Developments in Japan continued where the American Civil War had left off in 1865, and Choshu had prepared its military well.

Having gained the upper hand on three fronts, Choshu was now in the position to redirect troops back to the main theatre of war in the southeast. Because the Shogunal headquarters were at Hiroshima, the capital of Aki, this is also referred to as the Aki front. This is where the vanguard of the Shogunate army stood, traditional samurai from the domains of Hikone (the former "Red Devils" of the Ii) and Takada, the domain ruled over by the Sakakibara, also ancient followers of the Tokugawa. Hikone fielded altogether 1, 887 fighters, of which 711 were mounted samurai organized into sections of nine men on average. These were accompanied by numerous retainers and servants and joined by 160 artillerymen with 16 mostly outdated field guns, 382 infantry armed with muzzle-loading muskets organized into platoons numbering 25 men each (implying that they were not trained to operate in a coordinated manner on a larger scale), only 65 men armed with modern Western rifles organized into five (!) units, and 320 pikemen organized into tiny units of between nine and fifteen men. More than half of the Hikone contingent was made up of traditional samurai armed with bladed weapons. Less than one third were equipped with firearms, of which only very few were of the latest manufacture. Traditional organization into very small units ruled out the application of modern tactics. Takada provided 1, 000 troops organized in a similar manner (among these were 60 mounted samurai, 300 to 350 musketeers, 260 footsoldiers armed with lances, and 50 gunners with eight guns). Around 2, 400 men remained at Hiroshima, most of them probably non-combatants (after Totman 1980: 187 & 504).

This column was supplemented by troops from Kii and 2, 000 soldiers of the Shogunate army (three infantry battalions of 400 men each, 35 cavalry, one battery of six or eight horse-drawn guns, 50 engineers (*sakujikata*), and headquarters staff).

These troops, perhaps 7, 000 men in all, lumbered down the coastal road running from east to west. The vanguard consisted of 450 mounted samurai from Hikone and 150 fighters from Takada. It was a sight as from a bygone age. Two hundred and fifty years previously, the forbears of the Lords Ii and Sakakibara had ranked among the noble *Tokugawa shi-tenno*, the four loyal feudal cornerstones of the house of Tokugawa. At Kyoto in 1863 and 1864, the Choshu rebels had been defeated using traditional arms and armour – so why should one have modernized? By the Oze River, also known as the Battle of Geishuguchi, the Hikone and Takada contingents blundered straight into an ambush and found themselves under attack from several directions. The cavalry took to their heels almost immediately, only to be fired upon from both sides of the road with rifles and hand mortars. The proud samurai threw away their arms and red armour, abandoned their horses and ran. Some of them managed to acquire boats and thus made good their escape. The Hikone and Takada camps which had been constructed behind the vanguard were overrun. Losses were severe – Hikone had lost ten or twelve guns, two of them of modern American manufacture, large numbers of muskets, horses, and a considerable amount of ammunition. The paychest and most of the rice supplies were also lost. Takada losses consisted of eight guns and ammunition. The number of dead samurai is reported to have been "high". Commander Tokugawa Mochitsugu, the daimyo of Kii, was left with no choice but to deploy the Shogun's modern infantry battalions. These were reinforced by his best troops under *hohei bugyo* (commander of infantry) Takenaka Shigemoto as well as 300 modern troops from Shingu armed with Minié rifles under their *daimyo* Mizuno Tadamoto, and several field pieces. 200 samurai from Kii and 200 riflemen from Ogaki completed the Shogunal force. The ensuing fight for the village of Ono was remarkable in that for the first time since the Japanese Middle Ages non-samurai were mostly fighting non-samurai. On the Tokugawa side stood well-trained and (thanks to the fighting in Mito) experienced soldiers, while the Choshu troops consisted of militia partly composed of townspeople and even social outcasts. Choshu fighters again occupied the heights on both sides of the road, but this time the infantrymen and gunners of the Shogun and the Shingu troops under their valiant prince stood firm. Taking heed to guard their flanks, they counter-attacked and pushed the enemy back several kilometres. Over the next few days, the Shogunal forces controlled events. Choshu was employing between 700 and 1, 000 troops, while the Shogunate had 1, 500 troops in the field at all times, these soldiers being constantly rotated and replaced by fresh troops. The numerically inferior force faced the problem of having to fire more rounds, which would eventually tell on them in the form of decreasing ammunition supplies. This in turn would eventually force the soldiers into earlier retreat in order to maintain and clean their weapons,

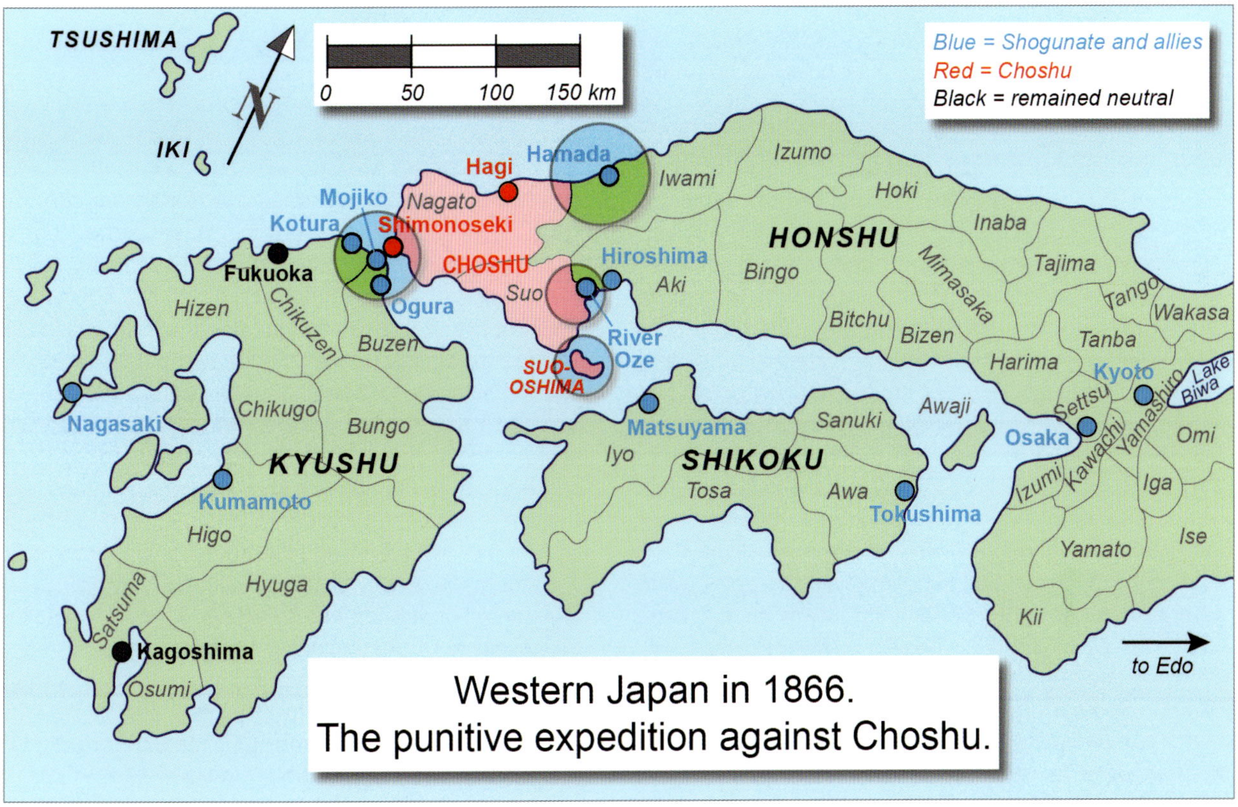

Western Japan in 1866.
The punitive expedition against Choshu.

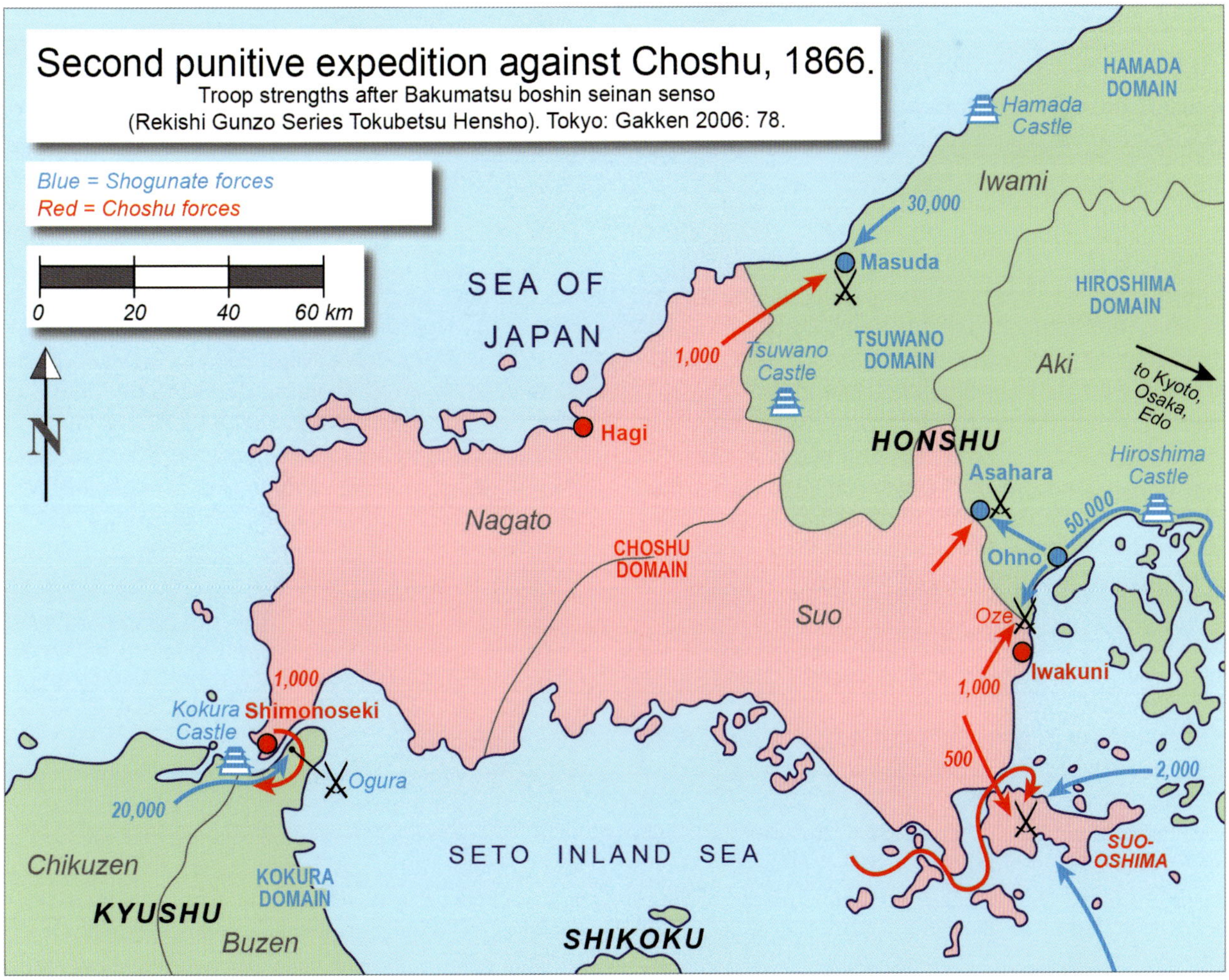

Second punitive expedition against Choshu, 1866.
Troop strengths after Bakumatsu boshin seinan senso
(Rekishi Gunzo Series Tokubetsu Hensho). Tokyo: Gakken 2006: 78.

making them vulnerable to enemy counterattacks. The Shogunal forces were supported by a naval bombardment from ships anchoring off the coast. Eventually the front line froze as both sides erected barricades, while the Shogun's generals quarreled over the most effective strategy. This benefited the Choshu troops, since the Shogunal attack had now entirely lost its initial momentum. Choshu had managed to hold its ground against a numerically superior force mostly consisting of troops of good quality, but the troops in this area were at the end of their tether. Food and ammunition were running low, and replenishing supplies was problematic (as would also be the case on several fronts in 1868). Choshu troops therefore frequently resorted to plundering. Another problem was the care of the wounded, who did not always receive adequate medical treatment. During the fighting Choshu had often ruthlessly burned villages and small towns to screen the deployment of its troops and to surrender only scorched earth to any advancing foe. After all, Choshu was fighting for its very existence.

While the Shogunal high command was busy arguing over what to do next, Choshu made the best of a month's respite by tending to its supply problems and increasing the number of troops on the Aki front to altogether five infantry battalions plus artillery and auxiliaries.

On the opposing side, the troops from Kii were not idle. Tokugawa Mochitsugu, now commander-in-chief, returned to Hiroshima. He ordered all samurai from Kii to equip themselves with firearms, and promptly procured 500 Minié rifles. He also scrapped the ancient feudal military organization and reorganized his men into battalions (*daitai*) of several companies each (*shotai*). Even the old military standards (*uma-jirushi* and *gunki*) were abolished because their presence on the battlefield had enabled enemy artillery to target the commanders. In the shortest of time, another large domain more or less successfully geared up its military from the 17th to the second half of the 19th century. Mochitsugu also asked the Shogun to dispatch the 2, 000 to 3, 000 modern infantry who had remained at Osaka to him, and to send modern firearms so that they could be distributed among the allied troops under his command. In both requests he was disappointed, however. An obvious notion would have been to take advantage of naval superiority by landing troops in the enemy's rear, but only one bungled attempt was made. By the end of the war, only Satsuma and Choshu troops and their allies were capable of successfully mounting marine landing operations under fire.

After a good deal of delaying, the Shogun's troops finally advanced again in September 1866. The largest Battle of the war ensued. Again, the spearheading infantry battalions stood their ground, and Mizuno Tadamoto's Shingu samurai fought with distinction. The traditionally-armed contingents from Hikone, Takada, Kii, Akashi, Miyazu and Ogaki had been given rearward duties and were in charge of securing the long supply routes along the coast.

Two Choshu battalions fell upon these troops, cutting the Shogunal army in two. Takada alone lost 68 men dead and wounded in one day. Once the Choshu troops realized that the typhoon rains had soaked the enemy's old-fashioned gunpowder, they attacked and fired volleys at point blank range. The unfortunate samurai from Takada, reduced to brandishing their useless swords, were routed. Artillery positions were speedily overrun and a large amout of booty was seized. Not counting the Shogunate's losses, the seven allied domains alone lost 150 men against Choshu's three dead and 16 wounded.

One week later the new Shogun Tokugawa Yoshinobu agreed to an armistice (his predecessor Iemochi had died unexpectedly in July). After two months, the war had come to an end. Choshu had evaded punishment, while the Shogunate itself had been made to look ineffective and foolish. It had failed to subdue even a single rebellious domain. Important domains especially in Kyushu (Satsuma, Fukuoka, Saga, Yanagawa, Kurume) had reacted sluggishly to the Shogun's summons or ignored them completely. They could no longer be counted on either as allies or subjects. To make matters worse, hoarding large amounts of rice to keep the troops fed had caused prices to soar, which led to civil unrest in many areas.

Choshu had lost less than 300 men killed in the entire war. Shogunal losses are difficult to ascertain as figures vary. The six Shogunal infantry battalions, numbering altogether 2, 400 men, lost between 150 and 200 dead, and between 350 and 450 wounded. Losses sustained by the domains allied with the Tokugawa, especially Hikone, Takada and Kokura, amounted to several thousand. It cannot be said that the Shogunal army fighting on the Aki front had lacked courage or skill. The Choshu troops had simply proved themselves superior since they were better led and equipped, and their efficiency was outstanding. As a result, hundreds of Japanese daimyo and their advisors had seen a single domain defeat the mighty Shogun and now began to wonder which side to take in the conflicts that would surely not be long in coming.

It remains a matter of speculation whether morale among the 21 allied domains would have been higher if the Shogun himself had conducted the campaign, as might have been expected of a military ruler. It later transpired that the reason for the Shogun's absence had been a lack of funds – there was simply not enough money to raise and equip the appropriate retinue of 3, 000 men, and so the Shogun had stayed put in Osaka. Once again old-fashioned social convention had proved painfully counterproductive.

Im military terms, several conclusions could be drawn from the failed punitive expedition against Choshu of 1866. The first was that the Shogun's new infantry battalions were in the position to stand up to the tactically and technologically efficient modern *shotai* fielded by Choshu. The contingents armed and organized in the traditional manner, i. e. the old-fashioned Tokugawa samurai and the troops of the allied domains which had not modernized their armies, had proved entirely worthless. The death ride of the red Ii samurai into a hail of bullets at the outset of the war had become proverbial for a historical turning point. The Tokugawa were also forced to recognize that even domains with a long record of loyalty could no longer be relied upon to lend their support unconditionally, or even respond to the Shogun's call to arms. The Shogunate therefore took the correct decision to quickly try to enlarge the modern contingents of its own armed forces. It also realized that it was pointless to continue to demand obsolete troops from its unwilling daimyo and vassals, opting instead for raw recruits and money. The creation of a national army, or at least an army for those parts of the country still loyal to the Shogun, appeared the only way to prevail in the great civil war that was now on the horizon.

"In this sign, conquer!" – the Battle of Toba-Fushimi (3rd–6th January 1868)

Among the noteworthy things about the pivotal four-day Battle of Toba-Fushimi early in 1868 is the contrast between its size – 20, 000 troops were involved, of which the comparatively small number of between 400 and 900 were killed – and its huge historical significance. This one battle broke the determination of former Shogun Tokugawa Yoshinobu to continue to resist against the upstart powers from the south and west. Only because individual domains and samurai refused to abandon the Shogun's lost cause did the Boshin War last into the following year. Even while the Battle of Toba-Fushimi was still raging, Japan received a new Imperial government and embarked on a path of radical modernization. In a matter of only a few years, Japan abolished the old samurai caste and entered the colonial world stage.

The Battle of Toba-Fushimi was preceded by a final round of struggling for political control at Kyoto. To alleviate the pressure exercised by Satsuma, Choshu and the influential faction headed by Iwakura Tomomi at the Imperial court, Shogun Tokugawa Yoshinobu stepped down after only 15 months in office on 9th November 1867. Political power was transferred to the Emperor while Yoshinobu himself along with his household troops and advisors retired to Osaka. The question now arose what was to become of the former Shogun's estates, whose value amounted to several million *koku*. Since the office had been held by the Tokugawa for such a long time, it had become virtually impossible to clearly distinguish between office and personal property. The Tokugawa's enemies demanded that large parts of the estates be returned, and eventually even all of them. This was an intolerable provocation in the eyes of the Tokugawa samurai who lived off these very lands. As always, Yoshinobu resorted to tactics, yet Satsuma skilfully increased its provocations. Imperial decrees were issued against Yoshinobu, some of them clearly acts of forgery. At Edo, Lord Satsuma encouraged wild *ronin* to attack members of the Tokugawa party from the security of his local residence. The Shogunate retaliated. On 25th December the Satsuma residence was torched by fighters from the Shonai domain – war now appeared almost unavoidable.

Yoshinobu still held the right to travel to Kyoto for negotiations at the Emperor's court – in fact, he had been summoned to do so. At Osaka on 2nd January 1868, he gave in to his most loyal allies, the daimyos of Aizu and Kuwana. We do not know how strongly he himself was in favour of war, but in view of the heated political atmosphere a strong advance guard appeared advisable. He thus dispatched a large part of his troops (altogether 15, 000 men) in two columns to Kyoto via two country roads. The travelling distance was about 55 kilometres. These troops were not an army marching to war however but a substantial vanguard, a security force rather than a fighting force. Yoshinobu told Aizu that under no circumstances were they to become involved in any fighting against Satsuma at Kyoto.

Troop types and strengths of the modernized Tokugawa army in the second half of 1867

Type	Japanese name	Description
French-trained élite troops	denshutai	2 infantry battalions, cavalry, artillery (less than 2,000 men), mostly non-samurai
Modern infantry armed with Minié rifles	hohei	7,760 men organized into battalions of 400–500 men each
Artillery batteries and artillery guards	*taihotai-shojutai, sappei-gumi*	3,000 men fit for action out of altogether 5,000; mostly equipped with light 4-pounders, organized into 7 ½ battalions; supported by 2 infantry battalions who also saw to the supply train and logistics.
Rifle units	okuzume jutai	4 battalions of high-ranking samurai
Rifle units	yugekitai	5 battalions of middle-class samurai
Rifle units	jutai	17 ½ battalions of lower-class samurai
Cavalry	kiheitai	4 ½ squadrons with Western equipment
Irregulars	shinsengumi; mimawarigumi	300 to 500 traditional samurai serving as police force in Tokyo (swords, lances, a few rifles)

(Totman 1980: 346 ff.; not all "rifle unitrs" were armed with firearms throughout)

On paper the Shogun´s army added up to 24,000 men, but their availability and combat readiness varied considerably ("paper soldiers"). This was aggravated by limited funds, which effectively did not really allow for the maintenance of such a large number of troops. For this reason, the quality of both equipment and supplies varied greatly. Even before Toba-Fushimi, most of the *jutai* units were disbanded. 37 commanders and their deputies received letters of cancellation, which caused volent protests and looting at Edo even though many were encouraged to join the infantry and generous bounties offered. Again, the samurai proved firmly set in their ways, and they were much more expensive to maintain than the simple but adaptable non-samurai recruits. In a few months they could be sufficiently trained to become modern infantry capable of swiftly annihilating any unit of traditional samurai sent against them. The Shogunate command promptly devised to enlarge the less expensive *hohei* modern infantry to 6,000 men, but until January met only with limited success. There was neither enough time nor money to make up for two hundred lost years. The Shogunate troops were to be supplemented by forces from allied domains, but their number was hard to foresee in view of the unstable political situation:

Troops with mixed equipment (lances, swords, rifles; some artillery)	*kumi*	Troops supplied by vassal domains whose armies had undergone different degrees of modernization

The Battle of Toba-Fushimi, 3rd – 6th January 1868
to Kyoto
Toba Road
Takeda Road
Katsura
Nishikikoku Road
Toba (village) 3.1.
Fushimi (small town) 3.1.
Shimo-Toba 4.1.
Tominomori
Yodo-Senryomatsu 5.1.
Yodo Castle
Uji
Ponds
Yamazaki
Hashimoto
Yodo
retreat
Hashimoto-Hachimangu 6.1.
Kizu
Kuzuha
Otokoyama Hill with Hachiman Shrine
to Osaka
Shogunate forces
Shogunate allies who changed sides in the course of the battle
Imperial forces
Important bridge
Action
Castle
Imperial forces' advance

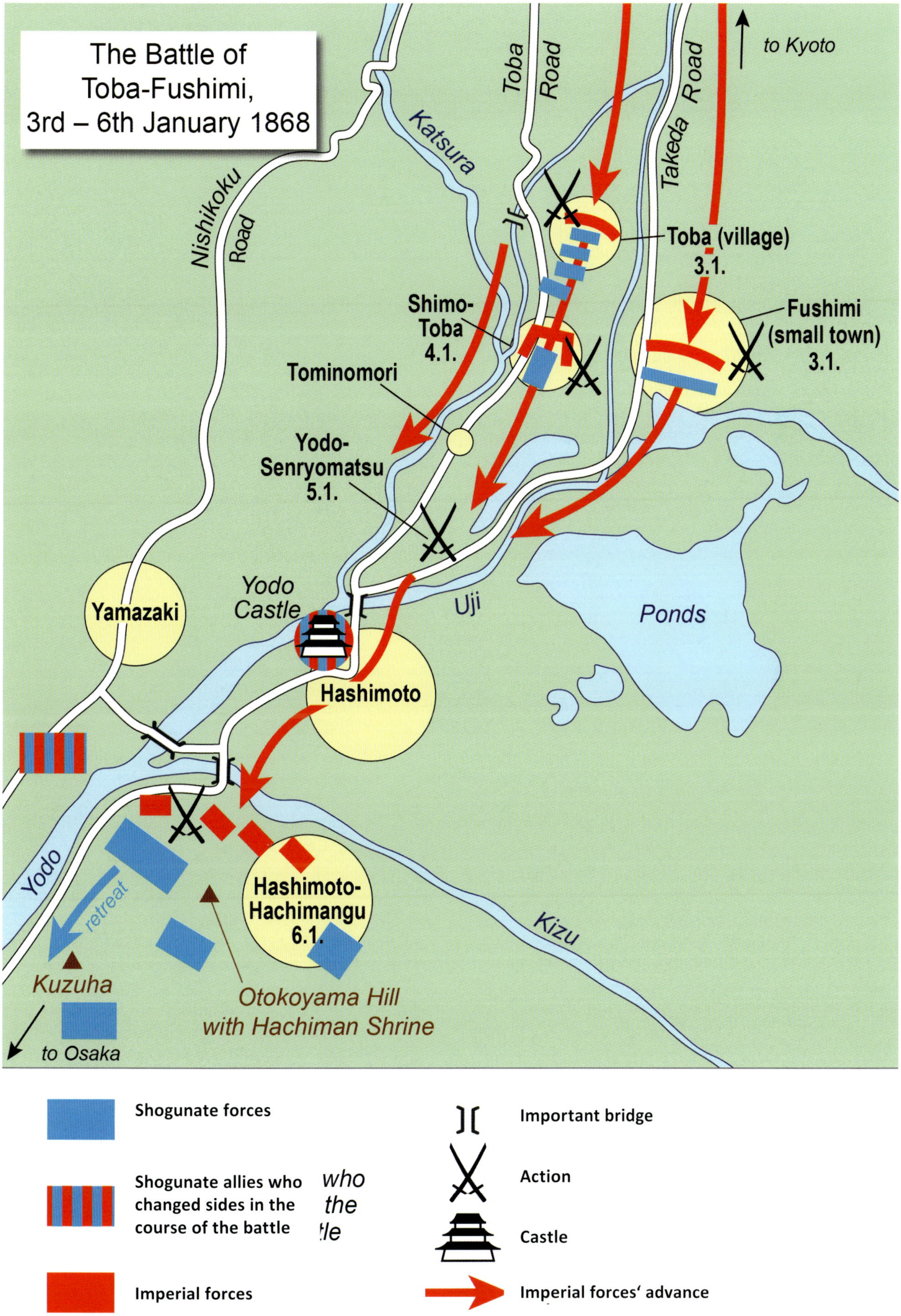

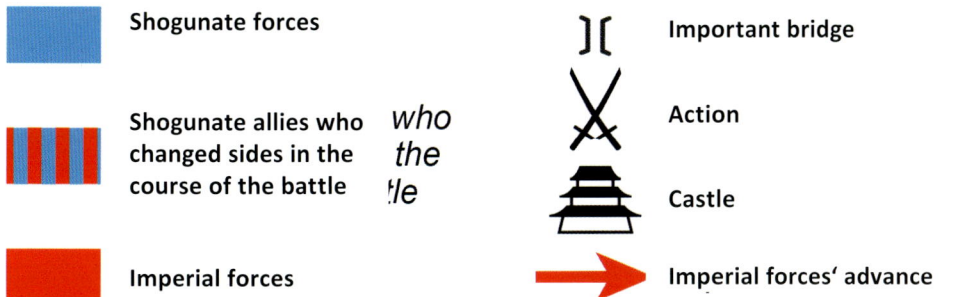

The first day (3rd January 1868)

The former Shogun divided his troops into two columns, while the Yodo samurai guarded their castle on the river of the same name. 1,000 men from Tsu and 500 men from Obama were also stationed in rearward positions along the river.

The first Tokugawa column consisting of four infantry battalions (among them the crack *denshutai*, who for some unknown reason had been equipped not with their usual breech-loading Chassepots but with obsolete muskets), a small unit of engineers, the 400 men of the Mimawarigumi (a former police unit from Kyoto) and samurai from Kuwana and Matsuyama took the country road to Toba. The Aizu troops and the Shinsengumi marched along the Takeda Road to Fushimi, a suburb of Kyoto where an advance guard had occupied the large complex of buildings holding the offices of the local magistrate. This deployment of forces meant that although the troops with the highest morale were present at Fushimi, they were only armed with few and outdated firearms. The village of Toba and the former castle town of Fushimi were only situated 10 km away from Kyoto.

The Satsuma and Choshu troops (later to be joined by units from Tosa) established a line of defence controlling the Toba and Takeda Roads. The Koeda bridge, the Jonan-gu shrine and the town of Fushimi served as fortified strongholds. Artillery positions were established at the Jonan-gu shrine in Toba and the Mikamiya shrine at Fushimi.

Toba

On the afternoon of 3rd January, a sunny but cold day, the Tokugawa troops encountered the Satsuma forces at Toba barring the road ahead with wings extending left and right. Twice the Shogunate army's commander courteously demanded that the road be cleared. At around 5 pm the battle for Koeda bridge commenced when Satsuma troops, only numbering about 900 men in this area, opened fire, putting the Shogun's mounted envoy Takigawa Tomoshige, who had been sent to negotiate with the Emperor, to ignominious flight. Although the army's deputy commander (*rikugun bugyo-nami*) Okubo Tadayuki was officially in command, affairs got out of hand when the Shogunate troops on the road were fired upon. Without waiting for orders or a ranking officer to take charge, they counterattacked immediately out of the line of march. The attack was directed against carefully prepared positions, and the infantry had not even bothered to load their muskets. The Mimawari samurai, some of whom were wearing their traditional armour, led the attack armed with lances, followed by two infantry battalions under Tokuyama Kotaro, a deputy commander of infantry (*hohei bugyo-nami*). The first battalion was repulsed by heavy fire from the front and the flanks. The next battalion also advanced in close order instead of spreading out – it too was fired upon from three sides. Two precious Shogunal battalions had now been severely mauled for no apparent gain. Evidently the local Tokugawa commanders had relied on their troops' numerical superiority (2,000 or even 2,500 Tokugawa men against 900 Satsuma fighters), but they lacked support from their cavalry and artillery. Both columns' operations remained uncoordinated, each obeying its own commander as the various samurai contingents fought in the traditional manner while the modern infantry mechanically performed their drill movements. It did not occur to any of the officers to execute a flank attack, e. g. via the Nishikoku or Tamba-guchi Roads, which would have been promising. Narrow roads, some crossing marshy terrain or winding through settlements, prevented the Tokugawa troops from exploiting their numerical advantage. The Tokugawa soldiers clung to every inch of ground, sustaining heavy losses from the four (eight according to some sources) Armstrong guns positioned at the Jonan-gu shrine. Kuwana troops, bringing their own guns, finally came to the Tokugawa's rescue by circumventing the grimly contested bridge. Long after dark, the Shogunal troops retired to Shimotoba. The Shogunate army's predicament was aggavated by a crisis in command. While Takigawa had fled the field (he later returned, only to disappear again for good a short while later), the commander-in-chief, former Shogun Yoshinobu, was lying on a futon at Osaka with a head cold. Most of the Tokugawa troops were well-trained and had fought courageously, but there was no one available to lead them properly.

Fushimi

At Fushimi, 800 Satsuma troops had blocked the road to Kyoto at the Mikamiya shrine and positioned riflemen and nine field guns on the heights commanding the road. On the previous day a vanguard of 200 Aizu troops had landed their boats at Fushimi and occupied the local magistrate's offices in the town centre. The Satsuma troops had a Gatling Gun at their disposal, but whether it was employed remains unclear. The Satsuma forces were reinforced by two Choshu infantry companies (125 men), and by a further four from Tosa under Yamada Kikuma, Yoshimatsu Hayanosuke, Yamaji Motoharu, Kitamura Shigeyori and Futagawa Motosuke, in accordance with a secret deal struck by Satsuma behind the Tosa rulers' backs. The Tosa artillery contingent was recalled at the last moment. Lord Yamauchi of Tosa was unwilling to abandon his domain's neutrality. The population of Tosa had become deeply divided, the rift between the factions running between east and west. The die was cast only after Toba-Fushimi. Henceforth Tosa would become the third largest contributor to the new Imperial army. For now, 1,400 Satsuma, Choshu and Tosa troops held the town of Fushimi.

When the sound of gunfire drifted over from Toba, diplomatic exchanges at Fushimi also ceased abruptly, giving way to furious street fighting. The Shogunate force consisted of 900 Aizu samurai, 150 Shinsengumi samurai under Hijikata Toshizo[52], one half battalion of infantry, several smaller units of samurai from Hamada and other domains, and the local magistrate´s force together with its four guns. Altogether the Shogunal troops totalled around 2,000 fighters. If one considers the enemy´s superior armament, they did not possess any superiority of note, and they would receive no help from the thousands of Tokugawa troops to their rear. One and a half further Shogunal infantry battalions played no part in the street fighting, and the engineers, cavalry reinforcements and the four guns which had been promised all failed to show up.

The fighting around the large office complex belonging to the local magistrate at the southern edge of Fushimi was particularly intense. Hijikata´s men attempted several assaults with bladed weapons but stood no chance against Satsuma´s guns. Satsuma and Choshu firmly held their positions, the training of the troops, which had begun several years previously, now paying handsome dividends. They stormed the Aizu battery which had been guarded by men armed with lances and succeeded in disabling three of the four guns. At around 8 pm a shell hit the ammunition store in the office complex. The ensuing blaze forced the Tokugawa troops occupying the buildings out into the open. Several civilian houses in the vicinity also caught fire, clearing the line of fire for Satsuma snipers. The fighting intensified. The Aizu commander, Hayashi Gonsuke, continued to direct his men despite wounds from three bullets. Hamada troops provided relief for the beleaguered Tokugawa. The firing eventually ceased at around 1 am, both sides withdrawing from the burning town. The Shogunate troops beat a disorderly retreat to the bank of the Uji river, where the infantry had established a bridgehead. They were now without a leader, as Takenaka Shigemoto had chosen to extend his own personal retreat all the way to Yodo castle. The ignoble desertion of two high-ranking samurai commanders in one day was unprecedented in the history of the Tokugawa.

Kyoto

On the same day, a meeting was called at Kyoto between representatives of several domains and those of the Imperial court. A number of daimyo refused to take up arms against the former Shogunate, claiming that the conflict was a private feud between Satsuma and Choshu, and Aizu and Kuwana. Eventually Iwakura Tomomi, a courtier of the anti-shogunal faction, managed to push through the dispatch of troops to Otsu on Lake Biwa to the east of Kyoto in order to protect the capital in case Tokugawa reinforcements approached.

The second day (4th January 1868)

Toba

The second day of the battle saw the arrival of Tokugawa reinforcements in the form of two fresh battalions of infantry armed with breech-loading rifles. The enemy dispatched four relatively fresh companies from Tosa whose positions in Fushimi were taken over by the exhausted Satsuma and Choshu troops. Several fresh Satsuma companies arrived from Kyoto. The Shogunate forces were thrown back 300 metres, losing two guns. The modern *denshutai* infantry lost its commander Sakuma Nobuhisa, an energetic *hohei bugyo* officer who had been trained by the Shogunate´s French military advisers. Battalion commander (*hohei kashira*) Kubota Bizen no kami was also among the fallen. Aided by Kuwana artillery, the lance-armed samurai from Aizu had a field day when they got to grips with some Satsuma riflemen before these had time to reload. The samurai wreaked havoc among the infantry, carving up the enemy with cold steel. Eventually the Shogunate force in the Shimotoba area retired to defensive positions fortified with rice sacks filled with earth. Again, poor leadership took its toll: the Tokugawa troops failed to post sentries to guard the flanks, enabling the numerically inferior enemy to envelop the position and surround it almost completely. After his batteries´ ammunition was exhausted Oyama Yasuke (Iwao), the Satsuma artillery commander, drew his sword and led his men to the attack to overwhelm the enemy at bayonet point. After sustaining further losses, the Tokugawa infantry finally retreated to a prepared position fortified with earth-filled *sake* barrels at Tominomori 750 metres to the south.

Fushimi

The brave Tokugawa troops who had faced rifles and artillery armed only with sword and lance were also forced to retreat further on the second day. Although the order arrived from Yodo to once more attack Fushimi, the local commanders refused to obey, pointing out that their troops were too exhausted. Meanwhile the enemy approached the Tokugawa positions under cover of dense fog. On the third day, contact with the Toba contingents was established. Satsuma and Choshu not only pursued the retreating Tokugawa force, but they also dispatched troops to both flanks.

Kyoto

It could be argued that the most decisive event of the entire Boshin War occurred on the second day of the Battle of Toba-Fushimi. A few kilometres away, the Emperor appointed Imperial prince Komatsu Akihito *sei´i taishogun* (supreme military commander-in-chief). The 21-year-old prince, who up to now had lacked all opportunity to gather military experience in the field (he later became a professional soldier), was not intended to actu-

---

52 cf. "Shinsengumi – shining heroes, or gang of thugs?", p. 77

For German-speakers, an excellent, lavishly illustrated Japanese-German bilingual source exists for the Battle of Toba-Fushimi: the *Nishiki no mihata* ("Picture book of the Boshin War").

It was written by Noguchi Shoichi and Tomioka Masanobu, translated by P. Ehmann and published by Azuma Kenzaburo (Toyodo), Tokyo 1907. The work was composed in cooperation with persons involved in the events of 1868. The illustration is a detail from plate IV, showing the entrance to Toba village on 3rd January 1868. On the left, Tokugawa infantry and artillery have deployed, marking their position with their Hinomaru standards. On the right, the Shogun´s envoys are attempting to negotiate the right of passage on the road to Kyoto with Satsuma officers. The marshy terrain and reeds growing in this area with its many streams and raised trackways are clearly discernible.

The uncoordinated Shogunal attack on Toba saw the 19th century fighting alongside the 16th.

In the foreground modern infantry can be seen taking casualties, while the samurai of the Mimawarigumi led by their commander Sasaki Isaburo are charging towards the enemy, many wearing full armour. Kuwana reserves have taken up position in the background. In the middle background, the Tokugawa envoy is seen making his ignoble escape.
(*Nishiki no mihata* 1907, plate VI)

ally command at Toba-Fushimi but assumed only nominal command. Satsuma's, Choshu's and Tosa's private armies were thus elevated to a completely new status. These troops now formed the Imperial army, the only force in the country officially entitled to carry out the Emperor's wishes. Anybody resisting it was a rebel against Imperial authority and outlawed. To promote the army's new status, Iwakura Tomomi had produced two large Imperial banners, the *Nishiki no mihata*. These were presented to the prince along with a sword (*setto*) as a sign of his authority to punish the enemies of the Emperor. On the same evening the new *sei'i taishogun* together with his new banners marched to the southern outskirts of Kyoto accompanied by the samurai of his bodyguard, a half-platoon of Satsuma troops and a contingent from Aki (Hiroshima/Geishu), the fourth domain after Satsuma, Choshu and Tosa in the Boshin War to throw in its lot with the western coalition.

The third day (5th January 1868)

The Shogunal troops were continually pushed back and forced to abandon their positions at Tominomori. At around 2 pm they approached Yodo castle from the north. The Toba and Fushimi columns merged at Yodo-Senryomatsu and succeeded in repulsing the pursuing enemy. Lance-armed samurai units from Aizu and Ogaki hid among the reeds and ambushed Choshu and Satsuma troops, causing 30 casualties. One Choshu *chutai* (half-battalion) had to be withdrawn. Boggy terrain with its single roadway proved an obstacle which was difficult to negotiate for the Imperial troops. The narrow causeway prevented the attackers from fanning out and outflanking the enemy. Both sides sustained casualties, especially among the unit commanders, who, clad in their conspicuous attire, became easy targets. Exhausted Aizu units had to be replaced by fresh troops, e. g. from Ogaki. Eventually the Shogunate forces retired across the so-called Small Bridge across the Uji in the direction of Yodo castle, setting fire to the village to the north of the bridge as they did so. During the withdrawal the *denshutai* infantry stood like a rock, which earned the praise and admiration of their Aizu comrades. Satsuma, Choshu and Tosa guns were positioned north of the river and began a systematic bombardment of the barricades erected by the enemy outside Yodo castle. In the four days of the battle, the Imperial artillery performed outstandingly and proved more decisive than that of the Shogunate, which more often than not simply did not materialize where it was needed.

Yodo was situated on the far bank of the Uji river and was easily accessible via the Small Bridge. The castle's governor was Inaba Masakuni, daimyo of Yodo, a *fudai* lord and old and faithful ally of the Tokugawa. Inaba was a member of the Tokugawa's Elder Council, the top body of the shogunal government. Yoshinobu trusted him infinetely. To the Tokugawa troops' great alarm and dismay, they found the castle gates locked. The daimyo himself was at Edo. In his absence, his retainers had decided that it was unwise to confront Imperial troops and promptly changed sides. This was a truly dramatic decision for the castle's garrison to take, but they were no fools. They had watched the Shogunate troops steadily losing ground. When the *sei'i taishogun* arrived from Kyoto and his two new banners were seen flying above the enemy ranks, the decision was taken. "In this sign, conquer!" – as from now, Yodo was an Imperial stronghold, and the garrison enthusiastically welcomed the Satsuma, Choshu and Tosa troops within its walls.

Bowed and battered, the Shogunal army continued its march south across the Great Bridge crossing the Kizu in the direction of Otokoyama and Hashimoto, where villages had been fortified in advance. Two mounted French observers were noted watching the crossing of the bridge.[53] The Tokugawa dead and wounded were either transported to Osaka by boat, or taken to the nearby Choen-ji temple. Among the dead was Inoue Genzaburo, long-time commander of the sixth unit of the Shinsengumi. The strength of the Shogunate forces now amounted to between 3, 050 and 4, 300 effectives, who were faced by 3, 500 Imperial troops. The most active troops, those from Aizu, had sustained casualties sufficient for them to be rotated away from the front line. A feeling of downheartedness was now spreading rapidly among the troops and their commanders.

---

53 cf. *"Jules Brunet, true 'Last Samurai'"*, p. 157

A Satsuma battery in action on the second day of the battle. Both infantry and artillery wore the same type of uniform. There were no mounted troops. Satsuma troops were recognizable by their high conical helmets with red *agemaki* (silk cord knot), and white brassards worn on the right arm. (*Nishiki no mihata* 1907, plate XII)

A study of Shogunate soldiers (Tokugawa, with Kuwana ranks forming the background) fighting Choshu troops. While the modern infantry have deployed several ranks deep and are firing regular volleys, samurai armed with sword and lance are attacking head-on. Interestingly, some have taken off their wooden helmets and are holding them like small bucklers. (*Nishiki no mihata* 1907, plate XI)

The other side of the road: a platoon of Choshu infantry return fire. Reinforcements are moving up to relieve the troops engaged. Allied Tosa troops can be seen on the left. (*Nishiki no mihata* 1907, plate XI)

After decisions have been made at the palace of Kyoto, Imperial *dainagon* (regent) Kuga Michihasa personally paints the characters *sei'i taishogun* ("Commander-in-chief") onto a silken banner measuring 400 x 90 cm. Two slightly smaller banners he has painted with *gunji sanbo* ("Staff officer's war flag"). *Gunji* referred to a staff officer whose rank roughly equalled that of a major. Both standards were intended for officers appointed from the court nobility, while the proper staff work was done by professional officers from Satsuma and Choshu. (*Nishiki no mihata* 1907, plate XIV)

The flag bearers accompanying the Imperial commander-in-chief were a vital element designed to inspire fear and confusion among the Shogunate troops. Apart from the three war banners, the two Imperial banners made of Nishiki brocade and emblazoned with sun and moon badges, several large flags showing the Imperial chrysanthemum were carried. The Imperial flag bearers of the 1868 campaign are described in a contemporary source: "… and I see a red silk flag, with the Mikados's [= the Emperor's] emblem upon it, slowly advancing, carried erect, high in the air, by the gigantic wrestlers of his Majesty, surrounded by a number of samurai and attendants, all wearing green-coloured trousers." (Cortazzi 2002: 137). The practice of hiring Sumo wrestlers as standard bearers dated back to the 16th century. (*Nishiki no mihata* 1907, plate XVI)

The new commander-in-chief Prince Komatsu Akihito, also known as Ninnaji-no-miya and other names, on the march from Kyoto to the Toba-Fushimi battlefield, surrounded by the samurai of his bodyguard. The young prince had until recently been a monk, hence his closely cropped hair. (*Nishiki no mihata* 1907, plate XVI)

The Imperial banners

Altogether 17 different Imperial banners were in use during the Boshin War between the battles of Toba-Fushimi and Hokkaido. Every corps bearing such standards could demonstrate its legitimacy for all to see and indicate that any resistance to its advance was an act of rebellion against his Imperial majesty. In 1888 all surviving banners were painted by artist Ukita Kasei and thus preserved for posterity. The first ever Imperial standard is said to have been presented to a general by Emperor Go-Toba. An Imperial banner commonly displayed a sun or moon disk in gold or silver on a background of red brocade. The emblems were either applied to the fabric, or painted on. The Imperial banners displayed at Toba-Fushimi, both spectacular to behold and decisive for the battle's outcome regarding their psychological impact, had already been manufactured in 1867 by anti-shogunal courtier Iwakura Tomomi. This was a long time before the appointment of an Imperial prince as commander-in-chief of the combined Satsuma and Choshu forces, making them the official Imperial army and thus the only legitimate armed force in the field. The precious materials had been discreetly purchased in Nishiki, the brocade manufacturers´ quarter of Kyoto, and then made into the the two main battle flags emblazoned with sun and moon emblems respectively. The new banners were seemingly miraculously produced on 4th January and are often referred to as *Nishiki no mihata* or *-gohata*, "beautiful" or "sublime banners from Nishiki". The precious silk brocade is richly decorated with elaborate patterns and shot through with gold and silver threads.

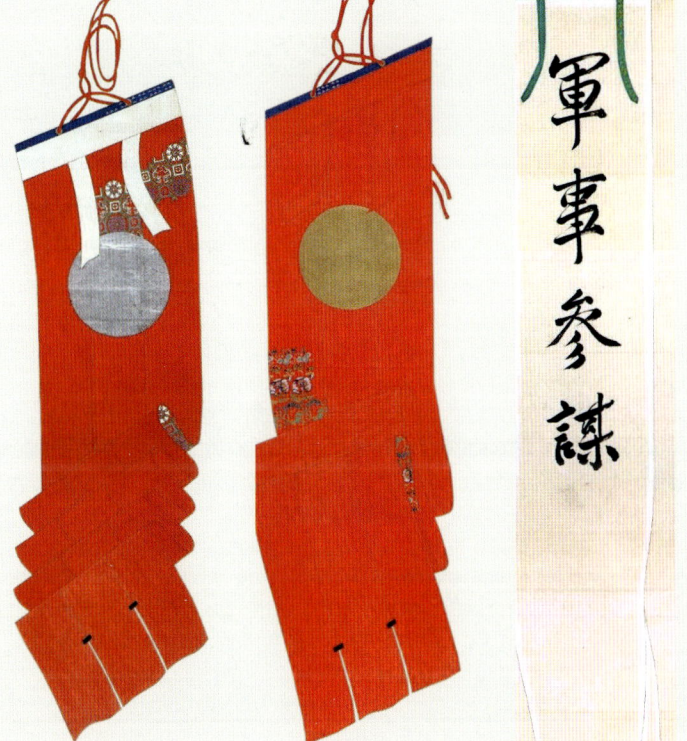

1. Imperial moon banner
2. Imperial sun banner
3. *Sei'i taishogun*´s war banner

Banners 1–3 were suspended from crossbars imitating the ancient style preceding the 16th century

4–6. represent Western style flags displaying the Imperial chrysanthemum badge for military units

The banners were painted by Ukita Kasei in 1888. (https://www.digital.archives.go.jp/DAS/pickup/view/category/categoryArchivesEn/0600000000/0602000000/00)

1   2   3

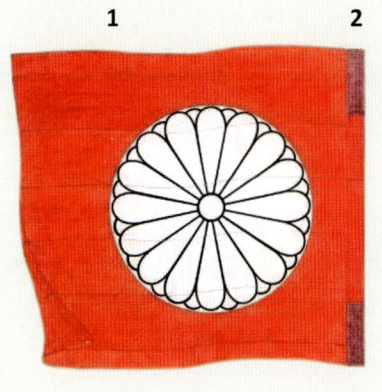 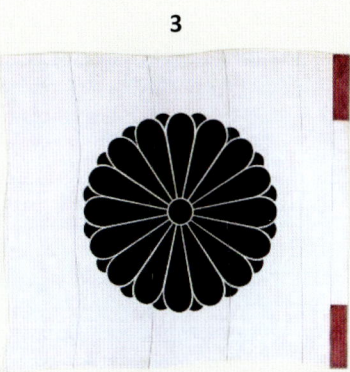 

4   5   6

The fourth day (6th January 1868)

The Battle of Hashimoto

In the early hours of the fourth day of the battle, Imperial troops were ferried across the Kizu (the Great Bridge had been burned by the retreating enemy). The artillerymen from Tottori and their pieces failed to make the crossing and were replaced by 140 men from Hiroshima/Aki who had come from Kyoto as part of the *sei'i taishogun*'s entourage. The Imperial commander-in-chief was visible riding among his troops and continued to boost their morale.

Satsuma's forces numbered 15 companies, each down to about 90 infantry. Choshu had 4 ½ half-battalions and an independent company as well as a further three companies from Iwakuni and Tokuyama at its disposal. The Imperial vanguard caught up with the retreating Shogunal column, and a firefight ensued. The Shogunate troops stood and fought and managed to prevent the enemy from reaching their encampment. Their current position on both sides of Mount Otoko with its Ichimizu-Hachiman shrine appeared safe enough for the time being. On the western side of the mountain was the town of Hashimoto. Most of the Shogunal troops, including the remaining Shinsengumi under Hijikata, encamped in and around the local guesthouse and its attached brothel. Cover was provided by the mountain in the east, while the Yodo river gave protection to the west. The far bank was occupied by friendly troops from Tsu. 500 troops from Obama and some Miyazu artillery stood on the Kusuha plateau to the south. The remaining Aizu artillery had taken up positions in the western sector in order to provide flanking fire in the case of an Imperial attack.

It was all to no avail. The defensive action against Imperial troops was already in full swing when at noon a new situation presented itself. To the west of Hashimoto was situated the frontier post of Yamazaki on the far bank of the Yodo. This was garrisoned by 983 samurai from Tsu, a large domain in the provinces of Ise and Iga. Tsu gunners also operated the artillery position at Takahama. The Tsu contingent comprised this battery, infantry, traditional samurai, and various auxiliaries. These supposed allies of the Tokugawa suddenly began to take the Shogunal troops under fire from across the Yodo. Visibility was good, no mistake possible. In fact, these troops had received a visitor during the previous night: an Imperial envoy had persuaded them to recognize his master's authority. The Tsu commander of the day, a relative of the daimyo named Todo Uneme, despatched a letter to his former ally in the morning in which he expressed his regret: "We will never forget the grace of the Tokugawa, but I have no choice but to obey an Imperial order." Indeed there had already been dissent among the Tsu samurai for a while over divided loyalties.

It was the last straw. Although the valiant Shogunate garrison of Obama attacked the Tsu positions, the situation

The bitter end of Tokugawa hopes on the fourth day of the battle: while Satsuma and Shogunate troops are engaged in combat in the left background, the turncoat Tsu artillery opens fire on its former allies from across the Yodo river. The Imperial envoy in his richly decorated court attire can be seen looking on from behind the foliage on the right. (*Nishiki no mihata* 1907, plate XXVIII)

was hopeless as the Tokugawa troops found themselves under attack from all sides. Sasaki Tadasaburo, the commander of the Mimawarigumi, was mortally wounded. The Shogunal troops broke and fled along the Yodo river in the direction of Osaka, which they had left only five days previously. Many of the fugitives threw their rifles or blades into the river. The Imperial pursuit was only half-hearted – the Imperial troops were themselves exhausted, and the numerous Shogunate troops stationed in and around Osaka were still a force to be reckoned with.

Max von Brandt, envoy of Prussia and the North German Confederation, witnessed the flight of the defeated shogunal troops. For him an opportunity presented itself to purchase a few souvenirs:

"It was a strange spectacle to see the armoured men armed with bows, arrows and lances who formed the majority [of the fugitives]. One might have believed oneself back in the Middle Ages, and sure enough I was witnessing the funeral procession of ancient feudal Japan. [...] During this retreat I managed to purchase between eight and ten helmets of most peculiar appearance with hare´s ears, buffalo horns and grinning face masks from their owners, who seemed quite happy to exchange their uncomfortable headdress against a handful of coins."

(von Brandt 1901: 173 f.)

Compared to the fierce nature of the fighting, losses remained fairly light. *The official Book of Martyrs of the Bakumatsu Revolution* gives 112 fatalities and about 250 wounded for the Imperial side (dead: Satsuma 72, Choshu 38, Tosa 2), and more than 300 dead for the Tokugawa army (Tokugawa 163, Aizu up to 138, Kuwana 25, Ogaki 10, Hamada 5, and 29 Shinsengumi fighters). The number of wounded was approximately twice as large. Several units are not mentioned however, and so the above list is probably incomplete. Other estimates suggest that the dead amounted to up to 900, with a large number of wounded (Tokugawa: 400 wounded, Aizu 150, Kuwana 60, and 230 wounded Imperial fighters). Unsurprisingly, the highest death toll was paid by the bravest troops armed in the traditional manner, the men of Aizu, and the veterans of the Shinsengumi.

Why did Tokugawa Yoshinobu lose the battle despite a numerical superiority of three to one?

It should not be forgotten that only a part of the Shogunate troops fought with devotion. The Aizu and Kuwana samurai fought ferociously, and some of the modern infantry proved their worth. If the number of French-trained *denshutai* soldiers had exceeded 900 and had the Tokugawa commanders possessed both strategic talent and a plan, victory would have been within their grasp on the first or second day before the arrival of the Imperial banners. There was a sufficient number of troops to envelop the enemy at Toba and Fushimi and

Yodo castle.
(detail from an *ukiyoe* woodblock print by an unknown artist, 1870)

attack them from several directions. Instead, only parts of the available troops were employed, and this only half-heartedly. They were concentrated on the country roads and in the narrow streets of Fushimi, both of which were unsuitable for the deployment of large numbers of troops. This fighting ground was ideal for an enemy whose weapons were clearly superior, and whose confidence was high.

Large troop contingents were held back at Osaka, and the 15, 000 troops involved in the campaign were forced to occupy and secure a corridor spanning no less than 50 km between Osaka and Kyoto. This left a mere 5, 500 troops available for the march on Toba and Fushimi. Altogether 8, 500 Tokugawa troops eventually ended up taking part in the actual fighting, their effective strength still twice as large as the enemy's. In the final Battle of Hashimoto Tsu changed sides, which tipped the scales in that both sides were now more or less equally strong. However, the sheer momentum of the Imperial troops´ attack put the Shogunal forces at a serious tactical disadvantage (Totman 1980: 419 f.).

Regardless of these problems, the greatest drawback was the lack of motivation evident in the majority of infantry battalions, the contingents of some minor domains, and the commanders themselves. This problem might have been solved if Tokugawa Yoshinobu had taken the trouble to join his troops and by his presence had provided them with a souce of inspiration. Unfortunately, Yoshinobu was a politician, not a soldier, and it can be said that after his resignation as Shogun his lack of military talent was made all the more evident.

Those familiar with Japanese history will have noticed the ironic nature of the battle´s outcome: in 1600, the treachery of parts of the western armies (incidentally, at the instigation of the ancestors of the daimyo of Choshu, the Mori clan) brought victory to Tokugawa Ieyasu on the field of Sekigahara, leading to the founding of Shogunate rule in 1603. 268 years later, the Battle of Toba-Fushimi spelt the end of Tokugawa power for good, and this time it was the defection of the Tokugawa allies Yodo and Tsu which helped turn the tide.

Aftermath

On the evening of 6th January, the fateful news of his defeat reached a devastated Tokugawa Yoshinobu. During a dramatic council of war, the former Shogun seemed unable to make up his mind. Unsurprisingly, the Shinsengumi commanders urged their lord to renew the attack, while the Aizu commanders suggested continuing the fight from Edo. Yoshinobu was particularly unnerved by reports about the new Imperial banners. Having undergone the traditional education of a Tokugawa, he found the thought of having to appear before his ancestors and being called a traitor to the Imperial cause impossible to bear. He had been branded a rebel (*choteki*), and though he continued to delay for a few more weeks, his resistance had been broken. Henceforth his only wish was to be rid of the disgrace of treason and to preserve the existence and dignity of his house. Anyone willing to continue the struggle was clearly going to have to do so without Tokugawa Yoshinobu.

Yoshinobu then did what most of his contemporaries would have considered a despicable thing. Accompanied by only a few followers, among them Matsudaira Katamori of Aizu and Matsudaira Sadataka of Kuwana, he secretly left the castle of Osaka and boarded a ship to Edo. His army, including eight completely intact infantry battalions, remained behind. Eventually the soldiers began to realize that their master had deserted them. The Shogun´s army dispersed, and Osaka castle was burned to the ground. Few felt any obligation to a Tokugawa who had fled the field in such an ignoble manner. A large Aizu contingent began an orderly march to Wakayama and later headed east. Others, among them samurai and a few regular infantry, made their way to Edo, where some of them fought on. Some changed sides, or simply went home. The victors were able to seize "scores of rifles" and other equipment among the spoils of war. The fall of the house of Tokugawa had been anything but glorious.

The Tokugawa army at Osaka before the Battle of Toba-Fushimi in January 1868

Shogunate troops
12 infantry battalions at 400 to 500 men each (only four were engaged)
2 *denshutai* infantry battalions (900 men)
2 samurai battalions mostly armed with rifles (*okuzume jutai, jutai*) (1, 000 men)
6 guns (probably more)
Several very small cavalry units (which played no part in the fighting)
Engineers and workmen
Mimawarigumi (former police force armed with swords and lances) (400 men)
Shinsengumi (Former police force armed with swords and lances, and a few firearms; 1 gun) (150 men)

Allies
Aizu contingent, mostly samurai equipped with sword and lance, 2 batteries (1, 600 men)
Kuwana contingent, 4 companies (8 platoons) mostly of samurai equipped similarly to the Aizu men with 6 guns, 3 (!) cavalry, 40 pioneers and 30 princely retainers (altogether between 340 and 400 men)
Troop contingents from other domains: Matsuyama (between 160 and 320 men in 8 *shotai*); Miyatsu (250 men and some artillery); Takamatsu, Oshi (500 troops garrisoning Osaka castle); Nagaoka, Kasama, Obama (500 men, 250 according to other sources); Yodo, Tsu (983 men); Hamada, Ise-Kameyama (200 men); Himeji (200 men); Kii (Kishu) and Hikone sought to avoid becoming engaged from the very beginning, while Ogaki only became involved late in the campaign. Yodo and Tsu changed sides on 5th and 6th January respectively.

Estimated total
Ca. 15, 000 men, of which 8, 500 were engaged. (*Numbers derived from various sources*)

(*Material from various sources*)

Order of Battle of the Imperial army at Toba-Fushimi, January 1868

About 5, 000 men were available altogether, nearly all of them infantry companies equipped with modern firearms. Only the Satsuma figures are known.

Deployment of Satsuma troop contingents on the first day of the battle:

Saigo Takamori *tokatsu* (commander)
1. Osaka road: 500 infantry; commander: Ijichi Masaharu.
2. Toba village: 250 men, 4 or 8 four-pounder guns; commander Nozu Shizuo.
3. Fushimi: 6 companies of infantry (800 men).
4. Reserves: 200 infantry.

(Source: *Pictorial Saigo Takamori* 1990, vol. 2: 39)

After the first day, several hundred Satsuma reinforcements arrived from Kyoto, raising numbers to around 2, 500, or slightly more. Strengths of the Choshu and Tosa contingents are estimated at 1, 500 and 400 to 500 troops respectively. The Choshu forces engaged consisted of both regulars and militia (Seibutai, Hachimantai, Kiheitai, Yugekitai, Yochotai, and Shimbu). On the third day two guns and their crews from Tottori (Inshu) became engaged, 140 infantry from Hiroshima/Aki fought on the fourth day. To this number must be added the Yodo troops who later changed sides, plus the 1, 000-strong Tsu contingent.

From Kyoto to Edo

In January 1868, the victors without delay began to clamp down on the daimyo of Takamatsu, Bitchu-Matsuyama, Fukuyama and Himeji, all of them from the west, for their siding with the Shogun. All were forced to submit to Imperial authority. This put all of western Japan firmly under the control of the new government, and in central Japan the vassals of the Tokugawa followed the example of the western domains and surrendered. Even Owari and Kii (Kishu), ruled by two of the three branches of the house of Tokugawa, quietly changed sides. The small princedom of Kuwana, which, locked between Owari and Tsu, would not have stood a chance on its own, took this step in the prince's absence. Still at Edo, the daimyo decided to continue the fight against the Emperor's forces. The power of the Shogunate, whose administration continued to work unabatedly, was now reduced to northeastern Japan, namely the Kanto region around Edo, the Tohoku region in northern Honshu, and Yezo/Ezo, as Hokkaido was known at the time.

An opportunity for the conquered domains to prove their new allegiance quickly presented itself. At Kyoto, plans were being drawn up systematically for the march on Edo, capital and residence of the deposed Shogun. The troops from Satsuma, Choshu and Tosa were now joined by more allies, contingents from Inaba (Tottori), Hizen (Saga) and Aki (Hiroshima) featuring prominently. An Imperial office of defence (*gunbo jimukyoku*) was established, a forerunner of the Ministry of War and later Defence Agency/Ministry. The Imperial government was not to be satisfied merely by declarations of submission, but demanded logistics, money, and men for the war effort against the rebels. 60 fighters for every 10, 000 *koku* were to be provided, the government agreeing to cover part of the expenses for rations and accomodation in the field. Regarding the troops´ quality and equipment, standards were made unmistakably clear – only rifle and artillery contingents were acceptable, supplemented by the necessary porters. Troops were ordered to do without unnecessary appendages: "Your troops are only to bring clothing and equipment which serve practical purposes" (Hoya 2020: 160). The presence of any supernumerary officers apart from the commanders themselves was frowned upon. For better or worse, the new Imperial army had bid good riddance to bow and lance, cavalry, samurai armour, and military pomp. Some daimyo like the Hosokawa of Kumamoto who up to now had continued to ignore calls for military reform ran into serious trouble in their attempts to comply with the Imperial government´s demands. The quality and reliability of such contingents was to remain brittle for a long time, leading to the decision to disperse the veteran Satsuma and Choshu troops to various columns in order to control and bolster the militarily less reliable contingents. The casualty lists of the entire Boshin War tend to confirm this corset function of the élite Satsuma and Choshu units. Altogether 190 domains provided the Imperial army with around 110, 000 fighting men over 18 months, of which 15, 000 hailed from either Satsuma, Choshu, and Tosa. These three contingents suffered a quota of altogether 40% of the overall casualties sustained by Imperial forces in the conflict (2, 500 dead out of 6, 600). The huge Kaga princedom by contrast lost only 280 killed out of a contingent of 7, 800 (3% casualties). Choshu and Satsuma on the other hand lost 18% dead out of their effective totals, rendering almost very fifth man a fatality (Jaundrill 2016: 92).

The new Imperial allies were called to arms in February, when an "Imperial campaign" (*shinsei*) was announced in order to bring the eastern "bandits" (*zokuto*) to heel. Prince Komatsu Akihito was once again proclaimed the army´s overall commander (*kangun*). Later it was said that he was the only person in the entire Imperial army to have worn full armour.

Propaganda was also to figure prominently in the campaign east. The effect of the sun and moon banners carried at the army´s head has already been discussed above.[54] To provide every individual soldier with Imperial recognition and legitimisation, each man was issued a small rectangular piece of Nishiki brocade resembling the Imperial banners. These tags, issued from 13th March 1868, were known as *kingire*. They were attached to the left upper sleeve, supplementing the badges worn to identify the wearer´s domain.[55] A song composed especially for the campaign, *Tokoton-yare-bushi*, was frequently sung by the troops on the march and accompanied by the bandsmen and corps of drums.

A naval landing in Edo was dismissed as too dangerous in the face of the numerically superior Tokugawa navy. Instead, the Imperial army marched east in three columns along three major highways. One column took the route along the Japanese Sea coast (Hokoku Kaido), while the second took the road through the central mountains (Tosando). The third column took the Tokaido road along the Pacific coast. A full-scale engagement was fought against 900 infantry from various Tokugawa regiments under Furuya Sakusaemon and Imai Nobuo who had left Edo of their own accord and now called themselves Shohotai. Furuya was defeated at Yashu-Yanada 75 kilometres north-west of Edo on 8th March.[56] The Shinsengumi corps[57] was beaten back on 6th March. The remainder of the march from Kyoto to Edo remained uneventful apart from a few minor skirmishes. However, highwaymen and bands of armed brigands counterfeiting for Imperial forces were quickly becoming a problem across a land where law and order were slowly giving way. A certain Sagara Sozo was able to convince both daimyo and peasants that he was an Imperial commander (in 1969, Sozo´s story was made into the film *Akage* ("Red Lion"), starring Mifune Toshiro and directed by Okamoto Kihachi; the movie succeeds in conveying the atmosphere of doom prevailing at the time, and the political, social and military conflicts that shaped it). But his luck ran out eventually - Imperial forces arrived and made short work of Sagara and his band.

At Edo, the old government´s hold on power was eroding fast. Many fled to the surrounding countryside, among them numerous well-to-do Tokugara samurai. Of the roughly fifteen infantry battalions quartered at Edo, numerous bands of stragglers remained to form the core of the new forces emerging. Their presence made the streets of Edo increasingly dangerous. Tokugawa Yoshinobu himself had abandoned all resistance and retired to the temple of Kann'ei-ji, where he stoically awaited judgement hoping for the Emperor´s mercy. Edo itself was swarming with infantrymen, discontent samurai and other armed men. If they decided to make a stand, Edo would be done for. Fortunately, Saigo Takamori, the most influential commander in the Imperial army, and

---

54   cf. "'In this sign, conquer!' – the Battle of Toba-Fushimi", p. 111

55   cf. "Other mons and standards", p. 68

56   cf. "Imai Nobuo (1841–1918) and the long road to an ordinary life", p. 163

57   cf. "Shinsengumi – shining heroes, or gang of thugs?", p. 77

Tokugawa leader Katsu Kaishu[58] were able to reach an agreement. Edo was handed over without a fight. On 11th April the castle changed hands intact, and Prince Akihito took possession of the former Shogun´s residence. The troops from the west remained mostly well-behaved in order not to antagonize the civilian population, which had been suffering all sorts of privations. Fukuzawa Yukichi, founder of Keio University, remembered Edo in the spring of 1868:

"When the invasion force arrived, it turned out to be very disciplined, and no unreasonable acts of violence occurred [...] Even in this skirmish, it seems the soldiers were very mild. They did not attempt to molest any civilians or harm other men not angaged in the fight. Some of the officers actually went around announcing that the populace need not be alarmed, as there was strict regulation and perfect control over the troops." (Fukuzawa 1966: 198 f.).

The Battle of Ueno, 15th May 1868

In April 1868, the new Imperial army had occupied Edo and seized the local castle. Shogun Tokugawa Yoshinobu had long since given up and retired to Mito, but his young samurai were by no means prepared to give up so easily. Former Shogunal retainers founded a militia, the *shogitai*.[59] This unit eventually numbered several thousand angry young men who took to picking trouble with the Imperial troops as the situation in Edo got out of hand. On 15th May the Imperial commanders were fed up – a battle would have to determine who was master of Edo. Command of the Imperial troops was entrusted to Omura Masujiro from Choshu.

The Shogitai´s positions were around and inside the large temple complex of Kann'ei-ji situated on Ueno hill in the northeast of the city. The 3,000 Shogitai were organised into units with high-sounding names such as Manjitai, Shinbokutai, Hoheitai (former Tokugawa infantry), Kurama Yukotai, and Yugekitai (presumably the remains of the five Tokugawa battalions of the same name). Smaller contingents hailed from the northern domains of Takada, Obama, Takasaki, and Yuki. These units were militarily insignificant, however. The Shogitai had also positioned four four-pounder mountain guns on Sanno hill.

According to the Imperial plan of attack, Higo, Tottori and Satsuma infantry (under Saigo Takamori) were to assault the Black Gate (*kuro-mon*, also referred to as the Hirokoji Gate), which from the city side formed the southern main entrance to the walled temple grounds of Kann'ei-ji. This was where the Imperial commanders expected the fiercest fighting to occur, which is why the crack Tosa Jinshotai corps was also positioned at this point in the Imperial line. These troops, commanded by Itagaki Taisuke, were distinguished by the red yak hair wigs which they wore together with their regular dark blue uniforms. Choshu troops together with units from Hizen (Saga), Kurume, Omura and Sadowara were to attack from Yanaka in the northwest. Their objective was the backward Yanaka gate. More troops from Hizen and Kurume were stationed on Hongo hill on the far side of the Shinobazu Pond. They were reinforced by units from Tsu, Fukuoka, and Okayama. This protected position served as a base for the Imperial reserves, which were gradually fed into the fight for the Black Gate. Hizen, Okayama and Tsu gunners dragged their pieces into positions on the same rising ground, which commanded Ueno from across the waters of the pond.

The defenders, who numbered between 3,000 and 4,000 men, faced 10,000 Imperial troops, of which 2,000 were to spearhead the assault. The new government had succeeded in reinforcing its Edo garrison on time. Omura, who conducted the course of the battle from the nearby castle, deployed troops all around Ueno in order to block any anticipated retreat of the Shogitai via the surrounding rivers and roads, especially those leading to Nikko and the Mausoleum of Ieyasu. Some fugitives were later rounded up on the Negishi Road, but many Shogitai made good their escape to fight another day. Some escaped through the abbot´s quarters and made for the sea, where they were evacuated by Enomoto Takeaki´s ships.

The six Armstrong guns of Imperial artillery on the far side of the Shinobazu Pond kept up a continuous fire, and with deadly precision. The whole of Ueno was within range. The defenders were only able to sustain a much weaker response from the Sanno hill to the south. Their headquarters were based at the Toshugu shrine, which stood several hundred metres away and remained unscathed. It is possible that Omura deliberately spared the shrine because all over Japan the Toshugu shrines were places of veneration for Tokugawa Ieasu (d. 1616), the ancestor of the deposed Shogun. His supporters would have been outraged and fought all the more ferociously if it had been hit. Instead, the Imperial gunners targeted Sanno hill, where today a statue of Saigo Takamori stands. This hill was roughly on the same level as the Imperial guns´ position. Although the Shogitai had sought to protect their positions with tatami mattresses, these were of course unable to contain the effects of the 2,5 kg shells fired by the Armstrongs. After the first barrage the Imperial artillery fired shrapnel, causing heavy casualties among the Shogitai.

The bombardment caused massive damage – the main buildings of the Kan'ei-ji as well as around 1,000 civilian houses in the vicinity burned down. The Imperial infantry was able to make good use of its superior armament. Some Choshu units were even equipped with repeating rifles. The Satsuma infantry were armed with Enfield rifles and presumably also brought their Gatling into action.

---

58 cf. *"Katsu Kaishu and Saigo Takamori"*, p. 153
59 cf. *"Shotai militia"*, p. 100

The march from Kyoto to Edo on the three most important roads leading from west to east was neither a triumphal procession nor was it a particularly pleasant experience for those involved. The army was under constant threat of ambush, and the men suffered from the bitter cold. In unusual candour these details from a painted scroll show that both officers and men were by no means uniformly dressed. The illustrations from the *Nishiki no mihata* which show the troops in smart and splendid uniforms probably show the desirable rather than the reality of the 1868 campaign. Imported wollen blankets, often dyed red or blue, sold like hot cakes among the troops, something that did not escape Dr William Willis´ notice:
"Among the Mikado´s forces one saw men dressed after the different fashions of Europe in native and foreign material of almost every description and colour there was besides every imaginable combination of native and foreign garments [...] Nearly every soldier possessed a foreign blanket which by day he wore as a cloak. I saw several men dressed apparently with no small degree of self-satisfaction in the old clothes or our marines and men of the line." (Cortazzi 2012: 160)

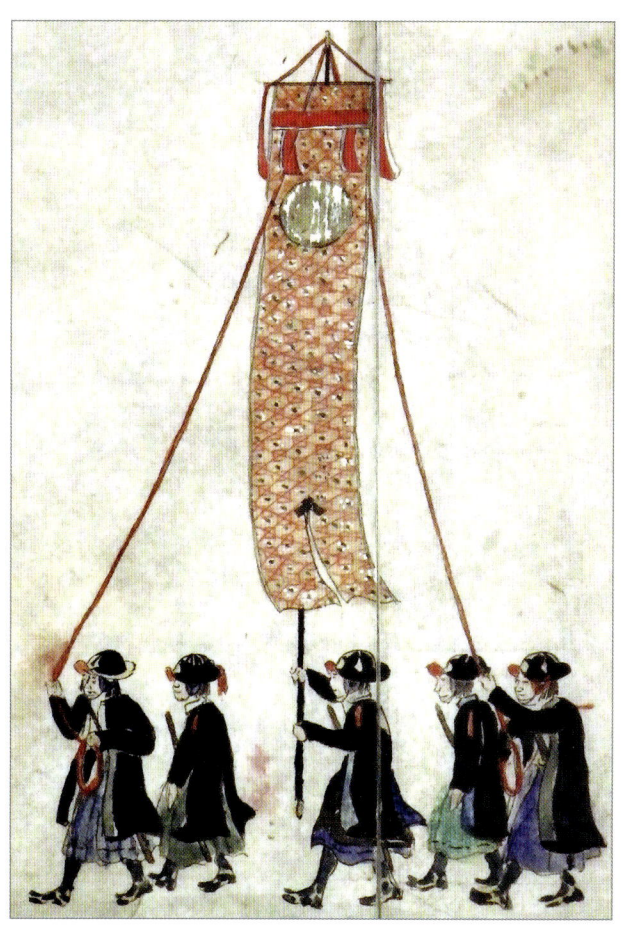

The persistent heavy rain which fell all that day caused problems for the Shogitai with their obsolete firearms, but the majoritiy of the defenders were armed with bladed weapons anyhow.

Two members of the Shogitai during the battle of Ueno on 15th May 1868.
Both wear civilian garb. One owns a musket with a short barrel, and a breastplate.
(*ukiyoe* by Yoshitoshi, detail, 1874)

The first assault on the Black Gate was conducted by a numerically inferior Satsuma force at around 7 am. They were repulsed with some loss by flanking fire from Sanno hill. Shortly afterwards the Imperial artillery fire on these positions began to take effect, and a diversionary Choshu attack on the north-western Yanaka gate brought some relief. The latter´s lack of local knowledge had been the cause of delay. Tosa also deployed its artillery, and its infantry opened fire on the Shogitai with its Snider-Enfield breech-loading rifles.

Eventually Saigo Takamori and his troops broke through the Black Gate, forcing the defenders to retire into the temple´s main complex. A running hand-to-hand battle involving swords, lances and bayonets developed in the courtyard between the gate and the halls of the temple. All the while the rain poured down on the comabatants. Most wounds were caused by small arms fire. Organised resistance collapsed at around 5 pm when the Choshu-led assault force broke through the back gate and attacked the main building from the rear.

A Shogitai unit commanded by Kasuga Saemon hid in the Iwaki area, while many of fugitives made their way to Aizu, the rallying point of the Tokugawa supporters.

The Boshin War´s front line moved northwards. Edo was now firmly in the hands of the new government at a cost of 100 Imperial dead. Of the Shogitai, at least 266 had perished.

The Battle of Ueno was to have a depressing postscript which showed the victors´ embitterment. The Shogitai having been denounced traitors to the Imperial cause, it was forbidden to recover and bury the bodies of their fallen. Any form of remembrance was at first strictly prohibited. Only after some time was permission granted to the priest Bukki from the temple of Entsu-ji (situated a few kilometres away) to cremate the corpses on the spot and to bury the ashes in the grounds of his temple. The spot of the Shogitai´s funeral pyre is marked by a monument erected in 1875, a time when emotions no longer ran so high. The weather-worn gravestones can still be seen today inside the Entsu-ji temple along with the bullet-riddled remains of the Black Gate, which was moved to this spot in 1907.

The Hokuetsu War in Nagaoka (May – August 1868)

Even before Edo passed firmly into government control on 15th May in the wake of the Battle of Ueno, there had been fighting in several places north of the capital, at Utsunomiya (120 km north of Edo) from 19th to 23rd April, and from 20th April onwards at Shirakawa (200 km northwards; the fighting was to last until 15th July), as well as in several other places.

The larger engagements formed the background to countless other skirmishes between Tokugawa loyalists and Imperial patrols. The latter were able to gradually extend their presence while the enemy irregulars lacked weapons, ammunition, supplies, and medical support. Most of these groups were eventually overwhelmed. Those who were not killed or went home continued to plod northwards, where the princedom of Aizu with its powerful castle of Aizu-Wakamatsu remained the hope that attracted Tokugawa stragglers from all directions like a magnet.

The Imperial government faced a much larger threat in the shape of 31 domains loyal to the Tokugawa, nearly all of which were situated in the Tohoku region (consisting of Echigo, Dewa and Mutsu provinces), and which also included Matsumae in Hokkaido. The so-called Northern Alliance (*Ouetsu Reppan Domei*) was formed in spring 1868. Its nominal head based at Shiroishi castle was the Ueno Kan'ei-ji´s former abbot. He was of Imperial blood and by his declaring himself Emperor provided the rebels at least with token legitimacy. This pretender ruled under the name of Tobu, while the lords of Sendai and Yonezawa, Date Yoshikuni and Uesugi Narinori, headed the alliance as governors general (*sotoku*). The most powerful member by far was Sendai (625, 000 *koku*), with Morioka as the runner-up (200, 000 *koku*). The two were followed by

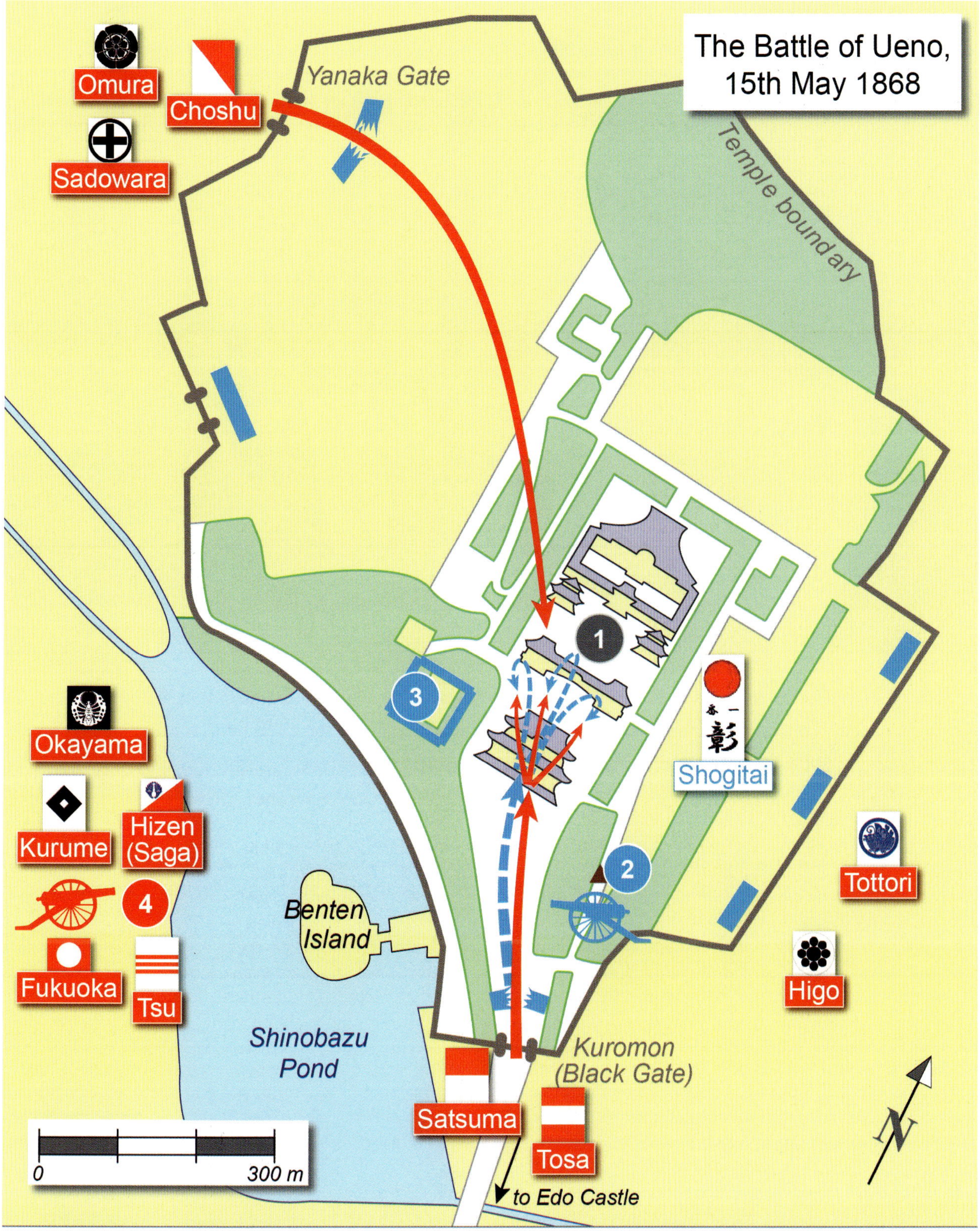

Wooded areas

Urban areas

Shogitai forcesi

Shogitai flight

Imperial breakthrough

1 Main building, *Kan'eiji* Temple

2 Sanno Hill (*Shogitai* artillery)

3 Toshugu Shrine (*Shogitai* headquarters)

4 Hongo plateau (Imperial artillery)

The various Imperial forces deployed are signified by their banners.

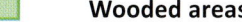

Monument erected outside the walls of Nihonmatsu castle in memory of the young samurai who fell in its defence. (Image: baku13, wikicommons)

Yonezawa (147, 000 *koku*), Nihonmatsu (100, 000 *koku*), Nagaoka (74, 000 *koku*), while Aizu (230, 000 *koku*) and Shonai (167, 000 *koku*), though not officially members, fought alongside the forces of the Northern Alliance. This happened after the alliance had failed to negotiate an amnesty for Aizu and Shonai. Altogether the alliance could muster about 50, 000 troops on paper, although in reality this number was never reached. After the shock of Toba-Fushimi many domains including Aizu and Yonezawa frantically began to introduce military reforms and attempted to come by sufficient numbers of modern arms. And although training methods were also brought up to date, most troops failed to come up to the standards of efficiency achieved by the south-western domains.

The so-called Hokuetsu War chiefly affected Nagaoka, which was situated on the coast of the Japanese Sea at the centre of the fragmented Echigo province. Both the duration and intensity of this conflict were to surpass all other episodes of the Boshin War. When it finally came to an end after months of vicious fighting, it had taken no less than 30, 000 Imperial soldiers from almost 40 domains to defeat 5, 000 enemies.

Together with other equipment, Nagaoka had acquired two Gatling Guns from the notorious Schnell brothers.

Meanwhile, an Imperial army under generals Yamagata Aritomo from Choshu[60][61] and Kuroda Kiyotaka from Satsuma was moving north-east along the coast of the Japanese Sea in the direction of Echigo. Its objective was to bring Nagaoka and its supporters into the Imperial fold. The Imperial force enjoyed vast numerical superiority, but the Satcho alliance forming its core was merely a partnership that happened to currently suit two age-old implacable rivals. Although Yamagata and Kuroda shared command of the Imperial column, they could not stand each other. The combat value of several contingents under their command was dubious. Yamagata was convinced that apart from the Choshu and Satsuma companies and battalions, none of the troops under his command had been sufficiently trained. He was right, as several instances of "friendly fire" were later to show.

Local allies did not prove to be particularly enthusiastic and actually went so far as to write a petition to the government asking it to take the fight somewhere else. Populous Takada (150, 000 *koku*) managed to turn out a mere 1, 000 fighters, whose marked lack of motivation

---

60 cf. *"The influence of foreign arms dealers"*, p. 48
61 cf. *"Choshu's Young Blades"*, p. 151

Silent witness of the Battle of Ueno in 1868: The Black Gate (*kuro-mon*), moved to the Entsu-ji temple in 1907.

The bullet holes still in evidence today show the intensity of the fighting.

The Black Gate viewed from the temple grounds.
To the left and right can be seen several grave markers of the fallen Shogitai fighters.

Banners of the Northern Alliance.
of 31 domains, measuring 237 x 114 cm (black banner) and 195 x 174 cm (white banner). Both standards were carried by Yonezawa, which was a member of the alliance. The badge resembles a five-pointed star but is in fact a pentagram. It remains a topic of discussion whether this is a symbol inspiring magical powers as contrived by Onmyodo sorcerer Abe-no seimei (d. 1005), or something entirely different in meaning. (Photographs with kind permission of Miyazaka Koukokan Collection, Yonezawa)

did nothing to improve the Imperial army's strategic position. In 1866 Choshu had heavily defeated the Takada samurai[62] and their disposition to serve Choshu as an ally was altogether limited. The Takada problem was solved by consistently deploying these troops in the forefront of the fighting right until the fall of Aizu. Nevertheless, these troops only lost 59 soldiers dead and 95 wounded in almost six months of heavy fighting. Communications and supply routes were utterly inadequate. The campaign would have failed if rations, ammunition and straw sandals had not been delivered by ship. Fortunately for the Imperial forces, Shogunate admiral Enomoto Takeaki preferred to employ his powerful fleet on the eastern coast and then around Hokkaido instead of achieving naval superiority off Nagaoka. An Imperial defeat at Nagaoka would have brought about the collapse of the new government's entire modernization scheme since most of its allies had joined the cause out of opportunism not conviction. In principle, all Imperial armies needed sufficient Satsuma and Choshu contingents to bolster their efficiency since most newly converted allies could not be trusted to fully apply themselves. That said, the fighting power of the Satcho troops still outmatched that of the other contingents by far.

Yamagata and Kuroda's objective was to seize the port of Niigata, which was instrumental in keeping the northern domains supplied. If all Echigo were brought under control, Aizu, Yonezawa and Shonai, the centres of resistance, would themselves be open to Imperial attack. Prince Makino Tadakuni of Nagaoka, whose troops were aided by 200 samurai from Kuwana (Prince Matsudaira Sadaaki of Kuwana owned land in the province), some *ronin* and Tokugawa stragglers as well as the Makino vassals, sent 2,000 fighters against the numerically superior Imperial force operating in the south of his domain; of these men, 800 were from Nagaoka itself. These troops were commanded by his highly competent supreme vassal Kawai Tsuginosuke, while the daimyo himself betook himself to safety in Aizu. His survival was essential as the focus of his samurai's loyalty.

Kawai inflicted heavy losses on the Imperial forces. His Gatlings were instrumental in this, firing up to 350 rounds per minute. The Nagaoka troops and their allies sustained 400 casualties, while on the Imperial side no less than 1,000 soldiers were killed. Their objective to force the Enoki pass failed, making this engagement the first Imperial defeat of the Boshin War. Still the Imperial forces retained the upper hand, bypassing the enemy's position by landing an élite force off a merchant vessel in the Nagaoka troops' rear. On 19th May, four days after the Battle of Ueno, these managed to take the castle at Nagaoka, which had been mostly stripped of its defenders. This move forced the Nagaoka troops to retreat,

---

62 cf. "The second punitive campaign against Choshu in 1866", p. 106

but as yet the powers of the Northern Alliance did not consider the situation an outright *casus foederis*. Aizu nevertheless dispatched 600 men, who were just like the Kuwana men equipped with firearms by Nagaoka. A short while later however, more troops from Aizu, Shonai and even 2, 000 samurai from Yonezawa[63] and other domains were marching in the direction of Niigata. Nagaoka had become the main theatre of the war.

Two months later on 24th July, the Nagaoka forces, aided by troops from Aizu, Yonezawa and other domains, succeeded in retaking the castle, albeit at heavy cost: Kawai Tsuginosuke was wounded and later succumbed to gangrene in Aizu. Nagaoka and its allies were only able to hold the castle for five days before Niigata was attacked by several thousand enemy troops in a concerted land and naval operation. Imperial soldiers commanded by Kuroda Kiyotaka arrived in two warships and four transports. They defeated the troops of the northern domains, among them the forces of Nagaoka, Aizu, Yonezawa, and Sendai. A large number of shells and heated solid shot were fired on the town, eventually causing the defenders to scatter. Nagaoka castle fell for the third and last time on 29th July. Nothing remains of this once proud edifice but two memorial stones near Nagaoka central railway station.

The embitterment and propaganda-induced resentment with which these fights were conducted is echoed by the Imperial reports after fighting in the region had ceased:

"Leaving at daybreak on October 14th soldiers from domains such as of Satsuma, Choshu, Aki, and Takanabe advanced on three routes along the inlet at Dekijima. There was a short artillery battle on the opposite shore of Heijima. From amidst a hailstorm-like shower of bullets, the soldiers eventually [...] reached the frontal coast in their small boats. After this advance, the traitors fell into disarray and abandoned their stronghold, and our army pursued them for almost a mile before surrounding Yonezawa's rebel troops on all sides. Not wishing to stop at this, Satsuma and Choshu troops, together with the conscripts and Takanabe troops fought hard, shooting and killing the traitorous senior vassal Irobe Nagato and and eventually obtaining the letter of military command by Uesugi Narinori from Yonezawa. Moreover, there were many dead among the rebels; the three ships *Settsu*, *Teibo* and *Chiwaki* launched attacks from the sea, giving the rebels no opportunity to get supplies. They were made to scramble into defeat, and riding the wave of victory the navy landed ashore. There, the two attacking teams merged, bringing peace to Niigata for the first time." (Hakoishi 2017: 128 f.)

Small northern domains realized that their game was up and began to defect to the Imperial side. By mid-August, the entire province of Echigo on the Japanese Sea coast was under government control. The Hokuetsu War, which had seen bitter fighting, was over. Nagaoka had made a huge war effort, fielding all of its 1, 500 samurai, more than one third of which were now either wounded or dead (266/317). The castle at Nagaoka together with 3, 000 housings had been burned to the ground. The men of Nagaoka had once more proved themselves samurai of the old school and fought bravely to the last (something which could not be said of all samurai involved in the fighting of 1868). They had not taken up arms to fight for a cowardly and weak ex-Shogun but to defend their homes. They had sustained huge losses defending their lord's castle. Thus, the emerging Imperial government was forced to acknowledge that another reason for abolishing the samurai caste besides its social and economic obsolescence was the fact that some samurai were still a martial force to be reckoned with!

The Hokuetsu War is also worthy of note in its mingling of tradition and modernity. The broken terrain of the battlefield had been dominated by modern firearms, with small contingents skirmishing at a distance from each other. Any troops caught in the open in dense formations took heavy losses. Artillery fire proved decisive in wearing down enemy troops and destroying fortified positions. The Imperial army had applied state-of-the-art modern tactics in successfully employing two landing forces, and generally by its skilled coordination of land and naval operations. And yet the samurai remained true to themselves, as the following episode from the diary of an Imperial samurai by the name of Mosuke shows. Mosuke fought in the so-called Akita War in the wake of Nagaoka's fall:

"I almost ran right into an enemy scout on the top of Mt. Tamasaka. Since only four or five *ken* (c. 25–30 feet) separated us, just as the enemy was trying to spin his gun around, I shot him in the waist, hitting him so that he fell to the bottom of a ravine. Afterwards, I took his rifle, his head and his long and short sword as trophies. [...] The heads taken at Kanayama were wrapped in straw and three sacks were forwarded [to headquarters]. Five were exposed for view at Yuzawa Inspection Point, two in front of the wholesale store, ten at Yokota and seven inside the temple. Yanagisawa Harima's head was pickled in salt and together with the captured long swords, spears and a battle pennant decorated with a large sparrow crest in bamboo was sent with a guard of seven or eight soldiers of various ranks on their way to the castle. After the fall of Yokota Castle, workers from the town had to clean up more than 80 corpses, of whom 50 were of samurai rank." (quoted after Hoya, n. d.)

The remaining troops who had fought at Nagaoka retired to Aizu, which was to become the next battle zone.

---

63 cf. *"The example of Yonezawa"*, p. 37

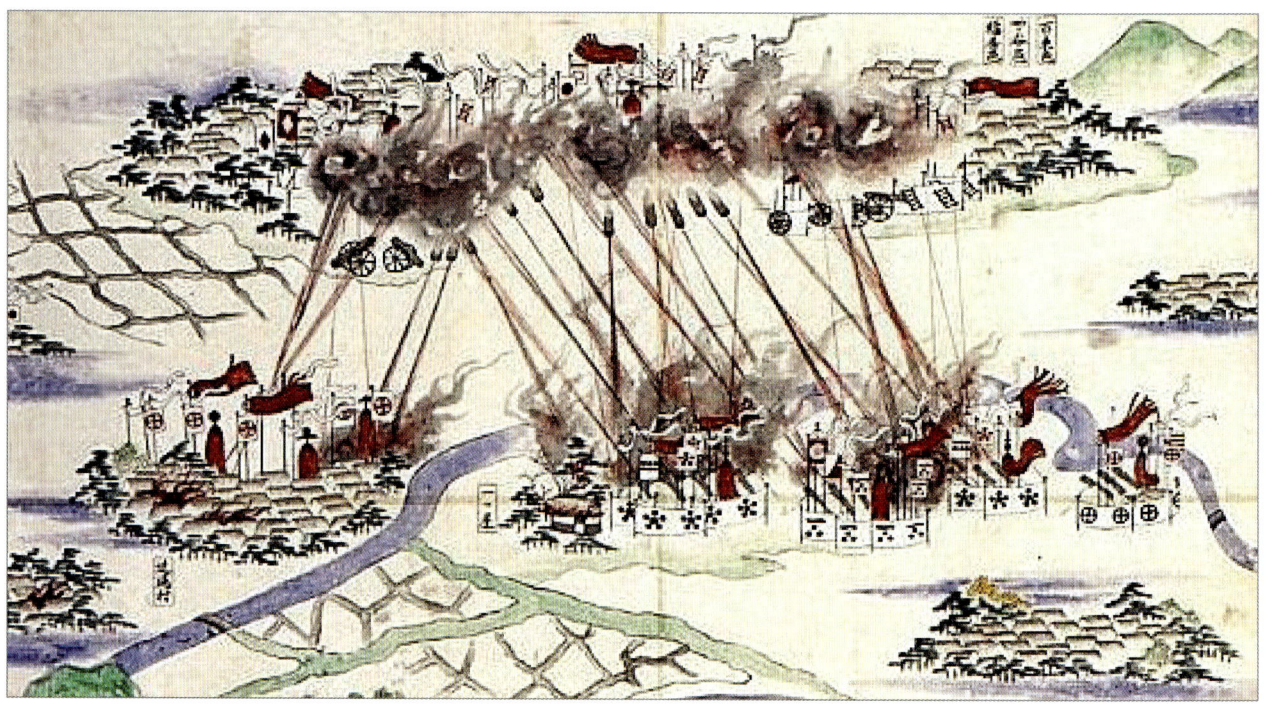

Nagaoka-jo kobo ezu ("Picture of the attack on Nagaoka castle and its defence").
The picture shows the far-flung military operations from the actions on the coast at Niigata to the surroundings of Nagaoka castle itself on the bank of the Shinano river. The painting was probably produced immediately after the Hokuetsu War and may have been commissioned by a member of the Maeda clan of Kaga, since Kaga troops feature prominently in the picture. The artist was clearly familiar with the local topography but certainly not an expert on modern firearms and the new military standards. Nevertheless, he must have been very impressed by what he saw or was told about since the number of guns depicted as well as their effect have been dramatically exaggerated. The Satsuma (detail: bottom left) and Choshu troops (detail: bottom right) are shown still using obsolete windsock standards along with traditional daimyo's *mon*, which would have been available to the artist from reference works. In principle the picture follows the archaic artistic tradition of presenting samurai warfare in the form of "wimmelpictures", rendering it almost naive when viewed against the background of a new time.

A common sight in the area north of Edo/Tokyo between April and autumn 1868: two Imperial infantrymen armed with muzzle-loading rifles and swords have dispatched two sword-armed samurai. (Alfred Umhey Collection)

A survivor from a different era: *uma-jirushi* like this personal standard of *karo* (chief retainer) Saigo Tanomo no longer possessed any military value in 1868. Shortly before the events of 1868 standards like this one were still proudly carried by Aizu´s forces on parade.

The bloody siege of Aizu-Wakamatsu
(6th October – 6th November 1868)

After defeating Nagaoka in Echigo the Imperial armies turned their attention to the hub and moral beacon of resistance, Aizu. Its fortress city of Aizu-Wakamatsu was situated in a broad valley basin surrounded by mountains. The fall of this stronghold before the onset of winter would prove a decisive blow for the Northern Alliance, since for inspiration the rebel cause looked up to Aizu and its lord Matsudaira Katamori, the former protector of Kyoto.

After the defeat of Toba-Fushimi, Aizu had made huge efforts to modernize its armed forces and create as many well-drilled and well-armed infantry units as possible in the short time available.[64] What was lacking in equipment and modernity had to be compensated by the Aizu troops' renowned efficiency with the sword and the lance. Altogether there were 11,500 defenders available, of which the most reliable were the Aizu samurai, while the peasant and urban militia were naturally less interested in the preservation of the ruling family than in the defence of their homes and property.

The defenders of Aizu-Wakamatsu in 1868

Civil servants and administrators	200
Genbu-tai (samurai veterans), 4 companies	400
Suzaku-tai (samurai aged 36–49 years), 12 companies	1,200
Seiryu-tai (samurai aged 18–35 years), 9 companies	900
Byakko-tai (samurai aged 17–18 years), 6 companies	300
Artillerymen for c. 50 pieces	300
Garrison troops and engineers	200
Total Aizu samurai fighters	**3,500**
Samurai from other regions	1,500
Armed peasants	4,500
Urban militia (townsmen, artisans)	2,000
Total other forces	**8,000**
Total defenders	**11,500**

(Source: http://www.aizue.net/siryou/gunsei.html)

After its surrender, Aizu handed over 2,845 rifles and handguns, and 51 artillery pieces. Even when allowing for equipment lost in action or abstracted, it is evident that less than half of all Aizu troops were equipped with firearms.

The rapid Imperial advance took Aizu, which had not completed its preparations for defence, by surprise. Since it was considered impossible to hold the castle indefinitely against modern artillery, it was decided to defend the passes through the surrounding mountains. Unfortunatley, the defending troops failed to occupy their designated positions on time, and to make matters worse the Imperial army unexpectedly turned up from the direction of Nihonmatsu in the east. Important bridges remained intact. The young samurai of the *Byakko-tai* corps were beaten at Tonokuchibara and retreated up Mount Imori. Hijikata Toshizo and his remaining Shinsengumi fighters were defeated in a similar engagement at the Bonari Pass. Already on 8th October the enemy had seized the town of Aizu-Wakamatsu and proceeded to set fire to the buildings. The sight of the burning town had tragic consequences: the fledgling young samurai of the *Byakko-tai* saw the conflagration from Mount Imori, and believing all was lost took their own lives. Other fatalities included around 200 wives and children of leading samurai, among them 21 members of the *karo* Saigo Tanomo's family (not related to the Saigo from Satsuma), who committed suicide to avoid capture and lessen the burden of the defenders. The first Imperial assault was beaten back, the attackers being expelled from the castle's courtyards. Later a troop of Aizu samurai under Yamakawa Okura (Hiroshi) who had been cut off succeeded in breaking through enemy lines by dressing up and counterfeiting as traditional lion dancers and jugglers. Their singing and dancing return proved a great boost for Aizu morale.

The core of the castle's defence was firm enough, even in the face of the huge Imperial numbers – the government had now mustered 30,000 troops for the siege. Again and again, small groups of men followed samurai tradition by making sorties to confront the besiegers in hand-to-hand combat. One of these actions developed into the slaughter around the Chome-ji temple. Twelve companies of altogether 1,000 samurai and *ashigaru* led by Sagara Kanbei, one of the daimyo's top retainers who had already fought at Kyoto in 1862, stood on the Aizu side. From the castle's gates, they swept into the town, driving Choshu, Ogaki and Bizen troops before them. The Imperial troops were eventually pushed out of the town and towards the temple, which was enclosed by walls on three sides. The Aizu troops stormed the temple, even employing artillery in the process. Finally troops from Tosa arrived on the scene. These soldiers were among the best in the Imperial army, and they managed to dislodge the Aizu troops from the temple. Choshu lost seven men killed and eight wounded, Bizen lost four dead and

---

64 cf. *"Samurai – the last battlecry of the old feudal élite"*, p. 82

The horrors of Aizu: in order to relieve the burdens facing the defenders, twenty-one women of the Saigo clan committed ritual suicide with their daggers. The gruesome scene, reconstructed at the restored residence of the Saigo at Aizu-Wakamatsu, depicts one of the hapless girls asking a bystanding Tosa officer to assist her with his sword.

seven wounded, Ogakai lost five killed and ten wounded. Tosa losses are unknown. Aizu lost 170 men killed and 93 wounded, 24 of which later succumbed to their wounds. The disparity between the number of dead and wounded is striking. Aizu was not in the position to provide medical attention for such the great number of wounded, and the enemy gave no quarter – it was not in the Imperial army's interest to care for enemy wounded.[65] Sagawa Kanbei's 63-year-old father was among the Aizu slain, as were many other samurai from the upper classes. Sagawa Kanbei himself was reputed to have helped himself to a little too much of the prince's traditional pre-battle tot of *sake*, forcing him to delay the sortie to sleep it off. He survived and later became a police officer under the new government.

Aizu was not able to prevent the enemy's systematic building up of forces in the area. Eventually the besiegers found a position from which artillery was able to fire shells into the castle itself. On 29th October alone, fifty pieces each fired fifty rounds at the castle and its grounds. The defenders had dug a deep trench lined with tatami mattresses in the vicinity of the main gate, where everyone apart from the men manning the defences took cover. The castle's buildings had either been destroyed or were in danger of collapsing.

Conditions inside the castle were appalling. There was not enough space for the many wounded, and when the castle's defenders finally decided to surrender, not a single piece of white fabric could be found to serve as a flag of surrender. Every patch had been used up for bandages. The flag eventually had to be sown together from rags. The *Aizu Boshin Senshi* chronicle recorded that in some field hospitals it became impossible to even lay down the wounded because the floor was littered with limbs and decomposing corpses. Men and women were literally pulverized by exploding shells. After the castle's surrender, British doctor Dr William Wills did everything

---

65 cf. "After the battle, or the experiences of Dr William Willis", p. 160

The main tower of Aizu-Wakamatsu castle in 1873 and restored to its full splendour today. Five years after the siege the damage was still clearly visible. (National Archives of Japan/Author´s digital archive)

in his power to ease the plight of the wounded but the thousands of casualties were simply too many. Willis nevertheless tended to the wounded until his medical supplies gave out.

On 6th November the besieged realized that it had become impossible to continue their resistance. Supplies and ammunition had all but run out. Prince Matsudaira Katamori himself together with his heir left the castle at the head of their troops, carrying a white flag painted with the characters signifying "surrender" (*kofuku*). He was taken into custody as the Imperial troops occupied what was left of the castle and town, and seized whatever booty was still worth the taking. The siege, which had lasted for one month, had cost the lives of 2,400 Aizu people, mostly from samurai families. 5,000 men, women and children finally surrendered together with Matsudaira Katamori.

The situation of the besieged had been so desperate that even women and children had fought in the castle´s defence. A group of *naginata*-armed young samurai women under Nakano Takeko had encountered Imperial troops at Namida bridge while seeking out a way to access the castle and fought bravely until their leader was felled by a bullet. The most well-known "Amazon" was Yamamoto Yae (1845–1932), who is even commemorated in the form of a one-year Japanese TV series ("Yae no Sakura", NHK 2013). The daughter of a hereditary expert of firearms from Aizu, she was completely familiar with this type of weapon. Knowing that firearms were now the decisive weapons on the battlefield, she chose not to fight with the *naginata* like the other women. Armed with a Spencer carbine, she stood on the castle walls alongside the men. She survived the siege and later moved to Kyoto, where she married the founder of Doshisha University. The memory of the Aizu wounded never left her: she later served as a voluntary nurse in the wars against China and Russia.

A grim fate awaited the defeated Aizu samurai. Choshu had not forgotten its humiliation at the hands of the Aizu samurai at Kyoto and could only just be dissuaded from more radical punitive measures. The domain was dissolved, and the gaunt figures of the samurai and their families could presently be seen marching in a trek which would take them to Tonami in the deep north of Honshu. Altogether 17,000 men, women and children suffered deportation. In this cold and unhospitable region, the available farmland officially yielded an annual gain of 30,000 *koku*, but in reality, it was much less (one quarter of the estimated yield was probably only ever achieved). The samurai and their families knew nothing about farming, and to avoid starvation and death from the bitter cold, many chose to emigrate to the United States. Later many samurai from Aizu also became military settlers in inner Hokkaido, which was systematically explored and settled during the Meiji period. For years, any descendants of Aizu samurai aspiring to a position in government

service could only choose between the police and the military. Prospects of promotion in the Japanese armed forces were nevertheless not good for men from Aizu. For decades, no Aizu soldier ever reached the rank of general. Between 1917 and 1920, the German prisoners of war interned at Bando camp in Shikoku made the acquaintance of Lieutenant Colonel Matsue Toyohisa, who served as the camp's commandant. Himself a man from Aizu, Matsue showed great kindnes and humanity to the prisoners in his care, for he knew the fate of the vanquished from experience, and was wont to refer to "the prison" that he himself was confined to. Although his superiors habitually bullied him, he continuously showed a samurai virtue not found among Aizu's enemies: *bushi no nasake* – a samurai pity.

Prince Matsudaira Katamori managed to avoid severe punishment. His son, who was born in 1869, was granted nominal princely rule over the small Tonami region, while Katamori himself settled in Nikko north of Tokyo. The historic town is the location of the most important Toshugu shrine, where Tokugawa Ieyasu, the ancestor of both the Tokugawa and Matsudaira, is venerated. Katamori became a Shinto priest, dying of pneumonia in 1892.

Sendai, Yonezawa and Shonai in the Boshin War

Sendai, the largest domain in the Tohoku region, surrendered even before the fall of Aizu. The example of Sendai, the home of the legendary Date clan, shows how centuries of idleness and stagnation can bring about a territory's defencelessness. Despite the military potential of no less than 33, 000 available samurai and an annual income of 625, 000 *koku*, Sendai had had the worst of five engagements with Imperial troops, the last at the Hatamaki pass, where it lost 46 dead to the Imperial army's seven. Sendai had also proved unable to dispatch auxiliary contingents to aid its allies Nagaoka and Aizu. As in so many other domains, the ruling samurai caste in Sendai was deeply divided over its attitude towards the new Imperial government; military measures remained half-hearted in consequence. In contrast to Aizu, Sendai got off lightly. Like many daimyo who surrendered, its ruler was forced to resign in favour of his heir, whose income was then curtailed by the reduction of territory. Sometimes a number of the prince's chief counsellors were nudged into taking responsibility – and then obliged to commit suicide. In 1871 the old domains were abolished in favour of provinces, which in turn were replaced by prefectures with a governor at their head. After the fall of Aizu and Sendai, the Northern Alliance had practically ceased to exist.

Yonezawa, which had sent many troops in aid of Nagaoka, made peace with the Imperial government on 19th October 1868. It was able to prove its loyalty by dispatching troops to fight against its northern neighbour, Shonai.

Shonai, situated in northern Tohoku, had vigourously fought against supporters of the Imperial cause in the region, and only capitulated on 10th November 1868 after Nagaoka, Yonezawa and Aizu had fallen. Due to its considerable financial resources, the modern armament of its forces (once again supplied by the ubiquitous Schnell brothers), and its ability to solve internal dissent to everyone's satisfaction, it was considered a particularly dangerous enemy by the Imperial government. Shonai's 2nd battalion under Sakai Gembai especially distinguished itself in the battles of Kiyokawaguchi and Tendo. In the wake of these engagements the princedom of Akita, one of the Emperor's few allies in the north, was threatened by enemy invasion. Élite troops from Hizen (Saga) had to be rushed in to stabilize the front with their Armstrong guns and Spencer rifles. When Shonai finally surrendered, it had remained effectively undefeated.

Last stand of the Shogunate party in Hokkaido – the surrender of Hakodate on 27th June 1869

Shortly before the battle for Hokkaido began, German merchant A. R. Weber visited the port of Hakodate, which is situated in the south of the northern main island of Hokkaido, or Ezo (Yezo) as it was called at the time. In his autobiographical work *Kontorrock und Konsulatsmütze* ("Merchant's coat and consul's cap") he gave a poignant description of the situation of the last Tokugawa army in Hakodate:

"The city was literally crawling with troops of the Taikun [i. e. the former Shogun], who seemed to look to the result of the oncoming battles with glumness rather than confidence. The outcome hardly appeared doubtful to me. The city's location was nevertheless ideally suited for defence. Access to the wide bay which extended far inland was only possible via a narrow gap in the rocks. To the entrance's right, covered by a high rock, lay Hakodate, entirely invisible from the Tsugaru Straits. To the left, the shore was craggy and inaccessible, making the eastern side the only promising target for an attack. Here, the bay ran close to the big ocean and was separated from it only by a narrow, sandy spithead. The water here was very shallow, making it impossible for large ships to approach the coast. The entire Japanese fleet was in the hands of the Taikun, and his admiral Enomoto enjoyed the reputation of being a capable and enterprising officer. […] Meanwhile operational plans were not restricted to merely reconquering lost territory, and the French officers who were employed in the army and navy as instructors were still proudly confident of victory. Cut off from all resources however the Northerners, as the Taikun faction

Goryokaku ("Five-pointed star fort") was erected between 1855 and 1866 to counteract a possible Russian invasion of Hokkaido. Following the ideas of Vauban, the polygon fortification with its five bastions and overlapping firing zones (permitting enfilading fire) was the most modern Japanese fortification of its time. In 1868/69 there was no tree foliage to impend vision. The city of Hakodate has meanwhile spread to the banks of the fortress´s moats. (wiki)

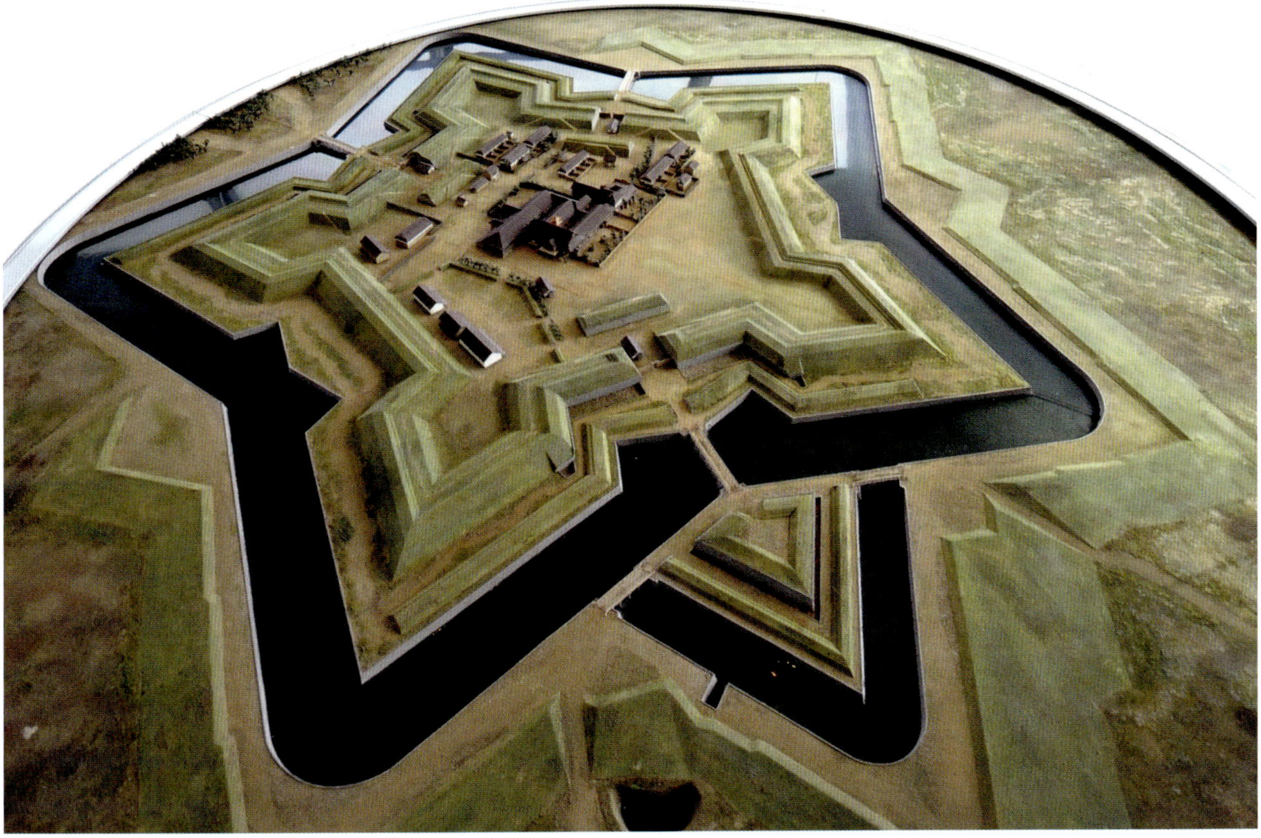

Model of Goryokaku fort as it appeared in 1868.
(Photograph with kind permission of Mr Kimura Tomoki, Goryokaku Tower, Hakodate)

Defendece of the ironclad *Kotetsu* employ a Gatling Gun, Port Miyako 1869

At the beginning of the battle for Hokkaido in 1869, the Imperial forces possessed the most powerful warship in Japan. The ironclad *Kotetsu* had been built in France and originally intended for the Confederate Navy in the American Civil War. Shogunal naval forces attempted to seize the vessel in a night raid as it lay anchored in Port Miyako. However, the attackers had neither reckoned with the ironclad´s low deck construction, nor with the Gatling Gun which the crew had mounted on deck. The sources confirm the presence of three of these weapons in the Boshin War: two had been sold to Nagaoka by the Schnell brothers, where they were employed by warlord Kawai Tsuginosuke against the Imperial army. The Gatling involved in the defence of *Kotetsu* was probably a weapon previously captured from Nagaoka forces. Illustration: Sascha Lunyakov.

The French military advisors and troop commanders with their Japanese comrades, Republic of Ezo 1869. Jules Brunet is seated second left beside Vice President Matsudaira Taro. Brunet insisted on the adoption of French-style-uniforms, a circumstance evident in this photograph. (wiki)

Flag of the short-lived Republic of Ezo which existed from January until June 1869. Its authenticity has been challenged since it was not flown by ships. The Northern Star superimposed on the Imperial chrysanthemum would have been an intolerable provocation to the Imperialists. (wiki)

was now called, were already suffering from a lack of funds which was growing daily worse, and resorted to all kinds of ruses to replenish their coffers."

(R. Weber 1973: 158 f.)

Weber´s assessment of Shogunal naval supremacy was to prove inaccurate, as we shall see.

Hakodate and its population of 28, 000 were protected by the fortress of Goryokaku ("five-pointed star fort"), the most modern Japanese fortification at the time. It had been built to guard against Russian invasion. Hokkaido was only accessible by sea. The small Imperial garrison of Hokkaido stationed in the Matsumae domain was expelled by surviving Tokugawa supporters who were willing to continue fighting and had arrived from Sendai by ship. After the defeat of the Northern Alliance these troops had retired northwards. Their evacuation from the Tohuku area had been carried out by the remaining steam-powered warships and transports of the Tokugawa navy under its admiral Enomoto Takeaki (1836–1908). Despite his young age, Enomoto was Japan´s most capable naval officer. Holding the second highest naval rank of *fuku-sosai*, he received his military training in Europe in the years 1862 to 1867. At Edo in 1868 he had refused to surrender his warships to the Imperial government.[66] He had been accompanied to Hokkaido by several French military instructors under Captain Jules Brunet[67] and the Tokugawa *hohei-bugyo* (general of infantry) Otori Keisuke, father of the French-trained *denshutai* infantry battalions. In contrast to Enomoto, Otori largely remained a military theorist whose repeatedly uttered *mata maketa-yo* ("We've lost again!") irritated many of his subordinates. Being a professional officer, the road to Hokkaido was Otori´s destiny, and he took it despite his doubts regarding the successful outcome of the campaign.

Enomoto and Otori were under no illusions. Simply resurrecting the Tokugawa Shogunate was out of the question. What they had in mind was an independent state either tolerated or recognized by the Meiji government, where Japanese men and women of the same political convictions as themselves could gather and live unmolested. This "Republic of Ezo" was proclaimed in 1869, and Enomoto was elected its first president. This move neutralized any claim of Imperial authority. The republic sought to establish international relationships, and for a certain time the German consul general Max von Brandt set about planning a German colony in as yet mostly unexploited Hokkaido, but his diplomatic superior Otto von Bismarck would have none of it.

The Japanese Imperial government however was not going to tolerate a division of the country.

---

66 cf. "Katsu Kaishu and Saigo Takamori", p. 153

67 cf. "Jules Brunet, true 'Last Samurai'", p. 157

Enomoto's forces consisted of a collection of samurai organized into different units, and infantry veterans, among them the French-trained *denshutai*, the Shinsengumi, the Shogitai, the Shohotai, and several other militias. Enomoto was assisted by the faithful daimyo Itakura Katsukiyo, Ogasawara Nagamichi, and Matsudaira Sadaaki of Kuwana.

The rifle units were organized into four regiments, each commanded by one of the French non-commissioned officers present (Fortant, Marlin, Cazeneuve, Bouffier). These units were referred to as *rejiman*, a Japanese loanword derived from the French *régiment*. The battalions were commanded by Japanese officers. General Otori Keisuke commanded the land forces together with Shinsengumi veteran Hijikata Toshizo, with Captain Jules Brunet acting as his chief of staff.

Land forces of the Republic of Ezo, Winter 1868 – early Summer 1869

President: Enomoto Takeaki

Commander-in-chief: *bugyo* Otori Keisuke; *bugyo nami*: Hijikata Toshizo; chief of staff: Jules Brunet.

First Regiment: 1st battalion of four militia companies and former *denshutai* officers; 2nd battalion of seven companies including Shinsengumi and Shogitai.

Second Regiment: 1st battalion of four companies of *denshutai* infantry; 2nd battalion of five companies of Ichirentai.

Third Regiment: 1st battallion of four Kasugatai companies; 2nd Battalion of four Gakuheitai companies.

Fourth Regiment: 1st battalion of five Shohotai companies; 2nd battalion of five Shohotai companies.

Field artillery under Seki Hiroemon (six batteries of four field guns each).

Coastal and fortress artillery: about 60 smaller batteries and emplacements with 1 – 2 older pieces of Dutch manufacture each.

Auxiliaries: three companies of engineers, and others.

Naval forces commanded by *bugyo* Arai Ichinosuke. Warships *Kaiyo-maru, Kaiten-maru, Takao-maru, Banryu-maru, Chiyogata-maru, Shinsoku-maru*; transports *Oe-maru, Chogei-maru, Hoo-maru, Nagasaki-maru, Mikaho-maru, Kaishun-maru*.

If we assume 400 men serving in each battalion, then according to this table the Ezo government ought to have had between 4, 000 and 5, 000 men available in its land forces. Headquarters were established at Hakodate with its Goryokaku fortress (garrison: 200), and at Matsumae in the south (garrison: 600). A further 400 troops were stationed in the north. Two mobile columns of 400 troops each commanded by Otori and Brunet respectively were to serve as rapid response forces if any urgent military crisis arose. Enomoto's forces were plagued by constant money shortages, and the local population could not help but ask themselves why their homeland had been chosen as the new area of conflict.

In 1869, the Imperial government dispatched a fleet and 7, 000 infantry to the north-eastern coast of Honshu.

Admiral Enomoto Takeaki (1836–1908) in Hokkaido (1868–1869).
(public domain)

The keys to successful invasion were naval attack and logistics. Fortune smiled on the Imperial troops when in 1868 Enomoto lost his most powerful battleship, the *Kaiyo-maru*, a brand-new Dutch-manufactured 2, 590 ton steam frigate with 26 heavy guns. This gave the Imperial navy the decisive edge over their opponents, for it owned an almost invulnerable vessel which was capable of outgunning any ship still in Enomoto's fleet: the first Japanese ironclad had been built by the French and named *CSS Stonewall*, had originally been intended for the Confederate navy in the Civil War. The Shogunate had attempted to purchase it from the US after the end of the war, but the ship held in Yokosuka harbour due to the US government's strict policy of neutrality.[68] Meanwhile however, the US had recognized the new Imperial government and handed the vessel over. It was rechristened *Kotetsu* and was now to form the spearhead of the Imperial navy. Enomoto contrived to neutralize this new threat with a lightning strike and dispatched his admiral Arai and three ships to attack *Kotetsu* at its moorings in Miyako harbour in northern Honshu. Bad weather interfered with the operation, and when Arai's *Kaiten-maru* (built at Danzig; 1, 920 t) was finally able to go alongside

---

68 cf. "The Battle of Ueno, 15th May 1868", p. 127
    cf. "The Battle of Ueno, 15th May 1868", p. 127

Gatling Gun on display at the Kawai Tsuginosuke Memorial Hall in the City of Nagaoka. According to various sources, Nagaoka domain´s leading retainer Kawai Tsuginosuke spent 6,000 or 10,000 gold ryo on a pair of Gatlings and is believed to have operated one personally. The original colour scheme of barrel and carriage has been carefully reconstructed.

The last Battle of the war was fought at Hakodate in 1869. Woodblock print artist Migita Toshihide (1863-1925) achieved lasting fame especially with his depictions of the Sino-Japanese (1894/5) and Russo-Japanese Wars (1904/5). Here he portrays President Enomoto Takeaki together with Vice President Matsudaira Taro. Both men are shown dressed in traditional Japanese clothing. The significance of naval combat is indicated in the background, while close combat with polearms was already mostly a thing of the past in 1869.

the enemy ship, it was discovered that the deck of the miraculous Imperial flagship was three metres below that of the attacking vessel. When the boarders had finally managed to clamber onto the *Kotetsu*'s deck, they were mown down by a Gatling Gun. Arai was forced to abandon the operation and lost one of his ships to boot.

Now that they had gained naval supremacy, the Imperial army began its landings north of Matsumae on 12th April 1869 with all the efficiency and confidence which they had gained in the course of their hitherto successful campaigning. Step by step Enomoto's and Otori's forces were pushed south via three routes. There were frequent skirmishes over barricades and fiercely contested mountain passes. In the end 2,000 Tokugawa loyalists had been killed, almost half of all troops originally available. Hijikata Toshizo was among the fallen. He was shot off his horse while leading his men; due to an earlier foot wound, he had no longer been good on his feet.

Eventually all that was left to Enomoto were 800 troops penned up in the fortress of Goryokaku and Hakodate harbour. As A. R. Weber had noted, this was a splendid position for defence. Enomoto's three remaining warships were anchored in the bay, and coastal batteries stationed at strategically important points offered further protection. Undeterred, the Imperial troops advanced across open country while their ships entered the bay, prepared for heavy losses. *Kotetsu* sported a 300-pounder Armstrong gun at its prow which destroyed everything in its path, while its armoured hulk was almost impervious to the enemy shells. All three Ezo ships were put out of action, and on 27th June 1869 the fortress of Hakodate surrendered to Satsuma general Kuroda Kiyotaka. The Boshin War was over, all of Japan under Imperial control. Most of the French military instructors boarded a French vessel and returned home.[69] Enomoto, Otori and Imai Nobuo[70] were imprisoned and threatened with capital punishment. They were later pardoned and released, and eventually all found themselves holding respectable positions in Japan's new post-war society.

Otori Keisuke's witty remark "It is easy to die; you can do so anytime you choose" is reported to have ultimately convinced Enotomo Takeaki that fighting to the death was not invariably a wise decision. There was no better way to express that the old days of the samurai had gone for ever – there was simply no lord left to sacrifice one's life for. To embrace a new era and recognize a new ruler and bear whatever they held in store was a new form of bravery the proud samurai of Japan still had to learn.

---

69 cf. "*Jules Brunet, true 'Last Samurai'*", p. 157

70 cf. "*Imai Nobuo (1841–1918) and the long road to an ordinary life*", p. 163

IMPORTANT CHARACTERS OF THE BAKUMATSU PERIOD

Monumental statue of Omura Masujiro, cast in bronze at Tokyo´s arsenal in 1893 and erected outside the Yasukuni shrine. The sculptor, Okuma Ujihiro, had travelled to France and Italy before creating the first Japanese monumental statue in Western style. The statue´s execution suggests that it was designed to assuage conservative misgivings about Japan´s opening up to Western influence. Omura, who like no other supported this policy, is depicted wearing traditional samurai costume and carrying two swords. Only the binoculars in his hand hints at his ambition to transcend old boundaries.

1860s Japan was full of fascinating, occasionally even eccentric figures. These could be found both among the rivalling Japanese warlords and the representatives of the Western powers. Many leading characters were young and reckless and prone to taking gambles. Some were truly flamboyant men; all were filled with vigour and idealism which brought about many dramatic situations. This resulted in plenty of interesting and exciting biographies, of which for space reasons only a few can be presented here. The lives of these men are a rich source of information about an era which ushered in the end of the samurai both as a social caste and fighting men.

Choshu´s Young Blades

As in Satsuma, the other major renegade domain, the rapid and violent changes characteristic of this epoch saw a new group of young samurai assert themselves as leaders of the Choshu domain. Those who survived later rose to become rulers of the new Japanese state. The five men presented here all came from humble backgrounds, Omura Masujiro only becoming a samurai in his adulthood.

Takasugi Shinsaku (1839–1867) was to play a hugely influential role in Choshu´s military reforms. Like so many of Choshu´s angry young men he was first strongly influenced by the radical philosophical teachings of Yoshida Shoin, but also witnessed as an observer the superiority of Western military technology during the Chinese Tai´ping Rebellion. His xenophobia drove him and Ito Hibumi to carry out a terrorist attack on the British embassy. Eventually however he and other "young blades" began to recognize that their true enemy was the Shogunate.

Takasugi Shinsaku became the founder of the *kiheitai* militia in 1863[71], a trailblazing unit fighting in the modern Western manner. The *kiheitai* accepted anyone willing to fight in its ranks, thus deliberately rejecting the received military monopoly of Choshu´s traditional samurai élite. The unit financed itself with the aid of wealthy merchants from outside the samurai caste. In a symbolic act, Takasugi cut off his *chonmage*, the samurai characteristic hairknot, and henceforth wore his hair cropped in the Western manner. In 1865 the brave and energetic Takasugi and his supporters became effective rulers of Choshu. By this time Takasugi, himself of slight build, had contracted tuberculosis, a condition which was not improved by his love of women and *sake*. Before his early death, he chose **Omura Masujiro** (1824–1869) as his successor not only as leader of the *kiheitai* but as commander of Choshu´s entire military – a truly splendid choice.

---

71 cf. *"Satsuma, Choshu and their allies"*, p. 61

Omura, a doctor´s son, was the oldest among the "young blades", and something of an intellectual. As a student of medicine at Nagasaki, he had learned his trade from the famous German doctor Philipp Franz von Siebold. A fluent speaker of Dutch and English, he became interested in military theory. Omura later designed the first modern Japanese Western style warship. Work as a teacher at various academies was followed by his gathering practical experience as a commander in the *kiheitai*, before he finally led the Choshu forces to victory against the Shogunate in 1866, and again in the Boshin War. When Omura was finally appointed deputy army minister in the new Meiji government in Tokyo, it took him only a few months to contribute significantly to the building of the new national military.

Omura despised the samurai and their small-time strivings to maintain the status quo. The sources record several remarks of his suggesting this dismissive attitude. As a reformer in 1860s Choshu, Omura had ruthlessly sold off samurai weapons and armour in order to finance the purchase of modern firearms. In November 1869 he was eventually set upon by a group of eight disgruntled samurai (most of them from Choshu) and died before a Dutch doctor was able to tend to his wounds.

Kido Takayoshi (1833–1877), also known as Katsura Kogoro (among other names), was the son of a samurai-turned-physician in Hagi. He was adopted by the Katsura family. After quarreling with his conservative family as a young man, Kido left the conventional school of his clan and joined Yoshida Shoin´s academy where he learned many new and radical ideas. He acquired an extensive and thorough military education by studying sword fighting technique at Edo, learning artillery technology from Egawa Tarozaemon, and visiting modern shipyards. He managed to survive the Shinsengumi´s massacre of their radical Choshu enemies at the Ikedaya tavern in Kyoto in 1864 by dressing up as a beggar and hiding under a nearby bridge. Here the shrewd Kido was fed by his Geisha lover with rice balls until the danger had passed.

Kido continued to work against the Tokugawa in secret, adopting several aliases in the process. He was a member of Takasugi´s *kiheitai* and instrumental in the sealing of the alliance between Satsuma and Choshu. He rose to become a statesman in the new Meiji government and was known for his moderation and reason. He vainly sought to prevent the invasion of Taiwan in 1874, which was one of Japan´s first steps towards establishing its own colonial empire. Kido died in 1877 from exhaustion, after an adventurous life and excessive alcoholism, tuberculosis (or beriberi) and an indefinable mental illness had finally got the better of him.

After he had been passed over in the question of Takasugi Shinsaku´s succession as Choshu commander-in-chief in 1867, **Yamagata Aritomo** (1838–1922) still managed a breathtaking military career. This had been anything but a foregone conclusion, for Yamagata was born the son of a lowly *ashigaru* from an impoverished samurai household. As a young *kiheitai* battery commander he had personally witnessed Choshu´s heavy defeat at the hands of the combined Western fleet in 1863. Yamagata spent the entire Boshin War holding the rank of a general and practically became the face of the new Japanese army under the Meiji government. He was promoted field marshal and became a prince in the newly established nobility. As such, he served as army minister three times between 1871 and 1878. He was Japanese prime minister from 1889 to 1891, and again between 1898 and 1900. Already in 1869, he had been sent from Satsuma to study in Europe together with Saigo Takamori´s younger brother Tsugumichi. He developed an intense interest especially in Prussian military affairs. In 1873 Yamagata introduced the German draft system in Japan and thus became one of the fathers of the Imperial Japanese Army as it existed until 1945.

Ito Hirobumi (1841-1909) as a young samurai in 1863. (photograph by Ueno Hikoma / Public Domain)

Ito Hirobumi (1841–1909), the last of the Choshu young bloods to be introduced, was also strongly influenced by Prussian and German ideas, albeit political ones. A count and four times Japanese prime minister, he was the father of the Japanese constitution and founder of the Conservative Party. Having studied in England as a young man together with four other Choshu samurai, he later turned away from the radical teachings of Yoshida Shoin. He was probably also plagued by remorse for having taken part in the foolhardy arson attack on the British embassy in 1863, and for his involvement in the murder of the headmaster of a Shogunate-friendly school. Ito´s change of attitude as well as his renouncement of xenophobia also contributed to the political change of tack of his mentor Takasugi Shinsaku. From political radicalism to statesmanship – Ito had come a long way. Only at the very end of his life did violence and radicalism once again catch up with him: in 1909 he was assassinated by a young foreign radical while visiting Korea.

Katsu Kaishu and Saigo Takamori

Katsu Kokichi (1802–1850), *hatamoto* of the Tokugawa, only succeeded in doing two things right in his entire life. For one thing, he decided to write an autobiography relating his more or less squandered but nevertheless interesting life. Concluding his narrative, he wrote: "Looking back upon my life makes my hair stand on end. An honest man should refrain from following my path." (Weber 2016: 72). His second great achievement was his son Rintaro (1823–1899), who by the name of **Katsu Kaishu** was to become one of the two saviours of Edo in 1868. Kokichi succeeded in keeping his son well out of his own villanies and proved a surprisingly loving and diligent parent. Even this notorious scoundrel holding the rank of *hatamoto* must have realized what precious hidden talents his young son possessed, and he was wont to defend his beloved boy against all reproof.

Rintaro, who at fifteen was already head of the Katsu family living in Edo´s Honjo district, dedicated himself to studying the Dutch language and Western military affairs at a time when profound changes were about to occur. When Commodore Perry in 1853 initiated the first of a series of events at whose end Japan was to become a modern country, Katsu Rintaro (or Kaishu, as he was known in adulthood) was able to make himself useful as a translator. Between 1855 and 1859 he taught at Nagasaki´s naval college and was one of the first Japanese experts on naval warfare. This knowledge secured him command of the first Western-type warship of the Tokugawa navy. The schooner *Kanrin-maru* had been purchased from the Netherlands and under his command took the first Japanese delegation to the USA, where for two months he was able to gather new impressions in San Francisco. His naval career continued to flourish after his return. He promoted the building of a large and powerful navy (i. e. the purchasing of Western-style warships and the building of artillery munition factories) and demanded that important posts should be awarded according to merit and expertise instead of kinship. He was a champion of military professionalism and considered the *hatamoto* of the Tokugawa "utterly useless". Whether he was actually referring to any specific person familiar to him is a different question.

This uncompromising attitude made him several enemies, and in 1864 he briefly lost his position, but the crisis of 1866 soon saw him back in office. Katsu Kaishu was now the uncontested supreme commander of the Tokugawa navy (*gunkan bugyo*). His twelve modern warships constituted the most powerful naval force in all Japan.

His actions in the fateful year 1868 were not attributable to personal weakness, although he himself admitted, "I despise killing and have never killed a man. Take my sword, for example. I used to keep it tied so tightly to the sword guard, that I couldn´t draw the blade even if I had wanted to." (Hillsborough 2011: 87). This attitude he shared with Saigo Takamori, who also never killed anyone in his life. In fact Katsu Kaishu was an expert swordsman. Yet one of his key merits both as an individual swordsman and as admiral and virtual prime minister was his capability to avoid bloodshed. In Edo, he addressed Kondo and Hijikata of the bloodthirsty Shinsengumi[72] with the words: "[Your mission in Kyoto] is no more than a personal battle. If you must fight again, do it on your own." (Hillsborough 2011: 186). Even though Katsu Kaishu showed considerable understanding for the Imperial faction´s ideas of reform and knew many of the protagonists personally, he remained loyal to his lord Tokugawa Yoshinobu as a samurai should.

Thus, Katsu Kaishu was not only a gallant soldier but also a diplomat and statesman who acted wisely and with foresight. He remained impervious to the more radical views of his time and based his actions on reason and careful deliberation.

Like Kaishu, **Saigo Takamori (1828–1877)** was renowned for his integrity. To this day his name is held in high regard, although he and Kaishu differed profoundly in character. Kaishu was a polite and accomodating man, while British diplomat Ernest Satow had a very different impression of Saigo Takamori when he first met the great man in Kyoto in 1867: "After exchanging the usual compliments, I began to feel rather at a loss, the man looked so stolid, and would not make conversation. But he had an eye that sparkled like a big black diamond, and his smile when he spoke was so friendly." (Satow 1983: 181). In time an excellent working relationship developed, which served both British interests and those of Satsuma, home of Saigo Takamori.

Nobody would have guessed that the little boy born to a poor samurai country squire in Kagoshima would one day as a politician significantly determine the fate of his homeland, and as a general not only lead the Satsuma forces in the battles of Toba-Fushimi and Ueno but also

---

[72] cf. "Shinsengumi – shining heroes, or gang of thugs?", p. 77

command up to 50, 000 soldiers during the Boshin War. It proved fortunate for Takamori to have been born in Satsuma at a time when great political and military changes were imminent. The key to his remarkable ascent in his clan´s samurai hierarchy lay in iron discipline and an unremitting desire for education. Young Takamori trained the use of arms more diligently than any of his companions, and he eagerly read any book he could lay his hands on. The samurai military *bu* and his intellectual *bun* virtues combined impressively in this young man. Daimyo Shimazu Nariakira of Satsuma, the great reformer (r. 1851–1858), became the focus of his loyalties. It was Shimazu who discovered Takamori´s talent and supported and encouraged him. His patron´s early death under dubious circumstances briefly stalled both Takamori´s confidence and his career when a suicide attempt failed, and he had to spend a total of five years in exile on southern islands. After returning to Kagoshima, Saigo doggedly continued to work his way to the very top of his domain´s samurai caste. Sources seem to indicate that he suffered from some form of depression, which however he could hold in check in order to serve a higher cause.

At Toba-Fushimi he twice visited the front line, exposing himself to considerable danger. It has been claimed that at the time he was again deliberately seeking death to follow his beloved lord Nariakira. Saigo survived again and continued to do his duty on this side of the grave. He led the Imperial army to the gates of Edo, and it was here that he and Katsu Kaishu wrote history together.

After the Shogun had retired into self-imposed captivity and the Tokugawa government had disintegrated, a contest for the possession of Edo became imminent in March 1868. Katsu Kaishu, who had been born in Edo, had decided to remain inside the city. Holding the newly created rank of *gunji toriatsukai* (commander-in-chief of all armed forces), he was the political and military leader upon whom everything now depended on the Tokugawa side. It was clear to him that any fighting in the streets would invariably result in the burning down of a large part of his city, which like all Japanese cities was built entirely of wood. Possibly the city would never recover its former status and Japan be ruled from the western domains. Saigo Takamori was concerned that a fight for control of the city would result in massive casualties even for his own side, and the political chasm between east and west would deepen still further as a result. A capital city left intact would be much more valuable to the new government than a smoking ruin. Nevertheless battle, fires, and the death of the enemy were still considered traditional outcomes of samurai warfare.

On both sides, there were those keen to fight it out the old way. Katsu Kaishu, the diplomat, promptly sent the most aggressive of his troops north to fight (and, ultimately, lose) against other Imperial forces. In spite of this clever ruse, things were on a knife´s edge in March 1868. Preparations were being made by the Tokugawa forces to set fire to the city´s south side to create an insuperable obstacle for the attackers. Saigo meanwhile had his hands full holding back the more hot-headed campaigners among the Imperial troops. Admittedly, the conditions under which the Imperial war council was prepared to accept the capitulation of Edo were extremely harsh. Among other things, the Imperial government demanded the heads of one hundred important members of the Tokugawa government and the surrender of all weapons, ships, and of the castle itself. The date of attack was fixed for 15th March. Things were clearly coming to a head. Saigo Takamori nevertheless was prepared to receive and listen to Katsu Kaishu´s envoy, and finally agreed to meet the man in person.

Katsu and Saigo, who were old acquaintances, met on 13th and 14th March 1868 on a Satsuma estate in Takanawa in the southern outskirts of Edo. For Katsu Kaishu, the stakes were high. He not only had to save Edo but also negotiate what was to become of his master Yoshinobu. He suggested that Yoshinobu be confined to house arrest in the friendly domain of Mito, and that the Tokugawa retain a part of their war materials, ships, and sufficient income.

Saigo Takamori (left) in conversation with Choshu officer Hayashi Tomoyuki during the Battle of Toba-Fushimi in 1868. (*Nishiki no mihata* 1907, plate X)

No mention was made of executions. In exchange for this, the Imperial forces would win the castle of Edo intact, which was after all the country´s most powerful fortress. Whoever held it controlled the entire city.

Thus, two wise and honourable leaders conferred among themselves over the avoidance of bloodshed and other damage threatening their common homeland. They talked about the future of their nation. First, it was agreed to suspend the Imperial attack. Saigo Takamori was clever enough to lay the final decision over any compromise in the hands of the Imperial government, thus bypassing the more aggressive of his field commanders. A decision in the Emperor´s name would be unanswerable in any case.

On 4th April 1868 Saigo and two Imperial envoys entered the castle of Edo. The following decision was announced:

1. Tokugawa Yoshinobu was to hand over the leadership of his clan and retire to Mito, where he was to remain in self-isolation.
2. Edo castle was to be abandoned and pass into the care of Owari (a Tokugawa domain, but now part of the Imperial army).
3. All warships and weapons were to be handed over; an "amount deemed appropriate" would be returned to the Tokugawa at a later date.
4. All Tokugawa vassals were to leave the castle and stay in the confinement of their houses.
5. Those who had supported Tokugawa Yoshinobu in his "rebellion" deserved "heavy punishment". However, by the grace of His Majesty the Emperor their lives would be spared.

All in all, this turned out to be a tolerable outcome for both sides, and a triumph of reason over hot-headed violence.

These conditions permitted those of the Tokugawa supporters inclined to continue the fight to escape north. On 10th and 11th April, they left the city, taking their best weapons with them. In fact, the astonished Imperial troops found that only 722 Japanese-made small arms had been left in the Edo arsenals. While the remaining Tokugawa garrison surrendered the castle without further ado, the navy under under Admiral Enomoto Takeaki had different ideas. On 11th April, one day before the ships were to be handed over, Enomoto sailed to Tateyama with eight of his ships. Threatened with sanctions for this violation of the agreement, Katsu Kaishu negotiated with Enomoto, who eventually returned. The fleet was divided between the two factions, Enomoto getting the better part of the deal by being allowed to choose the best four ships, while the Imperial admiral had to make do with the four oldest vessels. Enomoto´s squadron was to form the basis of the Tokugawa forces who fought on until surrendering in Hokkaido in June 1869.[73]

It remains remarkable that the Imperial forces were prepared to accept the Edo compromise in its ultimate form. Possibly they knew that the Imperial decision would prove too much for the proud Tokugawa warriors. The Imperial high command´s notion on 22nd April, according to which victory was "not yet entirely complete" was a massive understatement. The Boshin War had not been decided either on land or sea and dragged on for another 14 months. It was very sensitive to make lasting peace with those from the old Shogunate who had no will to fight.

That said, Katsu Kaishu had saved his city from almost certain destruction. In addition, he had managed to save Tokugawa Yoshinobu´s life. In September 1868 Edo was renamed Tokyo ("Eastern capital"), and in November the Emperor moved his household to the old Tokugawa castle. Edo/Tokyo had not just survived but even remained the seat of the Japanese government. It had even gained in reputation by becoming the Emperor´s place of residence.

Now that he was rid of all administrative and governmental responsibilities, Katsu Kaishu joined Yoshinobu in Mito. Evidently the Imperial government did not hold him accountable for the refusal of some elements of the Tokugawa army and navy to fully effectuate the Edo agreement. His knowledge in naval affairs and his humanity caused the new government to recall him in 1869. In 1872 he was appointed Vice Minister of the Imperial Navy and became Minister of the Imperial Navy in 1873. He served in this office until 1878. Without question he fully deserved the epithet "Father of the Japanese navy". In 1887 Katsu Kaishu was made a count and was one of the few former Tokugawa samurai to sit on the Imperial privy council. He died in 1899.

Of the two men presented in this chapter, Saigo Takamori was definitely the harder character to fathom. After adding great credit to his name in the Boshin War he became a full general in the new Imperial army and remained an important person in Japanese politics. He was instrumental in supervising the dissolution of the old domains and the creation of the new conscript army. It was however impossible to overlook the divergencies which separated him from other influential politicians of the early Meiji period. He was in favour of both the modernization of the armed forces, and Japan´s colonial ambitions in Korea. The Koreans had refused to recognize the Emperor Meiji, which had caused a national uproar in Japan, and Saigo was convinced that the Western powers would seize Korea if Japan did not beat them to it. He detested most Western innovations and objected to having his photo-

---

73   cf. *"Last stand of the Shogunate party in Hokkaido – the surrender of Hakodate on 27th June 1869"*, p. 142

The meeting between Saigo Takamori (left) and Katsu Kaishu (right) at Takanawa in March 1868.
The buildings had been occupied by Satsuma troops, who nervously eyed Katsu's voluminous bag. At the end of the conversation, Katsu produced a lacquered box containing Edo *sushi*, a well-known speciality even then. He presented it to his hosts in accordance with the Japanese tradition still observed today of bringing gifts (*omiyage*) in honour of the host. (painting by Somei Yuki, 1935)

graph taken. He resisted the building of a national railway network and insisted that the money would be better spent on the military. Strangely enough he did not seem to realize that a modern army was dependent on railways for transport. In 1873 Saigo resigned his public offices and retired to his home in Kagoshima. Here he founded a number of academies which attracted thousands of young men who shared his conservative views and found his old samurai ideals appealing.

These romantic die-hards eventually succeeded in bringing the new regional government in Kagoshima under their control. The government in Tokyo dispatched a naval squadron to empty the Kagoshima garrison's arsenal as a precautionary measure. The south Japanese powder keg finally blew when the government decided to abolish the samurai's time-honoured income in rice-based payments. Satsuma, which had been one of the cradles of the old system's overthrow, now became the region where in 1876/77 several tens of thousands of badly armed but highly idealistic former samurai fought against the new order. Saigo Takamori was persuaded to head the Satsuma Rebellion, although he was probably the only one to realize that the rising was doomed to fail against the new state and the army he himself had helped to create. The rebels failed to take the fortress of Kumamoto and were defeated at the Battle of Tabaruzaka. While the Imperial army was able to supply its units in the field with everything that was necessary, the rebels soon painfully began to feel the lack of even the most essential supplies. Eventually Saigo Takamori received a thigh wound at the Battle of the "White Mountain" (Shiroyama). Guarded by his most faithful followers, he chose to end his life in the true samurai manner.

The number of legends surrounding Saigo's death reveals how strongly his fate has continued to stir Japanese imagination. In his character the desire to leave bad old times behind and the wish to retain ancient traditions and values were merged. Saigo was caught in the insoluble

A great man and his dog: monumental statue of Saigo Takamori, erected in Ueneo Park, Tokyo, in 1898.

without military accoutrements to avoid embarrassment caused by his having fought both for and against the Imperial army. The modern viewer is confronted with the image of a modest and down-to-earth man who was immune to pomp and uninterested in monetary gain, and who impressed his contemporaries simply by his personality. He continues to impress to this very day.

Jules Brunet, true "Last Samurai"

The sources present Lieutenant (as from August 1867, Captain) Jules Brunet (1838–1911) as an intelligent, affable, and kindly man, who quickly felt at home in Japan and readily adapted to its culture. Good-looking and a remarkable 1, 85 metres tall, he quickly won over the hearts of his Japanese artillery recruits at Edo in 1867. Brunet was also a skilled draughtsman and painter; the watercolour sketches he made of the Shogunate soldiers during field exercises at Edo possess both a lightness and verve that make them appealing sources for the military historian. Even the Shogun Tokugawa Yoshinobu himself sat for Brunet at Osaka to have his portrait painted.

In 1867 Brunet was already able to look back upon ten years´ service in the French army, a few of which had been spent in the French attempt to establish the ill-fated Emperor Maximilian in Mexico. When Napoleon III sent the Shogun French military instructors along with the prized Chassepot rifles and field guns in November 1866[74], Brunet was already a member of the *legion d'honneur* and held a commission in the Horse Artillery of the Imperial Guard.

The French ambassador to the Imperial Court of Japan, Léon Roches, was at this time actively engaged in trying to counteract growing British influence by supporting the Shogun in his struggle against the renegade domains in the south-west of Japan. The most attractive offer the French were able to make apart from logistic and material support for the establishment of the naval arsenal at Yokosuka (1865–1876) was to grant the Shogun his long-cherished wish for military instructors, a wish the British had previously refused. After the disgraceful Choshu campaign in 1866 it had become clear to the Shogun that the building of a modern and powerful army was paramount. The French military mission was led by Captain Charles Chanoine and consisted of altogether 18 officers and NCOs. The four lieutenants and thirteen non-commissioned officers had been chosen from the infantry, cavalry, and artillery arms as well as the technical troops. They were to support the Japanese in their building of a modern army, and an independent armament industry. In January 1867, Captain Chanoine reported:

"In recent years, the Japanese have little by little adopted some drill elements from the Dutch, British, and French. [...] They are now willing to do everything the French way,

conflict between Japan´s rapid westernization, and the price it had to pay. Although modernization was deemed inevitable and necessary, many felt that the country had forfeited its very soul. Japan´s step into the modern world had come at a high cost.

Saigo Takamori had remained true to himself to the last. The dilemma he was faced with ultimately brought about his destruction, but he lived and lost his life in a manner he considered the only honourable way. The new government could not help but concede this, dangerous though the rising had been. In 1898 a huge bronze statue in his honour was unveiled at Ueno close to the place where he had fought valiantly against the Tokugawa´s Shogitai corps in May 1868. The statue shows a squarely built middle-aged man clad in an extremely casual short kimono carrying only one short sword and accompanied by his dog. This is probably how people would have encountered Saigo Takamori on his walks in his beloved home province of Satsuma during his last years. He is presented

---

74 cf. *"The Shogun makes a clean sweep – the new army"*, p. 23

Shogunate infantryman as painted by his instructor Lieutenant Jules Brunet in April 1867. (Alfred Umhey Collection)

but in order to follow up the desire with concrete actions, I believe it would be wise only to encourage reforms which are actually of use. We must make clear to them that the introduction of new uniforms alone will not create a new army." (Héon 2010: section 25)

Monsieur Roches, the French ambassador, actually went as far as to talk of "untrained bands of men which the Shogun continues to employ." Brunet, the officer responsible for inspecting the artillery, found the Japanese pieces in poor condition. The bores were deficient, and a maximum range of 1, 200 metres could only be sustained at the expense of target accuracy.

The French promptly set to work. As a first step, a cadre corps of 60 infantry officers, 20 artillery officers, a squadron of cavalry, and a battalion's worth of NCOs was brought up to strength and underwent training. There was no time to spare, and so the French concentrated on establishing an élite corps, the *denshutai*, whose conspicuous uniform is said to have been designed by Brunet. Between January and December 1867, around 1, 500 infantry, 300 cavalry and 250 artillerymen underwent training. The original objective of 12, 000 available troops had proved impossible to achieve in such little time.

Possibly Brunet was among the French officers who witnessed the Battle of Toba-Fushimi without becoming actively involved. The good account the French-trained Shogunal soldiers gave of themselves contrasted sharply with the rather poor way the Shogun and his highest representatives bore themselves. When Yoshinobu gave up the fight at Edo in March 1868, not only many of his samurai like Otori Keisuke and Enomoto Takeaki were disappointed but also Jules Brunet, who not only had faith in his Japanese soldiers but also held very firm ideas of military honour. This is where Western and Eastern military values touched – Brunet's disgust was shared by many of the Tokugawa's samurai vassals. The French government meanwhile recalled its ambassador Roches, declared itself neutral and summoned the military advisers to the port of Yokohama to bring them home. The Edo barracks and the countryside north of the capital however were still swarming with men willing to fight the Imperial army. Brunet decided not to abandon his faithful samurai and the men he had trained and prepared to follow them on their march north. He also considered it his duty to restore French military honour now that its military mission had failed. He wrote to his superior officer captain Chanoine:

"I have the honour of resigning my commission, which I shall presently submit to His Excellency the Minister of War. Under the pretence of travelling to see my old school friend Verny, director of the Franco-Japanese arsenal at Yokohama (to which you have kindly given your consent), I am actually travelling somewhere completely different. […] The Northern Alliance has renewed its request to me; the daimyo, friends of France, declare that they are in need of my advice […] I am under no illusions regarding the difficulties, which I am resolved to face with the determination either to die or to serve the interests of France in this country." (Héon 2010: section 57)

On 4th October Brunet and his companion corporal Cazeneuve, a cavalryman, boarded a ship to Sendai. Together with a part of the French-trained troops, who had come marching from Edo with the NCOs Fortant, Marlin and Bouffier, they sailed to Hokkaido with Admiral Enomoto's ships.[75] Brunet must have long realized that militarily decisive individual feats, let alone ultimate chances of success, were immaterial to a samurai code of honour. What counted, was faith and loyalty. This extended far beyond a feudal lord who had decided to step down, but also comprised a samurai comrades in arms. And Brunet was part of this comradeship. The samurai did not care overmuch about his military rank or nationality. To them, he was simply Jules Brunet. After his resignation had first been rejected, the French Ministry of War decided to grant him one year of unpaid leave in 1869.

---

[75] cf. *"Last stand of the Shogunate party in Hokkaido – the surrender of Hakodate on 27th June 1869"*, p. 142

The destination of Brunet and his colleagues was the northern Japanese main island of Hokkaido, where the followers of the former Shogun had retired by the end of 1868. The four French NCOs found themselves promoted to regimental commanders while Brunet himself took it upon himself to coordinate the staff work, especially the troops´ organisation and training. Again, he decided to implement French military doctrine and so had every officer promise him personal loyalty and the implementation of French drill and tactics. Among these principles was the rule to grant promotion by merit not birth. An unknown French officer described Brunet´s workload and pivotal role in the army´s workings as follows: "Customs duties, municipalities, fortifications, the army – everything was supervised and controlled by him. The fatuous Japanese are like puppets, and he enjoys seeing them dance to his music. [...] He has created a fine French Revolution in this brave new Japan. Commanders are elected, and personal merit not birth determines military rank. All this is a wonderful thing for this country, and he has done a great job if one considers the seriousness of the situation."

Possibly a single man´s part appears slightly exaggerated here, and there is a perceptible amount of Gallic arrogance in the words. That said, Brunet must have possessed the sensitivity necessary to persuade the conservative Tokugawa factionists to relinquish both their airs and graces and self-destructive red tapes. Instead, he prescribed modern ideas from abroad which they were forced to adopt for better or worse. It remains remarkable that Brunet never held any official military rank in Hokkaido – his personality was enough to give him all the authority that he required for his orders to be carried out. Sadly, it was all in vain. The power of the enemy was growing stronger both on land and sea. In June 1869, the last rebels laid down their arms at Hakodate. Brunet and most of his French comrades, one of which (Cazeneuves) had been wounded in the fighting, boarded the French gunboat *Coëtlogon* and sailed to Yokohama. Although the Japanese government demanded that its enemies should be punished, it was probably relieved when Brunet and his colleagues were quietly brought to France and diplomatic entanglements avoided.

In France Brunet´s popularity was such that he was only briefly suspended from duty. His only real punishment remained the fact that at the end of his 40-year soldier´s career he was still four months short of his official length of service. From February 1870, he fought in the Franco-Prussian War holding the rank of captain. He took part in the siege of Metz and, after being released from German captivity, in the fighting against the Paris Commune. After the war, his career continued to flourish; he was appointed Commander of the *Légion d'honneur*, served as military attaché in Vienna and Rome, and as chief of staff to his former commanding officer General Charles Chanoine, when the latter was French Minister of War.

He was eventually promoted to major general. Even the Japanese government finally forgave him and awarded the former "samurai" several highly prestigious decorations.

Brunet never returned to Japan. His old companions-in-arms Cazeneuves, Fortant, Marlin and Bouffier however had already returned to Japan by 1871 and found employment as lecturers at the military academy in Osaka and in other positions. France succeeded in preserving its strong influence in Japanese military affairs until the Germans gradually took over in the 1880s and 1890s. Nevertheless, lasting French influence after the fall of the Ezo Republic demonstrates that even the Shogunate´s former enemies were prepared to concede that the French officers had done their work well.

One of the reasons of the present author for adding Jules Brunet´s biography to the number of military lives discussed in this chapter is that it served as a model for a famous piece of Western popular entertainment culture. A blockbusting Hollywood production focusing on this particular period of Japanese history is Edward Zwick´s *Last Samurai* (2003). The movie thematizes and mixes at random various motives from the time of recurring samurai recurring rebellions against the new government. The plot has a fictitious American officer (played by Tom Cruise) and his sergeant serve first as military instructors in the new Japanese army before defecting to a rather romanticized group of renegade samurai; the story takes place in a very idyllic rural Japanese setting. The character of Captain Algren (Tom Cruise) is clearly modelled on Brunet, and naturally some French picturegoers were not amused by this cineastic form of cultural appropriation. Many will have found consolation in the fact that the film renewed a wider range of popular interest in this dashing and noble French "samurai".

After the battle, or the experiences of Dr William Willis

Figures assessing the losses sustained in the Boshin War between January 1868 and June 1869 vary between several thousand and well over 10, 000 fatalities. Many sources mention 8, 200 dead and more than 5, 000 wounded. Recent research suggests that the new Imperial army sustained as many as 6, 600 losses out of a total of 110, 000 effectives. The opposing side will have suffered many more.

Compared to the Boshin War´s historic impact or alongside the losses sustained in the preceeding American Civil War (1861–65) these numbers appear almost negligible. However, such an approach would completely ignore the appalling amount of suffering experienced by the casualties and discount the intensity and ruthlessness of the fighting, which became particularly evident in the battles for Nagaoka and Aizu.

Another question presenting itself is whether the dead outnumbered the wounded. The answer is possibly, yes. British doctor William Willis (1837–1894), who several times visited the front lines and himself tended to thousands of wounded, recorded the following in June 1868: "It is to be feared that a needless and cruel sacrifice of life characterizes hostile action on both sides, each justifying its acts by the conduct of its opponents. In the recent fight at Edo[76] all the wounded Ronin were beheaded, and I have learned from a reliable source that an unhappy doctor who lent his services to the Ronin was for doing so executed and his head exposed at a place called Sanya [...] in Edo. I have observed a significant absence of wounded prisoners and, notwithstanding assurances to the contrary [...] I am inclined to believe that a wounded prisoner has little if any compassion extended to him and is, as a rule, beheaded." (Cortazzi 2012: 122).

Even at Niigata in November Willis observed that he had up to then not come across a single wounded prisoner: "Wounded enemy soldiers are slain indiscriminately."

(Hoya 2020: 168)

The problem continued to haunt Dr Willis, who had been brought up in the slightly more humanitarian European tradition. He eventually appealed to the Imperial authorities to spare the lives of enemy wounded. The British doctor slyly remarked that the idea was of course not to show mercy to the enemies of the Emperor but to avoid "that all the great countries of the world would hear with horror" upon this Japanese practice (Cortazzi 2012: 137–8). Indeed, the brutal treatment of wounded enemies was simply a continuation of samurai tradition, according to which a warrior would rather put an end to his life than fall into the hands of the enemy alive. After all, what else could be expected from him but death? Since Japan under the Emperor Meiji was eager to gain the world powers´ recognition and respect, the treatment of enemy

Dr William Willis (1837-1894),
"Doctor of the Boshin War".

prisoners was gradually improved. Of all the important Tokugawa leaders taken prisoner only Kondo Isami and Oguri Tadamasa were executed, and later the German and Austro-Hungarian prisoners-of-war taken at Tsingtao during the First World War were mostly treated according to international standards. Only after World War One did nationalism and hyper-militarism gain more ground in Japan, which led to large-scale mistreatment and murder of enemy prisoners-of-war in Manchuria and during the Second World War.

Willis, who as a doctor with the British embassy enjoyed diplomatic status, was received at court because he had pioneered the treatment of wounded soldiers in the Boshin War. Already in early 1868 he had treated at Kyoto more than 100 Satsuma casualties of the Battle of Toba-Fushimi.[77] Not one of the wounded which he operated upon died. The Prince of Satsuma was so grateful that he wanted to give Dr Willis 2, 000 *bu* in silver, an enormous sum which the doctor politely declined. At Edo in June 1868, he treated 176 Imperial wounded from the Battle of Ueno and the fighting in the north, of which 120 came from Satsuma, 23 from Choshu, 18 from Tosa, five from Bizen, three from Tsu, and one from Omura. These figures clearly show which domains on the Imperial side bore the brunt of the fighting. On several occasions Willis expressed his admiration for the Japanese soldier´s capability to endure physical pain. Several of his patients who had been wounded at Toba-Fushimi were again wounded during the fighting in the east. "I was often struck by the fortitude with which pain was borne; yesterday, I extracted a bullet deeply lodged in the neck of a boy of 17; he exhibited no mani-

---

76 cf. "The Battle of Ueno, 15th May 1868", p. 127

77 cf. "'In this sign, conquer!' – the Battle of Toba-Fushimi", p. 111

Shogunate troops taking their ease during a field exercise near Mount Fuji in 1867.
(watercolour by Jules Brunet). From left to right: infantry with a samurai at centre holding a flag; to the right, two officers confer while their men enjoy a meal. To this day the surroundings of Mount Fuji serve as an exercise area for the the Japanese Self Defence Forces. (Alfred Umhey Collection)

festation of suffering whatever during the operations, which by his wish was performed without chloroform."
(Niigata, November 1868; Cortazzi 2012: 137).
Field hospitals were established at random wherever there was space. Most could be found in temples, where the modest priests even tolerated amputations being performed in full view of golden Buddha statues if there had not been sufficient time to surround them with curtains. Orderlies were often male, but these were occasionally assaulted or beaten by patients driven almost mad with pain. To solve the problem, married women were asked to tend to the patients, which immediately created the desired calming effect. Some patients were even taken care of by their girlfriends.

Another reason for Dr. Willis' considerable success was that his Japanese colleagues knew next to nothing about dealing with injuries caused by modern firearms, which formed the majority of wounds. Regarding the wounded after the Battle of Toba-Fushimi, Willis noted:
"I found on my arrival at the Satsuma *yashiki* [=residence] in Kyoto [...] over a hundred wounded men. Their injuries were almost exclusively the result of firearms. I notice this as it would seem to point to the comparatively little use that appears to have been made of the national weapon, the long two handed sword, in the late struggle. [...] I am inclined to believe that there must have been firing at comparatively close quarters between the contending forces. The statements of the wounded men are confirmatory of this view." (Cortazzi 2012: 103)

At Aizu several months later, Dr Willis saw the same: the wounds were almost all shot wounds but for a few injuries from spears or swords. There were no bayonet wounds. Max von Brandt, working on the other side of the front line, came to similar conclusions dealing with the wounds of two boatfuls of Aizu samurai after Toba-Fushimi: "All injuries had been caused by shot wounds, and most of these were severe, but none of these men, despite having been wounded 48 hours previously and having received no treatment since, uttered a single cry of pain." (von Brandt 1901: 183). Dr. Willis' and von Brandt's accounts demonstrate how ineffective old-style Japanese units armed only with sword and lance had become.

Historical depiction of the final battle for Hakodate in 1869.
Imperial warships have entered the bay while Choshu troops move against Tokugawa loyalists in the foreground.
Goryokaku fortress, threatened from the rear, can be seen towering over city and port.

Japanese surgeons tended to simply sew up shot wounds, often with fatal results. A large part of Japanese medicine was based on Chinese principles, which usually abstained from operations, instead relying on salves and ointments. Wills referred to this school as "the complicated and often mischievous system of medicine which had been borrowed from China." (Cortazzi 2012: 122). He spent every minute of his free time teaching Japanese doctors and orderlies, who proved quick in the uptake, the art and craft of Western medicine. This included probing for and removing bullets and bone fragments, applying splints to broken limbs, bandaging wounds effectively, and if necessary, amputating a shattered limb under hygienic conditions using brandy and chloroform. Dr. Willis also attempted to instil improved hygienic awareness and encouraged a more effective running of the military hospitals. He also made a point of caring for the many patients suffering from syphilis.

Dr. Willis had his most poignant experience on entering Aizu-Wakamatsu after its surrender. The town had been almost entirely destroyed in the fighting. The prince of Satsuma had asked him to go north and tend to the many wounded behind the lines. The British doctor obliged and betook himself on the arduous journey (Dr. Willis was an enormous man, measuring 190 cm and weighing 127 kg!). He was to treat no less than 1, 600 wounded (600 of these with his own hands, while the others were tended by Japanese doctors under his instructions). Of the 1, 600 wounded, 900 were from the Imperial army, while 700 were from Aizu, where too he had expressly asked to go. Among the many wounded were women, children, and elderly, for the Imperial artillery had fired its missiles into the city indiscriminately. Had it not been for Dr. Willis, no one would have cared for these people.[78] William Willis, who had worked for the British embassy since the year 1862, left the diplomatic service after the Boshin War and went to Satsuma, where he was received with open arms. In Satsuma´s capital of Kagoshima he established a modern hospital, where he treated thousands of patients, and also a school of medicine which was to become the basis of today´s School of Medicine of the University of Kagoshima. Willis was forced to

---

78   cf. *"The bloody siege of Aizu-Wakamatsu"*, p. 138

Satsuma troops evacuating wounded from the Toba-Fushimi battlefield.
Two men have been placed on doors removed from nearby buildings. (*Nishiki no mihata* 1907, plate XXI)

leave Japan in 1877, after the local government had cast doubt on his attitude towards his former patron Saigo Takamori´s rebellion. These doubts were entirely justified since Willis left no one in uncertain terms that his sympathies were with the rebels, who in his view lived up to their ideals and values, which was exactly what he was doing as well. Dr. William Willis died in his birthplace County Fermanagh, Ireland, in 1894.

Imai Nobuo (1841–1918) and the long road to an ordinary life

Imai Nobuo was born the son of a wealthy and respected *hatamoto* retainer of the Tokugawa. He was to become famous as the samurai who killed Sakamoto Ryoma, the architect of the pivotal alliance between Satsuma and Choshu (Satcho). Unbeknown to most, he also took part in almost all of the big battles discussed in this book and nevertheless managed to give his life a new direction in later years.

As a young samurai Imai Nobuo held an administrative post in the Yokohama magistrate´s office. Here he struck

Figurine of Hijikata Toshizo during his last fight in Hokkaido.
(Photograph with kind permission of Mr Kimura Tomoki, Goryokaku Tower, Hakodate)

Imai Nobuo wearing officer's uniform in Hokkaido in 1869. (public domain)

up many friendships with other young samurai, Furuya Sakuzaemon among them. An expert speaker of English, Sakuzaemon translated an illustrated infantry training manual, giving it the Japanese title *Hohei soren to zukai*. Imai studied sword fighting and jiu-jitsu and became an assistant instructor at the Shogunal Kobusho war academy.

Imai and other young samurai angrily watched Choshu's ever-increasing agitation against the Shogunate in the West. Together they offered the conservative Tokugawa authorities to raise a troop of "faithful and brave" samurai and fight the rebels. This proposition was turned down (Hellyer 2020: 174). Undeterred, Imai and two of his friends travelled to Kozuke province and began to raise a peasant militia (*noheitai*), which constituted a means of self-defence on a local basis. In times like these, such units were tolerated and even encouraged. Imai's pedagogic talent, the joy he took in teaching and training, was to resurface in different circumstances in later years. For the time being, he decided to join the Mimawarigumi police force at Kyoto in autumn 1867. In contrast to the Shinsengumi, the Mimawari consisted of samurai of noble breeding. These men were sons of Tokugawa vassals, not the rag-tag *ronin* who had been chiefly recruited for their strength and brutality. The plan to kill Sakamoto Ryoma may originally simply have been a dare common enough among young samurai at the time. Whatever its origins, Imai was part of the Mimawarigumi squad responsible for the murder of Sakamoto on 15th November, and he later boasted of having struck the death blow with his sword.

Imai was one of the four hundred samurai of the Mimawarigumi corps that took part in the three-day Battle of Toba-Fushimi from 3rd to 6th January 1868. The men were mainly equipped with sword and lance, and many wore old-fashioned armour. Hardly any members of the Mimawarigumi carried rifles. Following their defeat, Imai and his comrades were transported by boat to Edo, where the Mimawarigumi corps was disbanded. There was no longer any need for a police force at Kyoto, and to make matters worse Shogun Tokugawa Yoshinobu had decided to give up the fight. Imai and many of his comrades decided to go home and rejoin their families. However, after a short while Imai once again decided to leave his parents' home in Edo's Hongo district – he still had a score to settle with the rebels.

His old friend Furuya Sakuzaemon had meanwhile busied himself raising a new unit comprising of 370 survivors of the 11th and 12th Infantry Regiments, whose commanding officers Sakuma and Kubota had been killed at Toba-Fushimi. They were joined by men from the 6th Infantry, 70 samurai from Iwana, seven artillery pieces, and a well-filled paychest. This unit later became known as the *Shohotai*. Imai Nobuo was appointed its deputy commanding officer. The unit's rank and file were mostly men of peasant and city stock, with only a sprinkling of samurai. Once they had arrived in the area north of Edo, Furuya and Imai avoided attacking enemy troops carrying the Imperial sun and moon banners. On 9th March 1868 however, the Shohotai ran into a strong advance guard of the Imperial Tosando army at Yashu-Yanada in today's Tochigi prefecture. The Tosando army was the central contingent of altogether three Imperial columns rapidly advancing eastwards. The advance guard was composed of three units, totalling 200 men: one Satsuma company (120), a half-platoon from Choshu (30), infantry and engineers from Ogaki (50), and one field piece. Its commanding officer was Kawamura Yojuro from Satsuma.

So far, the local populace had been happy to provide both sides with supplies (although they probably had no real say in the matter). Then they sat down to watch the unfolding spectacle. Despite this audience, the Shohotai were caught completely off guard. Some of its dead were later found to have spent their last moments on earth in the arms of local prostitutes! In the dense morning mist the Satsuma soldiers and their allies crept towards the enemy camp with its 900 soldiers. The mist and the dark silhouette of the peasants who had decided to watch the show formed a solid grey wall which made it impossible for the sleep fuddled Shohotai to clearly make out the attackers. It was impossible to aim a rifle, which is why the Battle of Yashu-Yanada saw much fighting with cold steel, never a strong point of the Tokugawa riflemen. At nine AM it was all over. Shohotai losses were 62 men dead including four unit commanders, and eighty wounded. The Imperial force had lost only three dead and six wounded. The survivors fled to Aizu.

Even if one considers the random character of the Shohotai's composition and its alleged indiscipline, it remains surprising that 200 attackers were able to rout an enemy more than four times their number mostly in close combat. In the circumstances described above, rifles and artillery had proved of little use. The large number of Shohotai casualties indicates that they had sold their lives dearly. For an explanation, it makes sense to examine the fighting techniques of the Satsuma infantry, who in contrast to the Tokugawa infantry were born and trained samurai and were familiar with the sword from an early age. Every Satsuma rifleman carried his sword into combat. In Satsuma itself, the traditional sword fighting style was the *Jigen-ryu*, which concerned itself not so much with subtlety than with deadly efficiency. Its aim was to kill an enemy with one single slash of the blade. Physical strength, mental focus and technique made every Satsuma footsoldier armed with a sword a formidable enemy. After Toba-Fushimi many enemy dead were found whose own sword guards (*tsuba*) had been driven into their foreheads in a futile attempt to parry the blows of their Satsuma opponents. It is probable that the Shohotai experienced a similar onslaught at Yashu-Yanada, and broke.

Imai Nobou had once again been beaten, but after his arrival in Aizu (the haven of so many Tokugawa supporters) in April he managed to gather surviving Shohotai around him. From Aizu they marched to Echigo in support of beleaguered Nagaoka. Imai was involved in the fight for the local castle, which changed hands no less than three times.[79] Imai and the remaining Shohotai also took part in the defence of Aizu in autumn 1868. Together with most of the militia they succeeded in escaping from the besieged town and its castle and sailed to Hakodate in Hokkaido on board the Tokugawa steamer *Chogei-maru*. Imai commanded surviving Shohotai and *denshutai* soldiers in the last battles against the Imperial troops, his 130 *denshutai* riflemen firing 35, 000 rounds during the last battles around Futamataguchi. In June 1869 they finally laid down their arms. Imai later wrote a book about his experiences in Hokkaido entitled *The Dream of Ezo*.

Imai Nobuo was on the run. Not only had he boasted about having personally killed Sakamoto Ryoma, but he had also resisted and inflicted considerable harm on the legitimate Imperial army for no less than eighteen months. To everyone's surprise Imai was released from prison in 1872 and sent to Sumpu/Shizuoka. Why exactly he was pardoned is impossible to tell, but it is believed that Saigo Takamori in person put in a good word for him and other prisoners in order to encourage reconciliation between the two sides.

Much had changed since Edo had capitulated and received the new name of Tokyo. It had become the official seat of the Emperor and his government. Former Shogun Tokugawa Yoshinobu had been pardoned. Aged only 31, he withdrew into comfortable retirement at Sumpu, where already his great ancestor Ieyasu had spent the last years of his life. Even after their curtailment by the government, his estates were still worth some 700, 000 *koku*, while the house of Tokugawa itself was headed by Tokugawa Iesato (1863–1940), who was still underage at the time. The family exists to this day. The curtailment of the Tokugawa's position and wealth also meant that many thousands of samurai were left without income. To make matters worse for them the government set about gradually abolishing the entire caste in the course of the 1870s. In 1876, the wearing of double swords was outlawed. Many samurai henceforth sought employment in the army and police forces, or as civil servants, if the government permitted them. Others remained in Edo and became merchants or doctors. Many moved onto the estates of their former master in Sumpu, which was soon to become Shizuoka prefecture on the Pacific coast and turned to farming. In 1869, 250 samurai families had settled around Makinohara alone, while members of the Shogitai, who had made their last stand at Ueno, settled in nearby Numazu. It was the beginning of one of the great success stories of modern Japan – not least because of the hard work of the former Tokugawa élite, Shizuoka presently developed into Japan's greatest production area for green tea. Since green tea had become a fashionable drink both in the United States and Great Britain, Shizuoka provided one of the first of Japan's many important export products. Through their diligence and hard work, the samurai-turned-farmers were able to convert a wasteland into an important source of wealth, and to produce what was to become an international hallmark of Japanese culture.

A faithful Tokugawa veteran to the last, Imai Nobuo was given a small administrative post in Shizuoka. Old habits die hard however, and so Imai travelled to Tokyo as soon as the Satsuma rebellion broke out in 1876. Ostentatiously, he joined up to fight Saigo Takamori's rebels, but secretly he hoped to change sides and once again fight for his beloved old ways. This may suggest that Imai considered himself in Saigo's debt, but evidence is lacking. The rebellion collapsed before Imai could board a ship. He returned to Shizuoka, finally accepting the new order and his appointed place in it.

He was assigned two hectares of farmland among his former peers in Makinohara. Imai built a home for his family and together with seven or eight farmhands grew tea on one hectare of his patch. He laid down his swords for good, and later even refused to attend a Kendo demonstration. It is surprising that he was even baptized and henceforth led a pious life – after all, the Tokugawa had suppressed and persecuted the "evil religion" of the Christians for centuries. Imai frequently engaged himself in education and founded several schools. Surely, he was able to offer his students insight into the lessons learnt from his dramatic and turbulent life. He served as mayor before dying in 1918 at the age of seventy-six.

---

79 cf. "The Hokuetsu War in Nagaoka", p. 130

SOURCES AND FURTHER READING

Aoki, Takashi et al.: *Nihon no kassen-wo kaeta teppo, taiho, daizukan.* Tokyo: Yosensha Mook 2014.

Various authors: *Bakumatsu boshin seinan senso* (Rekishi Gunzo Series Tokubetsu Henshu). Tokyo: Gakken 2006.

Arima, Nariuri: *Bakumatsu-ni okeru seiyo kaki no yunyu.* In: Nippon Rekishi 120 (1958), pp. 2–13.

Bolitho, Harold: *The Echigo War, 1868.* In: Monumenta Nipponica 34, No. 3 (1979), pp. 259–277.

Boshinshoyo Kinki oyobi Gunki Shinzu (*Imperial Banners of the Boshin War*): https://www.digital.archives.go.jp/DAS/pickup/view/category/categoryArchives-En/0600000000/0602000000/00

Brandt, Max von: *Dreiunddreißig Jahre in Ost-Asien. Erinnerungen eines deutschen Diplomaten in drei Bänden. Vol. 2: Japan 1866–1875.* Leipzig: Wigand 1901. Online edition: https://oag.jp/img/1901/09/Dreiunddreissig-Jahre-in-Ost-Asien-1.pdf

Cortazzi, Hugh: *Dr Willis in Japan 1862–1877. British Medical Pioneer.* London and Dover, New Hampshire: Athlone Press 2012 (reprint from 1985).

Cortazzi, Hugh: *Mitford´s Japan. Memories and Recollections 1866–1906.* Revised edition, London: Japan Library 2002.

Craig, Albert M.: *Choshu in the Meiji Restoration.* Harvard University Press 1961. Reprint Lexington Books 2000.

Drea, Edward J.: *Japan's Imperial Army. Its Rise and Fall, 1853 – 1945.* Lawrence: University of Kansas Press 2009.

Ehlers, Maren A.: *Mountain Demons from Mito: The Arrival of Civil War in Echizen in 1864.* In: The Meiji Restoration. Japan as a Global Nation. Robert Hellyer and Harald Fues (eds.), Cambridge University Press 2020, pp. 113–136.

Esposito, Gabriele and Rava, Guiseppe: *Japanese Armies 1868–1877. The Boshin War and Satsuma Rebellion* (Men-at-Arms, 530). Oxford: Osprey 2020.

Fuess, Harald: *The Global Weapons Trade and the Meiji Restoration. Dispersion of Means of Violence in a World of Emerging Nation-States.* In: The Meiji Restoration. Japan as a Global Nation. Robert Hellyer and Harald Fuess (eds.), Cambridge University Press 2020, pp. 83–109.

Fukuzawa, Yukichi: *The Autobiography of Yukichi Fukuzawa.* New York: Columbia University Press 1966.

Gack, Valentin: *Aizu in der Meiji-Restauration. Vom Beschützer Kyotos zum "Feind des Kaiserhofs".* Dissertation, Tübingen 2017. Online: https://publikationen.uni-tuebingen.de/xmlui/bitstream/handle/10900/77949/Gack_Aizu%20in%20der%20Meiji-Restauration.pdf?sequence=1&isAllowed=y

Hakoishi, Hiroshi: *The Image of Prussia in Japan during the Boshin War (1868–1869).* In: Mutual Perceptions and Images in Japanese-German Relations, 1860–2010. Sven Saaler et al. (eds.), Leiden/Boston: Brill 2017, pp. 110–134.

Heath, Ian: *Japan and Korea: Organisation, Warfare, Dress and Weapons* (Armies of the Nineteenth Century: Asia). Foundry Books 2012.

Hellyer, Robert: *Imai Nobuo. A Tokugawa Stalwart´s Path from the Boshin War to Personal Reinvention in the Meiji Nation-State.* In: The Meiji Restoration. Japan as a Global Nation. Robert Hellyer and Harald Fuess (eds.), Cambridge University Press 2020, pp. 171–187.

Héon, François-Xavier: *Le véritable dernier Samouraï: l'épopée japonaise du Capitaine Brunet.* In: Stratégique, Institut de Stratégie Comparée No. 99, 2010, pp. 193–223. Online: https://www.cairn.info/revue-strategique-2010-1-page-193.htm

Hillsborough, Romulus: *Samurai Revolution: The Dawn of Modern Japan Seen Through the Eyes of the Shogun's Last Samurai.* Vermont et al.: Tuttle 2014.

Hillsborough, Romulus: *Shinsengumi. The Shogun´s last Samurai Corps.* Vermont et al.: Tuttle 2011.

Hoya, Toru: *A Military History of the Boshin War.* In: The Meiji Restoration. Japan as a Global Nation. Robert Hellyer and Harald Fuess (eds.), Cambridge University Press 2020, pp. 153–170.

Hoya, Toru: *Reading History from Historical Materials. Rifles in Bakumatsu History* (Global Focus on Knowledge Lecture Series, 3), n. d. Online: https://ocw.u-tokyo.ac.jp/lecture_files/gf_16/6/notes/en/06hoya_eng.pdf

Huber, Thomas M.: *"Men of High Purpose" and the Politics of direct Action, 1862–1864.* In: Conflict in Modern Japanese History. The neglected Tradition. Najita, Tetsuo and Koschmann, J. Victor (eds.), Princeton University Press 1982, new imprint, Cornell East Asia Series, pp. 123; 2005: pp. 107–127.

Jaundrill, D. Colin: *Samurai to Soldier. Remaking Military Service in Nineteenth-Century Japan.* Ithaca, London: Cornell University Press 2016.

Kimura, Sachihiko: *The Shinsengumi: Shadows and Light in the Last Days of the Tokugawa Shogunate.* In: The Tokugawa World. Leupp, Gary P. and Tao, De-min (eds.), Abingdon-on-Thames: Routledge 2021, pp. 1104–1124.

Meissner, Kurt: *General Eduard Schnell.* In: Monumenta Nipponica 4, No. 2 (1941), pp. 69 (395)–101 (427).

Mori, Mayumi: *Shogitai Ibun.* Tokyo: Shinkosha 2004.

Nakanishi, Ritta: *Japanese Military Uniforms 1841–1929. From the Fall of the Shogunate to the Russo-Japanese War.* Tokyo: Dainippon 2006.

Nishiki no mihata (Bilderbuch des Boshin-Krieges). Beschrieben von Noguchi Shoichi und Tomioka Masanobu. Übersetzt von P. Ehmann. Gedruckt und herausgegeben von Azuma Kenzaburo (Toyodo). Tokyo: Hokunkai 1907.

Noguchi, Takehiko: *Toba Fushimi no tatakai: Bakufu no unmei wo kesshita yokkakan*. Tokyo: Chuo Koron Shinsha 2010.

Ogura, Kazukuni: *Boshin senso emaki. Nishiki no mihata. Hamaguri gomon kassen-zu byobu* (Shukan e-de shiru nihonshi, 29). Tokyo: Shueisha 2011.

Orbach, Danny: *Curse on this Country. The Rebellious Army of Imperial Japan*. Ithaca und London: Cornell University Press 2017.

Oyama, Kashiwa: *Boshin no eki senshi*. 2 vols., Tokyo: Jiji Tsushinsha 1968.

Pettersson, Jan: *The Yonezawa Matchlock. Mighty Gun of the Uesugi Samurai*. Author´s edition 2017.

Pictorial Saigo Takamori, Okubo Toshimichi (2 vols); 1: *Bakumatsu ishin no fuun*, 2: *Shinsei Meiji no hikari to kage*. Tokyo: Gakken 1989, 1990.

Ravina, Mark: *The Last Samurai: The Life and Battles of Saigo Takamori*. Hoboken: Wiley 2005.

Saaler, Sven: *Men in metal: A Topography of Public Bronze Statuary in Modern Japan*. Leiden and Boston: Brill 2020.

Satow, Sir Ernest: *A Diplomat in Japan. An Inner History of the Japanese Reformation*. Rutland/Vermont and Tokyo: Tuttle 1983.

Smith, Thomas C.: *The Introduction of Western Industry to Japan During the Last Years of the Tokugawa Period*. In: Harvard Journal of Asiatic Studies 11, No. 1/2 (1948), pp. 130–152.

Sonoda, Hideo: *The Decline of the Japanese Warrior Class, 1840–1880*. In: Nichibunken Japan Review. Bulletin of the International Research Center for Japanese Studies 1, 1990, pp. 73–111.

Stahncke, Holmer: *Die Brüder Schnell und der Bürgerkrieg in Nordjapan* (OAG aktuell, 27). Tokyo: OAG 1986. Online: https://oag.jp/img/1986/09/oag-tb-027-Brueder-Schnell-und-der-Buergerkrieg-in-Nordjapan-Holmer-Stahncke-text.pdf

Steele, William M.: *Against the Restoration: Katsu Kaishū's Attempt to Reinstate the Tokugawa Family*. In: Monumenta Nipponica 36, No. 3 (Autumn 1981), pp. 299–316.

Steele, William M.: *Edo in 1868: The View from Below*. In: Monumenta Nipponica 45, No. 2 (Summer 1990), pp. 127–155.

Steele, William M.: *The Rise and Fall of the Shogitai: a social Drama*. In: Conflict in Modern Japanese History. The neglected Tradition. Najita, Tetsuo and Koschmann (eds.), Princeton University Press 1982, new imprint, Cornell East Asia Series, 123; 2005, pp. 128–144.

Ströhl, Hugo Gerard: *Japanisches Wappenbuch. Nihon Moncho*. Neu herausgegeben und bearbeitet von Wolfgang Ettig. Schmitten/Ts.: Tengu 2006.

Tokugawa Yoshinobu: *Sekimukai hikki. Tokugawa Yoshinobu-ko kaisodan*. Tokyo: Heibonsha 1966.

Tomkins, Tom: *Yokosuka. Base of an Empire*. Novato: Residio Press 1981.

Totman, Conrad: *The Collapse of the Tokugawa Bakufu, 1862–1868*. Honolulu: University of Hawaii Press 1980.

Warner, William Eugene: *Warships of the Late Tokugawa Conflicts (1853–1870)*. Charleston: CreateSpace 2019.

Weber, A. R.: *Kontorrock und Konsulatsmütze*. Neuausgabe mit einem Schlüssel und geschichtlichen Anmerkungen von Dr. Kurt Meissner. Tokyo: OAG 1973.

Weber, Till: *Samurai Armies of the Late Sengoku Period* (2 vols.). Volume I: *Anatomy of a Samurai Army in the 16th and 17th Centuries*. Volume II: *Castles and Sieges, Artillery, Heraldry & Clothing*. Revised and extended English edition. Berlin: Zeughaus 2022 (German originals in 2009 and 2012).

Weber, Till: *Katsu Kokichi, ein Samurai als Lebenskünstler und seine Abwege*. In: Ders.: *Tokyo. Eine Biographie*. Mainz: Nünnerich-Asmus 2016, pp. 72–75.

West, Michael: *Meiji Restoration Losers. Memory and Tokugawa Supporters in Modern Japan* (Harvard East Asian Monographs, 358), 2013.

Yamakawa, Kenjiro: *Aizu Boshin senshi*. Tokyo: Aizu Boshin Senshi Hensankai 1933.

Materials employed converting dates from the old Japanese and gregorian calendars:

https://homepages.cwi.nl/~aeb/go/misc/jdate.html

Japanese conversion software:

https://maechan.net/kanreki/

Samurai Armies of the Late Sengoku Period

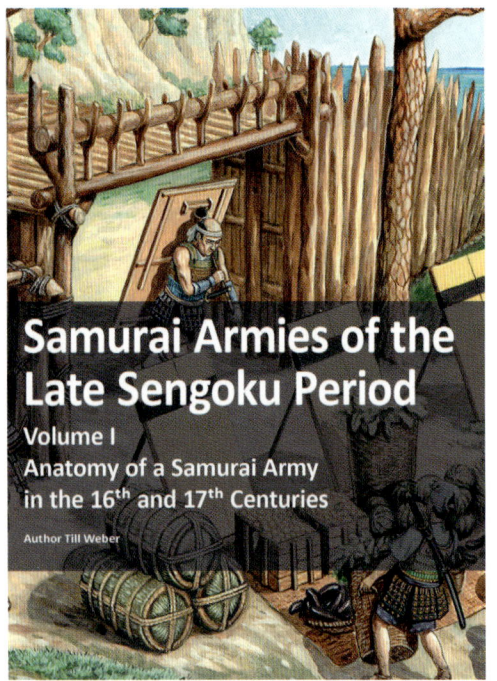

Volume I
Anatomy of a Samurai Army in the 16th and 17th Centuries

Author: Till Weber

The „Anatomy of a samurai army" details its composition, hierarchies, strengths and weaknesses as well as examining how it fought. Other aspects include:
- the differences between samurai and European warfare;
- the roles assigned to samurai and ashigaru in different armies;
- how these armies, some of which were over 100,000 strong, functioned;
- marching orders and camp facilities of the armies and;
- where each individual samurai stood in the order of battle.

The reader will discover what may seem to be abstract or strange ideas by way of the most detailed examples possible, in both word and picture, that are based on a variety of Japanese sources.
104 pages.
ISBN 978-3-96360-041-8

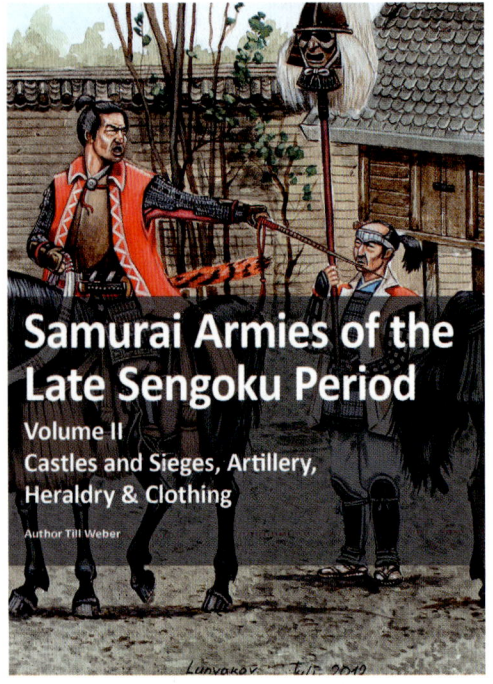

Volume II
Castles and Sieges, Artillery, Heraldry & Clothing

Author: Till Weber

The elegant, multi-storey main towers of Japanese castles, surrounded by massive fortifications, are widely known as symbols of samurai rule. However, the first of these tenshukaku were built only at the very end of the Sengoku period. Most fortifications were built of wood with earthen ramparts and ditches exploiting the natural environment.

The second volume of this series details these constructions as well as fortifications that were affected by major sieges: Fushimi, Tanabe, Otsu and Ueda in 1600, and Osaka in 1614/15. The author explains the sophisticated siege techniques and countermeasures employed by samurai armies of the period, and the Japanese artillery of the time.

A second focus is on the complex heraldry of leading as well as lesser known samurai families of the Sengoku period, illustrated by many colourful examples.

The third part offers an introduction to the world of traditional Japanese textile patterns and colours, their use, methods of manufacture in the pre-industrial age, and their special symbolism in the context of samurai history.

112 pages.
ISBN 978-3-96360-042-5

The books can be ordered online and are available at many bookstores.